Yale Studies in English/Volume 177

TOWARD *Women in Love*

THE EMERGENCE OF A LAWRENTIAN AESTHETIC

BY STEPHEN J. MIKO

NEW HAVEN AND LONDON, YALE UNIVERSITY PRESS, 1971

CONTENTS

ACKNOWLEDGMENTS

It does not seem possible, and it is probably not desirable, to write an academic book without various kinds of help and advice. I have certainly had my share. The earliest versions of the book were criticized by Martin Price, who gave me encouragement when it was most needed. Three anonymous readers of the version which was submitted as a dissertation suggested most of the subsequent changes. Portions of the later versions were read and criticized by David Gordon, Edward Casey, and Sheridan Blau; I tried to follow most of the advice they gave me. Elizabeth Schneider, Alan Stephens, and Marvin Mudrick have given me helpful advice about my academic vices. David and Joyce Brewster, by detailed criticism of another piece on Lawrence, helped me to clarify my chapter on *Women in Love*. Lee Baker assisted me in my research. Christopher Lauer helped me prepare the final manuscript and made the index. Merle Spiegel and Wayland Schmitt of Yale Press patiently helped me through final revisions. The secretarial staff of the English Department at the University of California at Santa Barbara typed large portions of the manuscript at various stages. And my wife has read through the entire manuscript at different times, offering criticism and encouragement.

The Academic Senate of the University of California at Santa Barbara granted me funds to get help with research and to travel to Austin and Berkeley. The staffs of the Academic Center Library at Austin and the Bancroft Library at Berkeley made their Lawrence manuscripts readily available to me. Where I quote manuscripts, I do so by permission of the Academic Center Library of the University of Texas at Austin and by permission of the director of the Bancroft Library of the University of California at Berkeley.

I gratefully thank all the above for their help. Any deficiencies of this book are, of course, my own responsibility.

S. J. M.

Santa Barbara, California
August 1971

A NOTE ON TEXTS

For convenience and consistency I have used the Viking edition
(Compass books) for *Sons and Lovers, The Rainbow,* and *Women
in Love,* and the English Phoenix edition for *The White Peacock*
and *The Trespasser.* The pagination of these two editions is identical, and one or the other is readily available to both English and
American readers. I am aware that some scholars find other editions of *The Rainbow* and *Women in Love* more adequate, but as
yet no fully adequate scholarly texts exist. The differences in
present texts do not significantly affect my work in this book.

LIST OF EDITIONS CITED

"The Crown." In *Reflections on the Death of a Porcupine,* pp.
1-100.
LH: The Letters of D. H. Lawrence. Edited with an introduction
by Aldous Huxley. London: Wm. Heinemann Ltd., 1956.
LM: The Collected Letters of D. H. Lawrence. Edited with an
introduction by Harry T. Moore. 2 vols. New York: Viking
Press, 1962.
Phoenix: The Posthumous Papers of D. H. Lawrence. Edited with
an introduction by Edward D. McDonald. London: Wm. Heine-
mann Ltd., 1961.
Phoenix: II: Uncollected Papers of D. H. Lawrence. Edited with
an introduction by Warren Roberts and Harry T. Moore. New
York: Viking Press, 1968.
"Pornography and Obscenity." In *Phoenix,* pp. 170-87.
"Psychoanalysis and the Unconscious" and *"Fantasia of the Un-
conscious."* New York: Viking Press, Compass Books, 1962.

The Rainbow. New York: Viking Press, Compass Books, 1961.

Reflections on the Death of a Porcupine. Bloomington: Indiana University Press, 1963.

Sons and Lovers. New York: Viking Press, Compass Books, 1958.

"Study of Thomas Hardy." In *Phoenix,* pp. 398-516.

The Trespasser. London: Wm. Heinemann Ltd., Phoenix edition, 1955.

The White Peacock. London: Wm. Heinemann Ltd., Phoenix edition, 1955.

Women in Love. New York: Viking Press, Compass Books, 1960.

A Bibliography of D. H. Lawrence. Edited by Warren Roberts. London: Rupert Hart-Davis, The Soho Bibliographies, 1963.

INTRODUCTION

Another book of criticism on D. H. Lawrence demands some explanation, especially since it deals with the novels about which most has been written. It does not, moreover, attempt to offer a radically different way of reading Lawrence or to deny that previous criticism has understood him. But of course I think it is different enough from earlier work to justify publication, and I will try to explain why.

Ever since Lawrence began writing he has been controversial. But for the last fifteen or twenty years the controversy has (with the exception of the trials of *Lady Chatterley's Lover*) increasingly focused on defining what sort of artist he was. Although no one can write of a novelist without taking into account the general validity of his ideas and attitudes, most recent critics are not mainly concerned with Lawrence's "message"—or at least they pretend not to be. Nor are they much concerned with his personal life. They want to describe and evaluate his work, according to criteria generally defended as aesthetic: why are his novels successful, why do they fail? I, too, am interested in these problems. But I found, when I tried to examine why I kept reading Lawrence, that certain patterns of conflict recurred in ways that the critics did not satisfactorily explain. I was particularly fascinated with Birkin in *Women in Love*, especially with his paradoxical role as an intellectual preaching anti-intellectualism. And, since Birkin is obviously Lawrence's most articulate voice in that novel, I wondered increasingly why Lawrence found this posture necessary and whether it had any determining influence on his art. This soon led me to look to his early work for answers—in short, to pursue a developmental approach. I was not surprised to find that the problem of Birkin's conflicting attitudes was intimately related to the problem of defining the senses in which Lawrence was a "religious" writer.

All the first five novels present evidence of a search for the most fundamental kinds of consistency, a basic search for coherence—not just of the worlds of novels, stories, and poems but of human life itself. It is ambitious to articulate such a search in novels; at first glance either philosophic system making or theology seems more appropriate. And, in fact, Lawrence wrote a good deal which seems to be both at once. But this sort of writing only emerged once he had found himself as a novelist, at the time when his novels were becoming most distinctly Lawrentian. This book is basically an attempt to understand what the term *Lawrentian* means and to correlate Lawrence's emerging ideas about the world with specific developments, both successful and not, in his art.

Again, this is obviously not a new approach. But it turned out to be different at least in its emphasis, and I think in some of its results. The most obvious difference is in the treatment of the first two novels Lawrence wrote: they helped clarify to me what sort of artist Lawrence became, and I therefore give them fuller treatment than is usual. They also proved interesting in themselves. I do not think, for example, that the second one, *The Trespasser,* is an aberration in Lawrence's career, despite its derivation from a friend's manuscript and its inferiority to most of Lawrence's other work. Throughout both my early chapters and those on the most important novels—*Sons and Lovers, The Rainbow,* and *Women in Love*—I argue that the differences in style and subject of each novel (all of which are more different from one another than is usual in even a developing novelist) are part of a larger struggle with problems of value which by their nature, or at least by the way Lawrence conceived them, are impossible to resolve. These problems can be approached in many ways; the extremes seem to be a psychoanalytic approach to Lawrence's neurotic personality and an affirmation of his religious and prophetic validity. Like most critics, I have tried to steer a middle course, though my biases are obviously more philosophic than psychoanalytic, more aesthetic than ethical. Throughout I try to relate aesthetic success and failure to Lawrence's basic struggle to clarify attitudes and ideas. My own struggle to identify these ideas and attitudes has led me to rather detailed analysis of two of Lawrence's most difficult expository works—"The Crown" and the *Study of Thomas Hardy*.

My interest in relating a developing mind to a developing art has also led to detailed discussion of many scenes that have been discussed before. It is futile to claim that all or even most of these discussions are justified by the degree of originality they display. But I hope they are justified by their relevance to my general argument or by their attempt at a kind of stylistic definition which I did not find in the criticism I have read. Since very little criticism of the first two novels exists even now, I felt a pleasant freedom in working out my own analyses. This happy state could not, of course, continue, and my treatment of the next three novels is obviously shaped in response to earlier work, to which I owe a great deal. Although I tried to avoid it, I occasionally found it necessary to argue with others. I hope that those who find me disagreeing with them in print will take this disagreement for what it most clearly is—a compliment to the force of their views.

1: THE WHITE PEACOCK

Of all Lawrence's books, the first is the one most consistently and pervasively concerned with nature. Everyone recognizes this, yet only Graham Hough is willing to call the "life of nature" Lawrence's "real subject," and even he does not seem particularly interested in pursuing the matter.[1] As Hough's analysis makes clear, the real subject is certainly not the only subject; a good deal of the book is concerned with the "human and social destiny" of the characters. Thus the book has at least two major concerns, perhaps even two kinds of life. What human destiny has to do with natural vitality is in fact one of Lawrence's major problems.

A writer's first novel is seldom his best, but it almost always reveals something about what his best will be. *The White Peacock*, as Hueffer pointed out to Lawrence, contains all the technical faults young novelists are accustomed to commit.[2] Yet it remains an impressive book in its own right, largely because of the life of

1. See Graham Hough, *The Dark Sun* (New York, 1959), p. 32. Hough argues that the "center" of the book is "displaced so that the circumference includes, not only the characters and their personal fates, but the whole life of nature which surrounds and flows through them. The characters are only forms into which this universal *mana* transitorily flows, and it is *mana* that is Lawrence's real subject." It is the transitory nature of this flow which seems to me most important. And are the characters only forms for it?

2. See Lawrence's "Autobiographical Sketch" in *Phoenix II*, p. 593.

nature which "surrounds and flows through" the characters. Lawrence did not quite know what to do with this flow, but he felt
strongly that it was important. Most of the technical faults can be
related to just this uncertainty, and most of Lawrence's successes,
both here and later, can be related to his attempts to cope with it.
These attempts are part of a gradually emerging effort to make
sense of almost everything implicit in a division between man and
nature.

The character who comes closest to capturing the natural life
and translating it into social and human terms is George Saxton.
At intervals throughout the book we encounter him mowing, and
in these scenes Lawrence effectively conveys George's temporary
possession of the natural flow about which Hough writes:

> George had thrown off his hat, and his black hair was moist and
> twisted into confused half-curls. Firmly planted, he swung with
> a beautiful rhythm from the waist. On the hip of his belted
> breeches hung the scythe-stone; his shirt, faded almost white,
> was torn just above the belt, and showed the muscles of his
> back playing like lights upon the white sand of a brook. There
> was something exceedingly attractive in the rhythmic body.
> [pp. 46-47]

In the early parts of the book George is heavy, muscular, brown,
and unsentimental to the point of cruelty. He appears to Lettie
Beardsall as a "great firm bud of life," and until his final decline
he is sexually attractive. Here we see him as almost the embodiment of natural force; the narrator's emphasis is upon his "beautiful rhythm" and the power which it conveys. In a later mowing
scene George's affinity to nature is emphasized again:

> Beneath us, the spires of the poplars in the spinney were warm
> gold, as if the blood shone through. Farther gleamed the grey
> water, and below it the red roofs. Nethermere was half hidden
> and far away. There was nothing in this grey, lonely world but
> the peewits swinging and crying, and George swinging silently at

his work. The movement of active life held all my attention, and when I looked up, it was to see the motion of his limbs and his head, the rise and fall of his rhythmic body, and the rise and fall of the slow waving peewits. [p. 218]

The deliberate comparison of George's movement to that of birds in swinging flight effectively dehumanizes him, almost reducing him to active life itself. But, unlike the first passage, this one evokes the loneliness of such a reduction. The backdrop is grey, and the peewits are crying (as they do a great deal throughout the book). Similar moments of pathos reappear frequently, and they tend to emphasize both the narrator's and the author's uncertainty about the value of natural forces.

Before long George leaves the land for good. He believes strongly that his departure for tavern-keeping is a vital loss: "I shall feel like that, as if my leading shoot were broken off" (p. 223). But George has rejected the pastoral life deliberately. Although forced off this land, he could have gone with his father to Canada and there continued his mowing. The choice is a rejection of the coherent natural rhythms we have just witnessed for a life both "human" and "social," and, as we judge from George's decline, the choice was a mistake. But it is not altogether satisfactory to think of this mistake as a simple rejection of nature; natural rhythms are not everything, as the crying peewits suggest. A brief look at Lawrence's first gamekeeper will show clearly that George is not simply all-too-human.

If George's ability to partake of and in a sense become a rhythmic natural force is appealing, Annable the gamekeeper makes a bad job of it, and Annable is obviously the most thoroughly natural man in the book. After boasting that he has required his wife to "breed" nine children in fourteen years, he answers criticism with a sort of primitive naturalism: "When a man's more than nature he's a devil. Be a good animal, says I, whether it's man or woman. You, Sir, a good natural male animal; the lady there—a female un—that's proper as long as yer enjoy it" (p. 131. It turns out that Annable is a Cambridge man who has taken to a

brutal life in the woods in bitter response to mistreatment by a
society woman. This makes his "natural" creed seem suspiciously
regressive and perhaps suggests that he has no important relevance
to George's more sensitive responses to nature. But to dismiss
Annable in this way is too easy, for he is powerfully portrayed,
he befriends the narrator, and his criticisms of the life-denying
behavior of upper-class women are at least partially borne out by
the book. What Annable does represent is a life totally amoral
and as animalistic as a sane man could attempt. This life soon
comes to an end, for in the eyes of the author it is clearly an
untenable extreme. The point is simply that thorough dehumani-
zation leads only to vigorous brutality; a man cannot completely
identify himself with natural processes and survive. The strain of
such a life upon wife and children is forcefully portrayed, so
there can be no doubt that traditional moral standards are also
operating and that nature offers no easy escape from them. Annable, then, offers an important perspective upon George's refusal
to keep farming, even though George's alternatives are not so
dramatic as Annable's. Life which does not somehow come to
terms with the "human" is at the very least incomplete. There is
something in George which Annable's bitterness had crushed and
which requires that George seek meaning for his life beyond the
hayfield.

What this something is gives George a great deal of trouble,
which his author in some degree shares. The pattern of George's
decline leaves some important questions unanswered. As a somewhat arrogant farm boy, George is awakened into consciousness
by the narrator Cyril and his sister Lettie. Lettie attracts him
sexually and impresses him with her cultural sophistication as
well, but he is not forceful or clever enough to win her. When she
marries a man of a higher class, George retaliates by marrying an
earthy, affectionate, sensual woman who unfortunately has no
sympathy with his yearning for culture. George continues to believe that to be deprived of Lettie is to be deprived of order in his
life, even though, as he meets her on increasingly equal terms
toward the end of the book, he shows himself both intellectually

and vitally superior to her husband. The more clearly he seems to recognize a real affinity with Lettie, the more gloomy he becomes, until finally he stops seeing her. Lettie in turn submits to the demands of family and class, escaping from her desire for George by skillfully dominating her husband and losing herself in her children. George makes money but finds this unsatisfactory as well. He takes up socialism, but with Lettie's help he comes to see through the limitations of socialist preaching. Still convinced of his incompleteness, he finally becomes an alcoholic, tormenting his wife and children until alcoholic poisoning reduces him to a wretched shell waiting in despair for death. Here the book ends.

Through all this George reveals a deficiency of will.[3] The natural vitality with which he is endowed and which his connections with the land help convey does not, apparently, extend to forceful and purposive action. His self-consciousness about his inferior mental agility, which allows Lettie and others to mock him at will, keeps him from mastering her as she seems to need to be mastered. The best he can do is to overwhelm her physically, as he does in a powerful scene of dancing.

> George continued the dance; her hair was shaken loose, and fell in a great coil down her back; her feet began to drag; you could hear light slur on the floor; she was panting—I could see her lips murmur to him, begging him to stop; he was laughing with open mouth, holding her tight; at last her feet trailed; he lifted her,

3. Julian Moynahan (*The Deed of Life* [Princeton, 1962], p. 11) explains this deficiency as a dissociation of values between the sexes.

Life is blighted because men and women, and the values Lawrence assigns to each sex, have been driven far apart and have no way of getting together again. The woman's value is order and form. It is associated with the home and the town. The man's value is sheer energy and animal vigor and is associated with the woodland and the farm. Women need men to invigorate and fructify the social and ethical orders they create. Men need women in order to channelize their turbulent and anarchic energies. Unfulfilled by man, woman becomes the white peacock, "all vanity and screech and defilement." Unfulfilled by woman, man gives way to the antisocial destructiveness of an Annable or the self-destructive, shapeless emotional vagaries of drunkenness.

clasping her tightly, and danced twice round the room with her
thus. Then he fell with a crash on the sofa, pulling her beside
him. His eyes glowed like coals; he was panting in sobs, and his
hair was wet and glistening. She lay back on the sofa, with his
arm still around her, not moving; she was quite anxious; the
father said, with a shade of inquietude:
"You've overdone it—it is very foolish." [p. 95]

But by the end of the book we can only wish that George had
overdone it more often. In this instance, after "laughing in a
queer way," Lettie recovers her composure. " 'You great brute,'
she said, but her voice was not as harsh as her words." Clearly she
enjoys being overwhelmed, and George's physical domination
here seems to be a model for more thoroughly sexual triumphs.
But Lettie is not to be won easily, and she discomfits him by
forcing him to display his clumsiness in a minuet. Her easy victory in the dance is typical of her victories throughout the book:
she capitalizes upon her superior sophistication and makes George
feel an inadequate bumpkin. And although George goes so far as
to surprise her by mastering sophisticated dances, he never manages to escape the feelings of inferiority which she has apparently
foisted upon him.

But this explanation does not go far enough. Not only does
Lettie make George feel inferior, but she also seems to reveal a
mysterious deficiency which was there from the first. None of the
obstacles she presents to him seem insurmountable, especially in
the face of his real successes in business, which reflect ability of
the type Lettie apparently admires. Nor is George insensitive; he
responds quickly and deeply to art, he enjoys intellectual discussion, and he even confesses in his cups to wanting to be a poet.
But when confronted with Lettie and her world he seems to
collapse, as if she had some mysterious power which he cannot
fathom. His own account of his failure is rather pitiful:

"You see, it's not so much what you call love. I don't know.
You see, I built on Lettie"—he looked up at me shamefacedly,
then continued tearing the shavings—"you must found your

castles on something, and I founded mine on Lettie. You see, I'm like plenty of folks, I have nothing definite to shape my life to. I put brick upon brick, as they come, and if the whole topples down in the end, it does. But you see, you and Lettie have made me conscious, and now I'm at a dead loss." [p. 235]

It is precisely this awakening to consciousness which has ambiguous value. If on the one hand George's natural vitality seems to lead toward it, on the other his quest for a more complete order somehow entails losing that vitality or letting it come to naught. If it is an intellectual or cultural order that he seeks, it is not clear that Lettie does not actually give it to him, for they become increasingly like-minded as the book progresses. Nor must George go without sexual satisfaction, for his wife seems eminently capable of providing that. What he does not get is real "possession" of Lettie, which would mean having both mind and body served by the same woman. This, perhaps, is the sort of order he seeks; if it is, the book makes it quite clear that neither George nor anyone else can attain it. It is difficult to resist asking why not, and it is this question that Lawrence does not seem able to answer.

George's failure seems, then, to involve more than an inadequate will. It is a symptom of a fundamental division in the book between the natural and the cultural, the objective power of nature and the personal power of man. Both George and Lettie attempt to integrate these forces, and both fail—George because he cannot use the former to inform or make meaningful the latter, and Lettie because she egotistically reduces her vitality to her feminine will. But in neither failure is a clear ideal implied. Of the two Lettie is the more self-sufficient, but she is also the more deliberately self-denying; George, on the other hand, seems more open to growth and change but less capable of using his flexibility. And although it is clear that each needs the other, it is not clear that a successful marriage would ever have been possible between them. We are impressed that some mysterious barrier would probably intervene, but, like George, we cannot tell what this barrier is.

The division in the book which this mysterious barrier represents can be made clearer by an examination of some of the attitudes of Lawrence's narrator, Cyril. His descriptions of nature are not all equally successful, and their failures indicate the same sort of breach between the natural and the personal that causes both George and Lettie trouble. They also provide evidence for Hough's suggestion that the natural is indeed a more fundamental value for Lawrence than the social world of character and culture.

If we look back for a moment at the first mowing scene, with its emphasis upon George's rhythm and power, Lettie's response seems telling: " 'You are picturesque,' she said, a trifle awkwardly, 'quite fit for an idyll.' " This is an inaccurate and inadequate way to characterize the quality of George's mowing; it is at once too self-conscious and too literary. Lettie, of course, is awkward because she does not quite know how to deal with her sexual response; her language is an attempt to hide it. But the frequent use of such language throughout the book cannot always be explained psychologically. Cyril is repeatedly falling into it, even after he embarks on fundamentally objective descriptions of nature, in which the book abounds. A look at one or two of these lapses should make clearer the pervasiveness of Lawrence's difficulty.

Here is Cyril recording a quick trip home through the countryside:

> I ran over the little bright brook that came from the weedy, bottom pond. The stepping-stones were white in the sun, and the water slid sleepily among them. One or two butterflies, indistinguishable against the blue sky, trifled from flower to flower and led me up the hill, across the field where the hot sunshine stood as in a bowl, and I was entering the caverns of the wood, where the oaks bowed over and saved us a grateful shade. Within, everything was so still and cool that my steps hung heavily along the path. [p. 6]

This is not startlingly good, but it is surely successful evocative writing. It is perhaps the most characteristic mode in which nature appears throughout the book, and its effectiveness implies an attitude which Lawrence values. Even though Cyril is describing his own movements the focus remains upon nature. not on Cyril. Yet a personal element is present, for nature is subtly personified. Water is sleepy, butterflies trifle (a particularly effective verb here), oaks bow and save. A touch of brilliance is evident in the sunshine standing as in a bowl; the image is not only strikingly apt, but it carries an intensity which teases analysis—perhaps because of its ability to capture the idea of light and suggest its condensation as a liquid.

In such a passage nature remains consistently in focus and is personified unobtrusively; we do not perceive it as a mere projection of the observer. Its success is due to the suggestions of latent possibility and meaning which these personifications carry. Unfortunately Cyril lets these possibilities become too explicit, completely changing the mood and also weakening the force of his description.

> The bracken held out arms to me, and the bosom of the wood was full of sweetness, but I journeyed on, spurred by the attacks of an army of flies which kept up a guerrilla warfare round my head till I had passed the black rhododendron bushes in the garden, where they left me, scenting no doubt Rebecca's pots of vinegar and sugar. [p. 6]

Like Lettie's response to George's mowing, this is self-consciously literary and, what is worse, self-consciously clever. In transforming the bracken into a siren the narrator makes himself an object of attention; nature becomes so openly personified as to imply a little drama, in which the narrator delightedly takes part. He also commands the attention of a guerrilla army, keeping himself in focus through an image that seems not only excessive but inappropriate. (Do flies strike swiftly from hiding, taking cunning advantage of cover?) In short, the narrator's involvement destroys the consistent narrative distance.

Cyril's lapse is of course common to narrators who are too conscious of their education or literary status, and it would be easy to dismiss it as simply the clumsiness of a young writer. But it may also be part of the fundamental difficulty implied by George's failure. Not only George but Cyril—and, since he gives no indication of realizing that this is bad writing, Lawrence—seems uncertain about the value of culture. Cyril is consistently at his weakest when he becomes involved in the sort of cleverness which implies that he has had experience with literature, that he knows a witty analogy when he sees one and can use it skillfully to color his writing. The fact is that he does not and cannot; he only draws attention to himself, without impressing us of the force or coherence of his presence. Nor does Lawrence in his later work master or even attempt to master the literary habits which Cyril cannot successfully employ. It soon becomes evident that such devices are for Lawrence false lights, representing values which he never accepted but which nevertheless tempted a young man not yet sure of his own path.

The success of the less literary mode of describing nature points in a more promising direction. As we shall see in later chapters, Lawrence continued to use and to attach increasingly more meaning to such descriptions. Even in this book they comprise the prevalent mode, and their success points toward Lawrence's later insistence on nature as a separate but vital presence. In *The White Peacock* no such clear insistence emerges, but the attitude which led to it certainly does. Perhaps another example will make this clearer:

The mare took her own way, and Meg's hat was disarranged once more by the sweeping elm-boughs. The yellow corn was dipping and flowing in the fields, like a cloth of gold pegged down at the corners under which the wind was heaving. Sometimes we passed cottages where the scarlet lilies rose like bonfires, and the tall larkspur like bright blue leaping smoke. Sometimes we smelled the sunshine on the browning corn, sometimes the fragrance of the shadow of leaves. Occasionally it was the dizzy scent of new haystack. Then we rocked and jolted over the rough cobblestones of Cinderhill, and bounded forward again at the foot of the enormous pit hill, smelling of sulphur, inflamed with slow red fires in the daylight, and crusted with ashes. [p. 240]

This passage is extraordinarily effective, and it uses only a minimum of personification. A sense of throbbing vitality is created instead by a series of metaphors which emphasize energy and movement. Elm boughs sweep (the only noticeable hint of personification), corn flows like a cloth pegged down but blown (again the visual aptness adds to the effectiveness), lilies are fires, the larkspur is smoke. Nature is presented as a feast for the senses, to which the rest of the passage adds smell and, depending upon individual preference, either touch or kinesthetic movement or both (the jolting over cobblestones).

What is important about both this passage and the earlier one is that literary success goes hand in hand with personal distance. There is no merging of observer and object, nor is there a simple response to nature's vitality, though vitality is surely present. Rather, nature seems to be sensed as a distinct presence which gives form and occasion to the observer's need for experience. The observer is susceptible to sensuous response, but he needs to objectify it; nature provides both the cause for such response and the material for making it coherent. The coherence can reside in any metaphorical device which suggests meaning or simply in consistency of sensuous adjectives. It fails when apprehension of the natural object yields to a literary comparison which itself demands attention. Subtle personification and vital metaphors provide means for expressing or implying a common ground, a connection between nature and observer which is real and important but does not approach identity. Too elaborate personification endows nature with a personal presence which the reader resists and which becomes an unpleasant form of pathetic fallacy. Sensuous imagery, on the other hand, implies nature as giver and observer as receiver, and even gratitude might be read into the relish apparent in the observer's persistence in noticing sensuous detail.

The uncertainty which is present in this stylistic lapse also appears in attempts by Lawrence and his characters to see larger meanings in nature. The yearnings which result from George's awakening into consciousness emerge as painful gaps in self-knowledge and seek both expression and fulfillment in natural forces. At an early stage in his final decline, George writes in a pathetic letter to Cyril: "Yesterday I watched broken white masses of cloud sailing across the sky in a fresh strong wind. They all seemed to be going somewhere. I wondered where the wind was blowing them. I don't seem to have hold on anything, do I? Can you tell me what I want at the bottom of my heart?" (p. 260). George's tendency to find in the movement of clouds a purpose which he lacks himself is consistent with his earlier "connections" with natural forces; it is also a fitting expression of his increasingly despondent state of mind. But it is questionable whether the sort of meaning he seems to see in nature is in fact there: is this a tendency in Lawrence to see in nature a coherence which man lacks, or is it simply an expression of George's mysterious inadequacy? In a scene of similar observation Cyril, always more articulate than George, points toward the former alternative by significantly emphasizing a natural order or purpose seemingly inaccessible to man:

> Across the infinite skies of March great rounded masses of cloud had sailed stately all day, domed with white radiance, softened with faint, fleeting shadows as if companies of angels were gently sweeping past; adorned with resting, silken shadows likes *[sic]* those of a full white breast. All day the clouds had moved on to their vast destination, and I had clung to the earth yearning and impatient. I took a brush and tried to paint them, then I raged at myself. I wished that in all the wild valley where cloud shadows were travelling like pilgrims, something would call me forth from my rooted loneliness. [p. 126]

This certainly emphasizes a meaning in nature from which the observer is dissociated. But once again there are stylistic difficulties which suggest that the loneliness of the narrator is the author's as well. The clouds are angels who sail in radiance to a vast destination, but there is nothing in the book to support either the angels or destination. If we take the balanced and impersonal mode examined above as a norm, this passage represents another movement toward pathetic fallacy, only here there is a yearning for a cosmic rather than a merely literary or personal order. If such a yearning could be accounted for by an analysis of the narrator's personality, it could not, of course, be used as evidence of Lawrence's uncertainty about man's relation to nature. But, as it turns out, Cyril's personality is the vaguest in the book.[4] His persistent loneliness is never explained, psychologically or otherwise. And although he strongly criticizes George for not being more forceful with Lettie, Cyril is totally and mysteriously inconclusive in his attitude toward Emily, whom he clearly might have married and who, as we shall see shortly, makes the only happy marriage in the book.

The mysterious disability of both George and Cyril, then, entails a vague yearning toward nature as an embodiment of a purpose or order which they themselves lack. In his failure to provide an explanation either in terms of these characters' personal problems or through nature itself, Lawrence himself is implicated in this yearning. The stylistic difficulties which appear in his expressions of it are evidence that he is groping for some principle of coherence. On the one hand, nature is firmly associated with an elementary sort of meaning, bound to the senses and vital; on the other hand, both Cyril and George look to this meaning for a larger order which does not seem to be there. Their yearnings are expressions of the mysterious ineffectuality which haunts them and which seems to have cultural associations, not only in George's aspirations but in everything we know about Cyril. For Cyril, too, seems to have had an awakening to consciousness which has crippled rather than enlarged him. He is characterized as George's "educator," but all he can do with his own education

4. Lawrence's letters reveal a growing dissatisfaction with Cyril, from a refusal to analyze him "as a *personnage*" to a vow to "stop his mouth." See *LM*, p. 25.

is disappear into France, leaving the "natural" home of his youth
for no evident reason and indulging, we assume, in intellectual
activity which only amounts to articulation of the melancholy
yearning we notice when he returns home. In fact, all Lawrence's
major characters are beset by a tendency to make melancholy
pronouncements about life and fate. Hidden in the gloom which
they generate are at least three possibilities about the ultimate
meaning these characters seem to seek in nature: it may be there
but somehow lost; it may not be there at all; or it may be there
and negative, as it often is in Hardy.

The second possibility may be readily dismissed;[5] the first and
third must be taken more seriously, especially the first. The
strong positive response to natural vitality which pervades the
book often verges on more comprehensive meanings, behind
which lies an attitude of reverence that George recognizes is lost
in tavern-keeping and horse-trading. But, as in the following passage, it is sometimes difficult to distinguish reverence from senti-
mentality:

> Below, in the first shadows, drooped hosts of little white flow-
> ers, so silent and sad; it seemed like a holy communion of pure
> wild things, numberless, frail, and folded meekly in the evening
> light. Other flower companies are glad; stately barbaric hordes
> of bluebells, merry-headed cowslip groups, even light, tossing
> wood-anemones; but snowdrops are sad and mysterious. We
> have lost their meaning. They do not belong to us, who ravish
> them. [p. 128]

The ravishing of nature later becomes much more distasteful to
Lawrence than he indicates here, where an indefinite longing and
fear are all that emerge.

> "Look at all the snowdrops"—they hung in dim, strange flecks
> among the dusky leaves—"look at them—closed up, retreating,

5. See p. 263, where Cyril, returning to Nethermere after his first absence, finds "the old symbols . . . trite and foolish." This is as close as
Lawrence comes to asserting that nature is meaningless.

powerless. They belong to some knowledge we have lost, that I have lost and that I need. I feel afraid. They seem like something in fate. Do you think, Cyril, we can lose things off the earth—like mastodons, and those old monstrosities—but things that matter—wisdom?"

"It is against my creed," said I.

"I believe we have lost something," said she. [p. 129]

Nowhere are we given Cyril's creed, for it is not yet formulated. In later books both the "holy communion" and the hatred of "ravishing" become integral parts of Lawrence's commitment to his own vitalistic religion. Here the issues drift away under the rubric of fate, slightly beclouded by an adolescent yearning which again prompts Lawrence to use personification in an obtrusive manner.

The formulations of fate which appear frequently throughout the book sometimes extend toward more inclusively negative attitudes. Here is Cyril, after a lush passage in which the earth is soothing, reassuring, "our . . . sympathy and hope":

A corn-crake talked to me across the valley, talked and talked endlessly, asking and answering in hoarse tones from the sleeping, mist-hidden meadows. The monotonous voice, that on past summer evenings had had pleasant notes of romance, now was intolerable to me. Its inflexible harshness and cacophony seemed like the voice of fate speaking out its tuneless perseverance in the night. [p. 194]

This note of "harshness and cacophony" repeatedly creeps into the book. Lettie, for example, realizing that her life is too cozy and meaningless, "clamours to be out in the black, keen storm" (p. 287). In describing George's honeymoon trip to the theatre to see *Carmen*, Lawrence uses this storm image to account for something essential about life: "The theatre surged and roared dimly like a hoarse shell. Then the music rose like a storm, and swept and rattled at their feet. On the stage the strange storm of life clashed in music towards tragedy and futile death" (p. 246). And

Cyril's response to a socialist speaker indicates another apprehension of gloom: "I felt a great terror of the little man, lest he should make me see all mud, as I had seen before. Then I felt a breathless pity for him, that his eyes should be always filled with mud, and never brightened" (p. 278).

But none of this amounts to anything like Hardy's persistent and relentless fate, which inexorably follows his characters to their unfortunate ends. Cyril's terror, in fact, is clearly meant as a rejection of any view that sees only evil or that, like Hardy's, insists upon a nature at best indifferent and at worst apparently malevolent. What Lawrence seizes upon in Hardy are the moments of vital response to nature; but, unlike Hardy, he does not reveal them as delusions or pastoral enticements which men foolishly pursue. In *The White Peacock* these gloomy notes about fate and life mainly reflect a groping toward an attitude which can accept natural meaning without reducing it to any of its pretty or sentimentally pastoral forms, an attitude which implies a search for coherent relations instead of tragic or alienated postures.

The state of Lawrence's philosophy at this time is summarized in a letter he wrote before beginning his final draft of *The White Peacock:*

I think there is a great purpose which keeps the menagerie moving onward to better places, while the animals snap and rattle by the way. So I laugh when I see their grimaces, if these do not hinder the march. I am sure I can help the march if I like. It is a valuable assurance.

But the folks who see the funny side of things suffer horribly at times from loneliness. It is a sad thing to be the only spectator at a farce. So religion is a most comforting companion; it's absolutely necessary to many who would drop and never recover without it; then love is next precious, love of man for a woman; one should feel in it the force that keeps the menagerie on the move . . . lastly, a passionate attachment to some work which will help the procession somehow is a safety against the loneliness . . .

You will see from what it pleases me to call my "philosophy," that I have still some religion left; I would give a great deal to fall in love; meanwhile, I keep up my confidence, writing this, that, and the other cultivating my soul, sure that it can give good help sometime to the march of the procession. [*LM*, p. 16]

This discussion of the great purpose exhibits the same vague uncertainty apparent in the novel. The hierarchy of values (religion, love, work) does not greatly change in later life, but love and work are increasingly defined by a new religion.

The other half of *The White Peacock*, in which the cultural values are central, is also best regarded as part of a search for coherence. In it Lawrence displays an interest in things social which is in some ways unique in his career but which is not of the greatest importance in his later development as a novelist. More important is a cluster of values which revolve around the figure of woman, values which have to do with education, morality, and motherhood—in general, the values of civilization rather than nature. All except perhaps those which are part of a traditional Protestant ethic express to one degree or another uncertainties similar to those we have been examining.[6]

6. Graham Hough sums up the general relation of "traditional European ethics" to the emphasis on the "natural":

From the point of view of traditional European ethics, his later answers were to be highly eccentric, but there is no hint of this in *The White Peacock*. Where George fails, for instance, he fails not only by the Laurentian code but also by a quite central and normal moral code: he hides his light under a bushel; his will refuses to accept the responsibilities of consciousness. The same is true, less markedly, of Cyril. Lawrence is not for the most part thinking in traditional moral terms but so far his presentation has nothing repugnant to them. [*The Dark Sun*, p. 32]

Although I attempt to pursue the hints of eccentricity a bit further than Hough does, this formulation seems generally adequate. It is not until his fourth book that Lawrence shows strong signs of attacking the usual Christian ethic, and the difficulties connected with replacing those parts of it which he finally rejected continue throughout his life.

Cyril's descriptions of the most sophisticated people in the book display an uncertainty similar to that which we examined in his descriptions of nature, and for much the same reasons. Only the scenes of natural description are on the whole successful, although occasionally or sporadically marred by self-conscious cleverness. Virtually all the gatherings at which sophisticated banter appears are weak, and the weakness cannot be accounted for by claiming that Cyril considers all educated people silly and shallow. Certainly we are meant to regard these conversations as shallow; they take place at parties and social gatherings, and we should not in any case expect profundity. But they go on a good deal longer than we like, and here literary references proceed unchecked. Freddie Cresswell, the best man at Lettie's wedding, is described as possessing "a drawling manner of speech, like a man who has suffered enough to bring him to manhood and maturity, but who in spite of all remains a boy, irresponsible, lovable—a trifle pathetic" (p. 225). This is not an unsympathetic view of Freddie, but Freddie's talk soon cuts off sympathy:

"Lord, a giddy little pastoral—fit for old Theocritus, ain't it, Miss Denys?"

"Why do you talk to me about those classic people—I daren't even say their names. What would he say about us?"

He laughed, winking his blue eyes:

"He'd make old Daphnis there"—pointing to Leslie—"sing a match with me, Damoetas—contesting the merits of our various shepherdesses—begin Daphnis, sing up for Amaryllis, I mean Nais, damn 'em, they were for ever getting mixed up with their nymphs."

"I say, Mr. Cresswell, your language! Consider whom you're damning," said Miss Denys, leaning over and tapping his head with her silk glove. [p. 226]

The dialogue goes on for quite a while, and Cyril's later remark that it is "whimsical affectation of vulgarity which flickered with fantasy" does not make it less painful to read. The book would

hardly have suffered for omitting this and most of the other
social scenes, for they seldom make thematic points which are
not better made in more intimate gatherings, and they almost
never reveal something important about the major characters,
being inhabited mainly by minor ones. The length and frequency
of dialogues like this one, together with Cyril's generally con-
descending attitude toward them, imply that Lawrence considered these social creatures foolish but clever. He must have at
least thought them entertaining, or he would not have put them
in. By doing so he reveals a rather adolescent yearning for high
life as well as a distrust of it—in short, an ambivalence toward
even the more trivial forms of social activity. As Lawrence's
career continues this distrust becomes more definite and acquires
ideological underpinning. Not until *Women in Love* do we again
meet people with aristocratic and university associations, and
then Lawrence clearly knows how to handle them. He makes
most of them objects for satire.

If these people and the awkwardness with which they are portrayed are of minor significance, the type of ambivalence they
seem to represent is not. It seems, in fact, to govern or at least
influence the whole portrayal of Lettie, who is the only figure of
social pretensions likely to impress the reader. Although Lettie,
like George, has in her childhood many vital connections with
nature, she very soon begins to theorize about her superiority to
him. In the following passage, for example, she criticizes him for
not responding with sufficient intensity both to sunsets and to
paintings of sunsets:

You are blind; you are only half-born; you are gross with good
living and heavy sleeping. . . . Sunset is nothing to you—it merely happens anywhere. Oh, but you make me feel as if I'd like to
make you suffer. . . . You never grow up, like bulbs which
spend all summer getting fat and fleshy, but never wakening the
germ of a flower. As for me, the flower is born in me, but it
wants bringing forth. Things don't flower if they're overfed.
You have to suffer before you blossom in this life. When death

is just touching a plant, it forces it into a passion of flowering.
[p. 27]

Lettie, who has reason to think she has overdone it, passes this
off as meaningless, it has too much predictive power to be dismissed. Apparently the natural vitality which George already possesses needs aesthetic awakening. Lettie attempts such an awakening, causes George (and herself) pain, and in the process leaves us
asking questions for which Lawrence provides no satisfactory answers.

Lettie's outburst implies that culture becomes a discipline for
broadening the soul, that aesthetic and intellectual endeavors lead
to a fuller life, superior in every way to George's natural sluggish-
ness or Annable's natural brutality. Although these are of course
traditional ideas, the particular force they have here, with the
more than metaphorical implication that a continuum exists between a fundamental natural vitality and the "highest" forms of
civilization, is unique in Lawrence's career. In his later works the
possibility of such a continuum soon ceases to be active; it is
replaced by the insistence that civilization's forms are no longer
capable of receiving life, or in more fervent moments by the
conviction that such forms actively produce death. But in this
book the possibility distinctly remains. Lettie's career is not
viewed entirely as a decline; her refinements on natural vitality
have an impressiveness which seems to carry out at least some of
the implications of her own analysis.

Lettie's wish to blossom is at least partially fulfilled. In doing so
she becomes more cultured than before and even takes on splendor.

Lettie stood between the firelight and the dusky lamp glow, tall
and warm between the lights. As she turned laughing to the two
men, she let her cloak slide over her white shoulder and fall
with silk splendour of a peacock's gorgeous blue over the arm
of the large settee. There she stood, with her white hand upon
the peacock of her cloak, where it tumbled against her dull
orange dress. She knew her own splendour, and she drew up her

throat laughing and brilliant with triumph. Then she raised both her arms to her head and remained for a moment delicately touching her hair into order, still fronting the two men. Then with a final little laugh she moved slowly and turned up the lamp, dispelling some of the witchcraft from the room. She had developed strangely in six months. She seemed to have discovered the wonderful charm of her womanhood.[pp. 251-52]

The reference to the peacock recalls the symbolic scene after which the book is named, when Annable compares a defecating peacock perched on a funerary angel's head (this sounds heavy-handed, and it is) to a woman, "all vanity and screech and defilement (p. 148)." Cyril manages to tone down the indictment by adding, in response to Annable's admission that his failure in marriage might not be entirely the woman's fault, the attribute of whiteness. The scene quoted above can be related in at least two ways to the earlier one. Lettie, who we know by now is not fulfilled, may be falling into a state of "vanity and screech and defilement" herself, and the references to the peacock may be meant to convey just that.[7] Or, as Cyril feels, the whiteness may indeed be redeeming. George Ford has in fact suggested that whiteness is "an evaluative test of [Lettie's] character"; for Ford, Lettie is "distinctly not evil."[8]

The passage clearly provides evidence for both views. Certainly Lettie is not evil, yet she is vain. Her whiteness is not an indication of moral purity but a reference to a form of sterility, or, if that word seems too strong, at least to a lack of commitment. The narrator later informs us that Lettie takes on "an ironical brutality" which, though "at bottom . . . quite sincere," leads to a "peculiar abnegation of self . . . the resource of a woman for the escaping of the responsibilities of her own life" (p. 280). This abnegation amounts to burying herself in her home and children

7. Moynahan, *Deed of Life,* p. 11.
8. George Ford, *Double Measure* (New York, 1965), p. 55. See also William A. Fahey, "Lawrence's *White Peacock,*" *Explicator* 17 (1958), item 17.

without giving up her domination of her husband. In the passage just quoted not even this much self-denial is present. Lettie is deliberately using the "charm of her womanhood" to maintain control over the two men. She obviously takes pleasure in her beauty, which is aesthetically arranged and manipulated to the greatest effect, to "triumph" over the men. The tone of the description is admiring but not uncritical; in the scene that follows Lettie directs her husband to kneel before her and rub her feet, and she rewards him with a "dear boy" and a touch on the cheek. George is immensely impressed by her sophistication; she sounds "wonderful in her culture and facility."

The attitude of the narrator in these passages cannot quite be explained by assuming that Lettie's natural vitality gains his admiration while her cultural attainments are consistently the target of his criticism. He is surely ambivalent about these attainments themselves. The description we have just examined implies that Lettie's natural beauty and even her womanhood have been heightened by her sophistication, even though that same sophistication tends to foster self-satisfaction, vanity, and unseemly domination of the male. Lawrence is uncertain about the attainments of "consciousness" itself.

This uncertainty crops up at regular intervals throughout his early novels, and it is taken up as well in his essays, many of which treat the problem of consciousness directly. Most of his later efforts at defining this idea strive to divorce it altogether from the culture with which it is here associated, but it may be argued that the divorce is never complete.[9] Here another complication emerges: the possessors of both culture and consciousness are mainly women, and women seem already to possess too many advantages.

Lawrence is even more openly and obviously ambivalent about Lettie's self-abnegation through devotion to her children. We have already noticed that the narrator regards this as an escape from the "responsibility for her own life." Lettie herself occasionally

9. I discuss this in detail later. See especially the section in chap. 5 on the *Study of Thomas Hardy*.

sees it as worse than that: "She was very contradictory. At times she would write to me in terms of passionate dissatisfaction: she had nothing at all in her life, it was a barren futility" (p. 287). And Cyril can get rather acid about it.

Like so many women, she seemed to live, for the most part contentedly, a small indoor existence with artificial light and padded upholstery. Only occasionally, hearing the winds of life outside, she clamoured to be out in the black, keen storm. She was driven to the door, she looked out and called into the tumult wildly, but feminine caution kept her from stepping over the threshold. [p. 287]

If the winds of life had achieved impressive substance throughout the development of the book, we might accept this as a Nietzschean pronouncement about an unfortunately safe existence and leave it at that. But the winds of life are not just unsatisfactorily vague; at times Cyril gives evidence of an entirely different attitude toward domestic life:

The baby turned with sudden coy shyness, and clung to her mother's neck. Meg kissed her fondly, then the child laid her cheek against her mother's. The mother's dark eyes, and the baby's large, hazel eyes looked at me serenely. The two were very calm, very complete and triumphant together. In their completeness was a security which made me feel alone and ineffectual. A woman who has her child in her arms is a tower of strength, a beautiful unassailable tower of strength that may in its turn stand quietly dealing with death. [pp. 288-89]

Both Lettie in her splendor and Meg with her child are triumphant; and in this passage Meg, at least, receives unqualified admiration. This admiration is more than evidence of Cyril's insecurity. In this book women have most of the advantages: they are culturally and intellectually superior, they are beautiful, they have strength of will, and they can stand up even to death in their role as mothers. All this begins to take toll on the less effectual males. Cyril finally bursts out in petulance:

A woman is so ready to disclaim the body of a man's love; she yields him her own soft beauty with so much gentle patience and regret; she clings to his neck, to his head and his cheeks, fondling them for the soul's meaning that is there, and shrinking from his passionate limbs and his body. It was with some perplexity, some anger and bitterness that I watched Emily moved almost to ecstasy by the baby's small, innocuous person.

Cyril feels not only neglected but envious.[10] And there is nothing to indicate that Lawrence does not share at least some of this envy, for the men have nothing to match this female power. Cyril cannot seem to choose between the roles of lover and child; he accepts neither and flees instead into his artist's isolation in France. I think we may take this flight as evidence of a lack of resolution on Lawrence's part between not only the spontaneous man and the cultured woman but man-child and woman-mother. This trouble with women takes an even more disastrous toll on the male protagonist in *The Trespasser,* and though Lawrence comes to various resolutions of these sets of value in the three books which follow, his heroes always illustrate intellectuality and masculinity in some form of conflict. The women always threaten to become mothers and falsely possess the men. Throughout his books he is concerned with defining the degree and significance of passion and sensuality, their relation to masculine domination and feminine submission (or vice versa, which consistently tends to have unfortunate consequences), and their ontological significance. He also analyzed history according to

10. While Lawrence was a teacher at Croydon he wrote some poems inspired by his landlady's baby which indicate strong sympathy for the mother's delight in fondling her child. The following passage from "Baby Songs Ten Months Old" comes especially close to Emily's raptures:

I can just see the nape of her white little neck—
My pale, wet butterfly, fluffy chicken.
The rest is a cloud of thistle down.
Soft, tickling brown. [*The Complete Poems of D. H. Lawrence* ed. Vivian de Sola Pinto and Warren Roberts, 2 vols. (New York, 1964), 2:863]

masculine and feminine principles [11] and wrote essays on the raising of children (though he had none himself).[12] This concern obviously has its literary beginnings in *The White Peacock.*

In the book the most pervasive (if not the most effective) evidence that some conflict involving masculinity is important is the feminine nature of the cultured narrator himself. This is a difficulty of which Lawrence was at least superficially aware, for he makes sporadic attempts to achieve ironic distance by allowing one of the minor female figures to call Cyril "Sybil" or "Pat" throughout the book. Cyril's most passionate sexual experience moreover, is homosexual, a rubbing of his naked body against that of the virile and beautiful George. We might even theorize that Cyril's loneliness is a function of his sensitivity to both sexes, which he cannot resolve by choosing one. But the value of this theory would be very limited, for the theme of loneliness, with its tendency to dissolve into an unspecified gloom about life, is too pervasive to be accounted for by sexual ambivalence. It seems to me both dangerously speculative and largely irrelevant, moreover, to deduce from this evidence that Lawrence himself was unable to face up to homosexual propensities and that this lies at the bottom of all his literary difficulties, as some critics have come close to doing.[13] Whatever Lawrence's personal sexual difficulties may have been, it seems highly doubtful that they will provide an adequate interpretation of his writing, for the values operating in his work are not reducible to formulations of sexual conflict.[14] What *The White Peacock* does allow us to say is simply that the cultural and social are strongly associated with the feminine, and

11. See the *Study of Thomas Hardy,* pp. 454-76; also the section on this book in chap. 5 below.

12. See "The Education of the People," in *Phoenix;* also *Psychoanalysis and the Unconscious,* and *Fantasia of the Unconscious.*

13. Notably John Middleton Murry in *Son of Woman* (London, 1931).

14. H. M. Daleski, in his *The Forked Flame* (Evanston, 1965), presents the best case so far for relating the two. But even though his basic approach is derived from the masculine and feminine principles of the *Study of Thomas Hardy,* neither he nor Lawrence limits himself to merely sexual meanings. What Daleski convincingly shows is that sexual meanings are intimately involved in the pattern of Lawrence's intellectual development

the vital and unconscious with the masculine, with the notable
exception that motherhood provides a direct access to vitality
which even nature cannot fully match. The men are left only with
failure in self-destruction (George), intellectual escape (Cyril),
and unquestioning service (Leslie, Lettie's husband).

It is convenient to summarize some of these problems as a series
of oppositions. Women have strength of will, men do not; its
absence in men leads to ineffectuality or self-destruction, whereas
its presence in women seems to imply egotism and excessive domination. Women have artistic sensitivity, men do not; men seem to
need awakening to the aesthetic, but women are in danger of
turning these propensities into a life-denying ornamentalism.
Both men and women can possess natural vitality, but women can
replace this with an equally natural maternity once childhood
connections with the land are lost, while men are largely set adrift
at the loss of these connections. Through all this is the persistent
implication that men need women for both sexual and intellectual completion, but these needs in women are, if present, less
intense. And there also persists an implication that coming to
consciousness, which seems to have strong aesthetic and cultural
associations, is necessary for completion, but that at some point
this process can (and in this book does) go wrong and descend
into artificiality and social silliness. The relation of this unfortunately vague "coming to consciousness" to "being" (fully capturing life) is never explored, but there are at least hints that the
two are related.

Most of Lawrence's later work is full of these oppositions. If
they indicate a fundamental dichotomy opposing the natural
male to the cultural female, such a dichotomy inadequately describes the weight given to the various values which appear or
even the way these values tend to be divided.[15] And it is only
slightly helpful to reduce all these oppositions to a groping

and that his novels may be analyzed according to this pattern. If sexual
meanings are fundamental, they are certainly not exhaustive.

15. Later, in fact, heavy emphasis is placed on female-natural, male-cul-
tural. See the section on the *Study of Thomas Hardy* in chap. 5 below.

toward a conception of the complete self, since they involve much more than a search for identity. I would prefer to regard them as elements in a larger search for coherence, in which man's nature comes to have a fundamental relation to his activities and to the natural world as well. But before we proceed to the next novel, where Lawrence makes a strikingly different sort of attempt to achieve this coherence, there is something approaching a resolution in this book which deserves attention.

There is one notably successful, unblighted marriage in the book, made by Cyril's old sweetheart Emily. Like Cyril, she has remained until the end of the book ineffectual and unimpressive in her sexual relations. Judging from her change in marriage, the trouble has been with Cyril and not with Emily.

> Emily, in her full-blooded beauty, was at home. It is rare now to feel a kinship between a room and the one who inhabits it, a close bond of blood relation. Emily had at last found her place, and had escaped from the torture of strange, complex modern life. She was making a pie, and the flour was white on her brown arms. She pushed the tickling hair from her face with her arm, and looked at me with tranquil pleasure, as she worked the paste in the yellow bowl. I was quiet, subdued before her.
> "You are very happy?" I said.
> "Ah, very!" she replied. [p. 316]

As one might guess from her escape from strange, complex modern life, Emily has married a farmer, who seems in every respect an ideal pastoral partner. Even though Cyril finds him too submissive, the portrayal of the marriage is convincing. There is no sense of an unfortunate herd-like existence attached to it, nor does one feel that Tom is the fleshy unflowering bulb which Lettie accused George of being. And in describing the marriage, Lawrence uses several of his favorite devices for portraying valuable relations. Emily's kinship with the room later becomes an argument for the fundamental ontological connection between man and even the inanimate object.[16] And Tom speaks dialect to his family but "good English" to Emily, foreshadowing the ability of Lady Chatterley's lover to express tenderness as well as to function with competence in more intellectual circles (abilities which Annable could not manage together, though he possessed them apart).

What seems to have happened is that, in the face of all the disaster he has wrought (with George in his most pitiful state), Lawrence, unable as yet to resolve the questions he has raised, reverts with grudging but real sympathy to a natural solution. This is not, of course, surprising, in view of the continued sympathy to nature evident throughout the book. He has also momentarily resolved the petulance about the power of maternity, for part of Emily's contentment lies in the fact that she is pregnant. Even though this cannot constitute a thematic resolution and Cyril must remind us that it is an escape, it is presented as a real alternative to the problems with which Cyril and the others have been struggling and cannot be compared with Lettie's similar escape from self-responsibility. Probably Lawrence intends for us to believe that Emily lacks Lettie's capacities for consciousness, and we as readers are supposed to identify more with the failures. But especially in the face of Lawrence's later works, where the marriage of a natural man to a more educated woman is at one point presented as a solution to most of the unresolved problems in this book, the intimacy and security of this farm cannot be ignored.

Finally, Lawrence is beginning to experiment with sexual response, and his experiments already hint that here both mindless vitality and self-consciousness may be overcome. What follows is an early encounter between Lettie and George.

"You ought to have been a monk—a martyr, a Carthusian."

He laughed, taking no notice. He was breathlessly quivering under the new sensation of heavy, unappeased fire in his breast,

16. See "The Novel" in *Reflections on the Death of a Porcupine,* p. 110.

and in the muscles of his arms. He glanced at her bosom and shivered.

"Are you studying just how to play the part?" she asked.

"No—but—" he tried to look at her, but failed. He shrank, laughing, and dropped his head.

"What?" she asked with vibrant curiosity. Having become a few degrees calmer, he looked up at her now, his eyes wide and vivid with a declaration that made her shrink back as if flame had leaped towards her face. She bent down her head, and picked at her dress.

"Didn't you know the picture before?" she said, in a low, toneless voice.

He shut his eyes and shrank with shame.

"No, I've never been in before," he said.

"I'm surprised," she said. "it is a very common one."

"Is it?" he answered, and this make-belief conversation fell. She looked up, and found his eyes. They gazed at each other for a moment before they hid their faces again. It was a torture to each of them to look thus nakedly at the other, a dazzled, shrinking pain that they forced themselves to undergo for a moment, that they might the moment after tremble with a fierce sensation that filled their veins with fluid, fiery electricity. She sought, almost in panic, for something to say. [pp. 28-29]

This passage contains a more thorough account of the quality of sexual response than is usual in *The White Peacock;* I have noticed only three or four similar passages in the whole novel. But it clearly foreshadows what came to be called psychic drama. Several descriptive devices common to that technique are already evident in this interchange: the insistence on the novelty of sensation, the location of sensation in a part of the body, the use of fiery and electric metaphors to evoke the quality of the psychic event. As this method developed in the later novels, the use of metaphor became much more imaginative, and the evocation of emotion became accordingly more precise. Here we still find

traces of the conventional labeling of the romantic novel: eyes
wide and vivid with a declaration, vibrant curiosity, shame, almost panic. Yet such connections do not destroy the scene's
effectiveness. The scene weaves together gesture and response;
conveys real interaction between George and Lettie; and, above
all, evokes the intensity, fascination, and disability that comes
with sexual attraction.

In Lawrence's second book, *The Trespasser,* it is precisely this
sort of relationship which becomes the center of attention. Not
only does Lawrence try to explore sexual attraction, but he attempts throughout to relate it to nature, even to the extent of
evolving a "nature-morality." He avoids some of the difficulties
of *The White Peacock* by simplifying the plot, reducing the number of important characters, and removing the narrator from the
action, thereby keeping his ineffectuality out of the reader's consciousness. But on the whole *The Trespasser* is inferior to *The
White Peacock.* It demonstrates the wisdom involved in the comparative neglect of direct sexual response in the first novel, for it
is impossible to read *The Trespasser* without feeling that Lawrence plunged beyond his depth. Yet only by such experiments
could he finally learn to swim.

2: THE TRESPASSER

In *The Trespasser* Lawrence further attempts to isolate and define the natural values which were implicit in *The White Peacock.* There is evident throughout a yearning toward an inclusive vision, a reintegration of not only man and nature but man and woman. But, as in *The White Peacock,* no final unity emerges, and the failure to find it is expressed as tragedy. And, again as in *The White Peacock,* both the difficulties of the characters and the difficulties of the novel emerge as groups of unresolved and conflicting values.

In *The White Peacock* the fundamental dichotomy of values seemed to be between the natural and the cultural, with complications caused by ambivalence toward woman's roles as wife and mother. In *The Trespasser* emphasis shifts to the sexual relation itself. The yearning for unity which we noticed in George and Cyril here becomes a central theme, and a tentative formula blending man and nature through passion emerges. But the vision of unity toward which this formula points is thwarted by the same sort of trouble with women that we noticed in *The White Peacock.* A more emphatic division between woman as mother and woman as lover takes place, and this division is finally enforced by associations with conventional morality. The male protagonist again appears mysteriously ineffectual, unable to cope with his failures, both real and imagined, with the two women in his life.

Even though these problems lead, as they did in *The White Peacock*, to literary inadequacies, certain clear advances in Lawrence's own search for coherence emerge.[1] Although the intensity with which the passion of the lovers is depicted is often only lush emotionalism, it represents Lawrence's first extended attempt at the psychic drama which was only touched upon in *The White Peacock*. It seems inevitable that at this stage in Lawrence's career such an attempt should largely fail; the ideas which govern it are not yet mature, nor are the attitudes it depicts quite coherent. But the direction in which these ideas and attitudes seek resolution does to some extent emerge, at least in the clearer definition of the problems.

In *The White Peacock* both George and Lettie have a natural vitality. There is only one character with similar vitality in *The Trespasser,* and he is from the first both more thoroughly and more consciously involved with nature than anyone in *The White Peacock.*

When he ran out on to the fair sand his heart, and brain, and body were in a turmoil. He panted, filling his breast with the air that was sparkled and tasted of the sea. As he shuddered a little, the wilful palpitations of the flesh pleased him, as if birds had fluttered against him. He offered his body to the morning, glowing with the sea's passion. The wind nestled in to him, the

1. Some critics (notably Hough) suggest that this novel, which is based on Helen Corke's diary, is an irrelevancy in Lawrence's career. The experience was not directly his, and certain elements in the novel, particularly the use of music, would certainly not have been present had Lawrence set out to write a similar story on his own. Fortunately Helen Corke used the diary herself in her novel *Neutral Ground* (London, 1934, but essentially completed in 1918), and even a brief comparison makes it clear that Lawrence transmuted her material into his own terms (as he did with Mollie Skinner in *Boy in the Bush*). The most obvious change is his willingness to explore the feelings of Siegmund; Miss Corke presents the island scenes from the woman's point of view. The whole pressure for vital-natural unities is Lawrence's as well, as is the treatment of passion generally. And Helena, as we might expect, is more harshly treated than Miss Corke's Ellis, even though both writers blame her for sexual inadequacy.

sunshine came on his shoulders like warm breath. He delighted
in himself. [p. 32]

This is Siegmund, whose tragedy the book depicts, on the morning after sexual consummation with his mistress Helena, with
whom he had fled to the Isle of Wight for a holiday. His communion with nature here sets the tone for most of his similar
experiences throughout the book; it is at once more complete
than anything he can manage with Helena alone and more ambitious than anything which appeared in *The White Peacock.* Out of
his emotional turmoil (a result, mainly, of the simple presence of
the sea itself, but further stimulated by a swim in which he cut
himself on a rock), Siegmund manages to create an interchange
between himself and the natural forces which surround him. He
not only responds sensually, reveling in the pleasures his body
brings, but he consciously seeks union with nature and offers his
body "to the morning." He senses nature as an animated presence, as the metaphors consistently indicate. (There is even an
ambiguous use of the participle *glowing,* which can refer equally
well to the morning or to Siegmund's body, to enforce our impression that the interchange is charged and important.) The relation implied here, while it falls short of unity, strongly emphasizes the likeness between Siegmund's body and the "body" of
nature, especially through the strong personification of natural
forces, which act as servants to Siegmund's delight in himself.

This delight seems at first narcissistic, but as the book develops
such a term becomes increasingly inadequate to describe it. Narcissism presupposes egotism, and Siegmund will provide evidence
of a humility so thorough as to make us wonder whether he has
any ego at all. His pleasure in his body is really a symptom of a
larger pleasure in life which he seeks, a pleasure also associated
with sex and thought of as a key to wholeness. And the mode in
which it is most consistently available in this book is the one we
have just witnessed: Siegmund in single confrontation of nature,
especially (but not exclusively) of the sea.

Siegmund's communion with nature is conveyed by two simple

methods: First, as we have just seen, natural forces are repeatedly
personified in order to interact with him directly. The sea is often
referred to as his "partner." Although neither so consistent nor so
insistent, such personification was not uncommon in *The White
Peacock.* The second method is more characteristic of *The Trespasser* alone. It is simply the obverse of personification, the metaphorical likening of the human to the natural: "She felt his body
lifting into her, and sinking away. It seemed to force a rhythm, a
new pulse in her. Gradually, with a fine, keen thrilling, she melted
down on him, like metal sinking on a mould. He was sea and
sunlight mixed, heaving, warm, deliciously strong" (p. 42). The
connections work, as it were, both ways. But this second mode of
comparison strongly implies union, and through it Lawrence
presses toward the religious or ontological formulations which
appear with increasing frequency in *The Rainbow* and *Women in
Love.*

> Presently she laid her head on his breast, and remained so,
> watching the sea, and listening to his heart-beats. The throb was
> strong and deep. It seemed to go through the whole island and
> the whole afternoon, and it fascinated her: so deep, unheard,
> with its great expulsions of life. Had the world a heart? Was
> there also deep in the world a great God thudding out waves of
> life, like a great heart, unconscious? It frightened her. This was
> the God she knew not, as she knew not Siegmund. . . . She
> listened for Siegmund's soul, but his heart overbeat all other
> sound, thudding powerfully. [p. 38]

Despite the somewhat querulous tone, this is more than an expression of Helena's insecurity. Siegmund is repeatedly likened to
the "heart of life," and toward the end of his stay on the island
he is addressed by his old nickname, Domine. Whatever his inadequacies (and they are considerable, leading to suicide), Siegmund's communions with nature are meant to reveal the "touch
of God" in him.[2]

2. God appears throughout the book in a pantheistic rather than an-
thropomorphic guise, as these passages imply. The characters seldom utter

But the touch of God, it seems, is incomplete without woman. And the passionate interchange between Siegmund and Helena is, after all, the center of the book. This sexual attraction is in turn described by metaphors derived from nature; Lawrence thereby displays a search for unity which contains both modes of passion. Although he is by no means clear about his ontology, he seems to be attempting articulation of a force which can provide a meaningful basis for man's relation to others as well as to the world.

Siegmund, "burning and surging with desire," is transformed by the firelight into a vital presence exerting hypnotic influence upon Helena. "He sat in the chair beside her, leaning forward, his hands hanging like two scarlet flowers listless in the fire glow, near to her, as she knelt on the hearth, with head bowed down. One of the flowers awoke and spread towards her. It asked for her mutely. She was fascinated, scarcely able to move" (pp. 27-28). If we take this passage alone, the flower metaphor seems merely a clever twist, an attempt at rendering an ancient situation with some originality. But it soon appears that for Lawrence it implies more than that:

> She had given him this new soft beauty. She was the earth in which his strange flowers grew. But she herself wondered at the flowers produced of her. He was so strange to her, so different from herself. What next would he ask of her, what new blossom would she rear in him then. He seemed to grow and flower involuntarily. She merely helped to produce him. [p. 28]

Lawrence does not consciously intend any phallic associations

---

his name, and when they do they are self-conscious as well as somewhat doubtful about his nature. It is not until *The Rainbow* that Lawrence makes an obvious attempt to define his rejection of Christianity. By the time he wrote his first two novels, however, he had read Schopenhauer and did not consider himself a believer. See *The White Peacock,* p. 58, and Edward Nehls, *D. H. Lawrence: A Composite Biography* (Wisconsin, 1957), 1:66-70. The fullest account of Lawrence's early reading is in Jessie Chambers, *D. H. Lawrence: A Personal Record,* 2d ed. (New York, 1965), chap. 4. See pp. 111 ff. for an account of Lawrence's reading of Schopenhauer and "the materialist philosophy."

here. He is seeking a pattern by which to capture the respective roles of man and woman in the sexual relation, and it is no accident that a natural metaphor presents itself, not only as a vehicle for sexual attraction, as in the first quotation, but as a means of analyzing the larger meaning of that attraction. We shall see shortly that the relationship of woman as earth (passive) and man as flower (active) is not one with which Lawrence is altogether happy, and it does not appear consistently throughout the book.[3] But at least it suggests a possibility for fruitful union, and it is this possibility which Lawrence takes up in a third extension of the same metaphor.

> Meanwhile the flowers of their passion were softly shed, as poppies fall at noon, and the seed of beauty ripened rapidly within them. Dreams came like a wind through their souls, drifting off with the seed-dust of beautiful experience which they had ripened, to fertilise the souls of others withal. In them the sea and the sky and ships had mingled and bred new blossoms of the torrid heat of their love. And the seed of such blossoms was shaken as they slept, into the hand of God, who held it in his palm preciously; then scattered it again, to produce new splendid blooms of beauty. [p. 50]

This is not quite successful, but it clearly indicates that the passionate experience which is the book's primary subject is meant, finally, to expand into a vision of unity: "In them the sea and the sky and ships had mingled and bred new blossoms of the torrid heat of their love." Beneath the vagueness we can detect a thrust toward the ontological, which underlies the intensity of this book and provides the motive force for its continued analysis of passion. It is passion which is meant to complete the "touch of God" we noticed in Siegmund. This is in turn related to the natural world which the lovers confront in the Isle of Wight. The flower metaphor carries, however vaguely, a sense of union which has

3. This relationship does, however, remain in Lawrence's mind, emerging as part of the male and female principles of the *Study of Thomas Hardy*. See the section on this book in chap. 5. below.

religious overtones and is itself a part of Lawrence's concern for a natural unity. Nothing in *The White Peacock* quite approaches this attempt to transcend and unite man and woman and man and nature.

But unity sought is not necessarily unity found, and as in *The White Peacock* literary uncertainty points toward uncertainty about value and relation. The vagueness of the passage quoted above, through which much of its possible meaning evaporates (What, for instance, can one make of either the hand of God or the fertilization of souls in the total absence of any formulation to explain them?), seems to indicate an uncertainty about the passionate experience it culminates. In short, we encounter once more the trouble with women which appeared in *The White Peacock*. But here the nature of that trouble is clearer. If Siegmund's responses to nature indicate a potential for religious experience, Helena's indicate a fundamental deficiency:

> After breakfast, while Siegmund dressed, she went down to the sea. She dwelled, as she passed, on all tiny, pretty things—on the barbaric yellow ragwort, and pink convulvuli; on all the twinkling of flowers, and dew, and snail-tracks drying in the sun. Her walk was one long lingering. More than the spaces, she loved the nooks, and fancy more than imagination . . . she knew hardly any flower's name, nor perceived any of the relationships, nor cared a jot about adaptation or a modification. . . .
> "That yellow flower hadn't time to be brushed and combed by the fairies before dawn came. It is tousled . . . " so she thought to herself. The pink convolvuli were fairy horns or telephones from the day fairies to the night fairies. The rippling sunlight on the sea was the Rhine maidens spreading their bright hair to the sun. . . . She did not care for people; they were vulgar, ugly, and stupid, as a rule. [p. 34]

This has a strong similarity both to Lettie's occasional tendency to regard nature through literary allusion and to Cyril's more frequent tendency to carry literary cleverness to the point of self-dramatization. Here again nature is seen not as an objective presence but as a form of self-indulgence. And Helena, who persists in "reducing" nature to her own terms, easily outdoes either Cyril or Lettie. Despite tendencies of his own to fall into habits similar to Helena's, Lawrence is even more sharply opposed to fancy than Wordsworth was. Of course, Helena's insistence that nature be pretty as well as friendly ignores conceptions of it as grand, powerful, impersonal, or cruel, all of which are, as we shall see, both present and important in this book.

Helena's escapism is further evident in her fondness for displaying her intellectual and especially her musical sophistication. But Lawrence's judgment of Helena's cultural accomplishments is less apparent than that of her fantasies about nature: "Helena belonged to the unclassed. She was not ladylike, nor smart, nor assertive. One could not tell whether she were of independent means or a worker. One thing was obvious about her: she was evidently educated" (p. 74). The evidence for her education is of varying sorts, and not all of it is clearly presented as false sophistication.

> "I assure you, it is only a fog-horn," she laughed.
>
> "Of course. But it is a depressing sort of sound."
>
> "Is it?" she said curiously. "Why? Well—yes—I think I can understand its being so to some people. It's something like the call of the horn across the sea to Tristan."
>
> She hummed softly, then three times she sang the horn-call. [p. 18]

Any attempt to picture this makes it seem like a scene from a comedy, especially when Helena must add a fourth horn-call to the initial three. And this is surpassed by her insistent argument that the pitch of the fog horn is E, not F sharp, as Siegmund believes. Unfortunately Lawrence does not indicate that his intentions here and in several similar scenes are satirical, and such arguments are surely the silliest parts of the book. They remind one of the social banter that comes off so poorly in *The White Peacock*, and they seem to indicate the same ambivalence toward cultural attainments that was present there. However, in this book the association of woman with culture has much less importance. Lawrence is much more consistently concerned with female inadequacies, which take on almost cosmic significance. Helena's failure to meet Siegmund's desire causes a major collapse in his quest for meaning.

Unfortunately, Siegmund relies upon Helena to fulfill his yearning for experience which can at once transcend the immediate and reduce it to some sort of order.

> When Siegmund had Helena near, he lost the ache, the yearning towards something, which he always felt otherwise. She seemed to connect him with the beauty of things, as if she were the nerve through which he received intelligence of the sun, wind, and sea, and of the moon and the darkness. Beauty she never felt herself came to him through her. It is that makes love. He could always sympathise with the wistful little flowers, and trees lonely in their crowds, and wild, sad sea-birds. In these things he recognised the great yearning, the ache outwards towards something, with which he was ordinarily burdened. But with Helena, in this large sea morning, he was whole and perfect as the day. [p. 35]

Once again we see that the sexual and the natural are meant to be related in some larger whole, but in expecting Helena to support such a relation Siegmund is mistaken. The whole described here is apparently achieved through passion the night before, and even then Siegmund had to take "a good deal of sorrow in his joy" because his partner could only manage to present herself as a "sacrifice." This sorrow soon outweighs the joy, and with it comes a doubt that destroys not only the whole but whatever Siegmund has of a coherent self. Though it is clear from the first that he is weak and excessively dependent upon Helena, her sexual failure is the immediate cause for his downfall. Helena, moreover, helps his destruction along by displaying a power which quite transcends her "whiteness" (she is described as "white" even more than Lettie is) and which startlingly empha-

sizes the disparity between male and female that haunts Lawrence's first two novels. Lawrence informs us that "psychically
she was an extremist, and a dangerous one."

In one rather startling scene of psychic extremity both Siegmund's and Lawrence's difficulties in achieving the sort of whole
just discussed emerge more fully. Helena reaches one significant
"ecstasy of love," in which she manages her own integration of
man and nature. In it her whiteness reveals itself as blackness and
directly foreshadows the dominant imagery of *Women in Love,*
especially as it is embodied in Gudrun:

> He pressed back his head, so that there was a gleaming pallor on
> his chin and his forehead and deep black shadow over his eyes
> and his nostrils. This thrilled Helena with a sense of mystery
> and magic.
>
> " 'Die grosse Blumen schmachten,' " she said to herself, curi-
> ously awake and joyous. "The big flowers open with black
> petals and silvery ones, Siegmund. You are the big flowers,
> Siegmund; yours is the bridegroom face, Siegmund, like a black
> and glistening flesh-petalled flower, Siegmund, and it blooms in
> the Zauberland, Siegmund—this is the magic land." . . . "They
> are all still—gorse and the stars and the sea and the trees, are all
> kissing, Siegmund. The sea has its mouth on the earth, and the
> gorse and the trees press together, and they all look up at the
> moon, they put up their faces in a kiss, my darling. But they
> haven't you—and it all centres in you, my dear, all the wonder-
> love is in you, more than in them all, Siegmund—Siegmund!"
> [pp. 59-60]

Helena soon swoons "lightly into unconsciousness." Upon returning she proclaims, "I have been beyond life. I have been a little
way into death." But her "peaceful happiness" almost immediately gives way to the realization that "she must be slowly weighing
down the life of Siegmund." And after witnessing this scene we
can hardly be surprised by such a realization.

The scene has a strong element of the demonic. It is as if Helena
can be released only into a kind of prurience when her passion is

finally stirred. Her compulsion to see Siegmund as a black and glistening flower is not only another instance of her tendency to reduce everything to fantasy but a foreshadowing of the tendency of all Lawrence's "cerebral" women to regard sensual experience as black, in a manner which Lawrence later described as pornographic.[4] Her view of the natural world, too, takes on this overluscious quality, and she collects all the kissing in the figure of Siegmund, whom she delights in having. This is female possessiveness with a vengeance. It is no wonder that Siegmund is overwhelmed at the transformation of his "brave little Helena"; "he was almost afraid of the strange ecstasy she concentrated upon him."

Siegmund's fear, however, soon gives way to another sort of realization.

> He felt stunned, half-conscious. Yet as he lay helplessly looking up at her some other consciousness inside him murmured: "Hawwa—Eve—Mother!" ... This woman, tall and pale, dropping with the strength of her compassion, seemed stable, immortal, not a fragile human being, but a personification of the great motherhood of women. ... She had never before so en-

4. Even Helena's fondness for German romantic poetry, which she chants to herself as she becomes ecstatic and which provides her with phrases throughout the scene, came to be regarded as a form of pornography by Lawrence:

> One of my most sympathetic critics wrote: "If Mr. Lawrence's attitude to sex were adopted, then two things would disappear, the love lyric and the smoking-room story." And this, I think, is true. But it depends on which love lyric he means. If it is the *Who is Sylvia, what is she?*—then it may just as well disappear. All that pure and noble and heaven-blessed stuff is only the counterpart to the smoking—room story. *Du bist wie eine Blume!* Jawohl! ... Sentimentality is a sure sign of pornography.... Away with such love lyrics, we've had too much of their pornographic poison, tickling the dirty little secret and rolling the eyes to heaven. [*Pornography and Obscenity,* pp. 180-81]

Lawrence was willing to allow, however, "My love is like a red, red rose." His criticism is based, of course, on the recognition of a repressed natural sexuality in such songs, a repression displayed by many of Lawrence's female characters. Gudrun is the fullest embodiment of the demonic force which such repression can achieve.

tered and gathered his plaintive masculine soul to the bosom of her nurture. [pp. 60-61]

Like Cyril, Siegmund does not seem sure whether he wants most to submit to woman as mother or to master her as lover. Once she displays sensual power of her own he is all too ready to be taken as child, yet throughout the book he complains that he is not "masterful enough." Like George, he seems to realize that the union he seeks requires a more forceful assertion, but, again like George (only more pitifully so), he is mysteriously incapacitated. It is not that woman as lover need preclude woman as mother; all men, I believe, are to some extent mothered by their women. But Siegmund cannot relate one role to the other, and Helena is certainly incapable of doing it for him.

The implicit pattern of coherence which we extracted from Lawrence's blending of the sexual and the natural flounders, then, on the same confusion about the female role that appeared in *The White Peacock*. And again the confusion—or perhaps actually the lack of resolution—belongs not only to the characters but to some extent to the author. We might deduce as much from a repeated tendency to explain the malaise which afflicts both Siegmund and Helena as simply an overdose of intensity, but the difficulty is even clearer in a scene with the sole function of explaining what is going wrong. For this purpose Lawrence introduces a new character, Hampson, who appears only here. Hampson is an old musician friend whom Siegmund has forgotten; he approaches Siegmund and offers a series of generalizations about women and life obviously meant to apply to both of them.

> "The best sort of women—the most interesting—are the worse for us," Hampson resumed. "By instinct they aim at suppressing the gross and animal in us. Then they are super-sensitive—refined a bit beyond humanity. We, who are as little gross as need be, become their instruments. Life is grounded in them, like electricity in the earth; and we take from them their unrealised life, turn it into light or warmth or power for them. The ordinary woman is, alone, a great potential force, an

accumulator, if you like, charged from the source of life. In us her force becomes evident.

"She can't live without us, but she destroys us. These deep, interesting women don't want *us;* they want the flowers of the spirit they can gather of us. We, as natural men, are more or less degrading to them and to their love of us; therefore they destroy the natural man in us—that is, us altogether." [pp. 69-70]

This indictment of women is strongly reminiscent of Cyril's outburst while watching Emily fondle her baby, and it anticipates the portrayal of both Miriam in *Sons and Lovers* and Hermione in *Women in Love.* It is at least clear that women need men to help them develop the "flowers of spirit" which (for reasons unstated) they need, while the natural man gets slighted and finally crushed. But the metaphors are confusing, especially that of the electrical accumulator. The nature of women's potential force is unclear, as is the way in which men allow it release.[5] Nor is there anything to help us discover how it is converted to flowers of the spirit, or why men are defenseless in face of a process which they apparently initiate. And this, unfortunately, is as close as we can come to a direct confrontation of Helena's destructive power. That the formulation is groping,[6] providing only the vaguest hints of what later became a theory of inhibition by "false concepts," together with the fact that a full explanation of Siegmund's help-

5. Later Lawrence makes this force somewhat more definite: "This is the desire of every man, that his movement, the manner of his walk, and the supremest effort of his mind, shall be the pulsation outwards from stimulus received in sex, in the sexual act, that the woman of his body shall be the begetter of his whole life, that she, in her female spirit, shall beget in him his idea, his motion, himself" (*Study of Thomas Hardy,* quoted in *Phoenix,* pp. 444-45). Yet precisely what this begetting entails—how much the woman provides, how much the man initiates, and, especially, how much he departs in another direction—is subject to redefinition throughout Lawrence's life. In this sense his problem with women was never solved.

6. What remains of earlier versions of the novel indicates that Lawrence had considerable difficulty with this scene and did much rewriting. Although the earlier versions are rather lugubrious, as Lawrence apparently recognized, they show the "dark powers" at an early stage of development

lessness requires more than we can glean here or elsewhere in the book, indicates that neither Siegmund nor Lawrence has come to a clear understanding of his attitudes toward women.

The vision of unity which was built upon the woman, then, finally comes to nothing. As it crumbles, however, some of the values upon which it is founded emerge more clearly. Apparently exacerbated, Helena has a fit of conscience; she feels "the crying of lives I have touched," and the possibilities of a real passionate union disappear altogether. She begins to "scourge herself" and rejects Siegmund, thrusting him away when he tries to comfort her sobbing. Siegmund in turn finds "death taking place in his soul," as a result of both Helena's rejection and his own conscience, which he cannot separate from his general feelings of

---

more clearly than the scene does in its final form. Hampson argues that "once you have found the eternal roaring night which is the very core of you . . . you don't easily come back into the blue rooms." This darkness undergoes elaborate metaphorical development:

> Now look here, we're each one of us like a house—a temple, if you like—built round a roaring dark space. This roaring dark space sets us going like machinery, miller and mill stones and mill machinery all rumbling and busy, but the ghastly black hole where the black water roars—that's the origin. Now you look too long in the black horror of the water-sluice, and you forget yourself, your mill and your grist—everything. All the rest seems clanking clattering foolery: there's the roaring black space.

This passage, the earliest version I found, is taken from a Holograph MS at Berkeley, pp. 133-34; see Warren Roberts's bibliography, E407a. (The Holograph MSS are hereafter cited as Hol.)

The point of all this seems to be that love will irrevocably draw Siegmund to "the dark roaring space whence his activity issues." Women "make us open the doors that were not made to open" in order to watch the "black raving of incoherent life-water as it pours darkly in us." The women "exult" and "kill us," meanwhile "gathering the experience" and "storing" it as "blood-wisdom."

This helps fill in what Lawrence meant by Helena's momentary vampirism, and it foreshadows a continuing fascination with both dark sexuality and the demonic. The identification of the roaring black space with life indicates as well that Lawrence has not yet emerged as a vitalist; his notions of vital force are still colored by a rather melodramatic gloom.

inadequacy. He presses his face against the turf, "trying to hide" (p. 84).[7] As they both recover from these agonies of disillusionment, a new vision emerges in Siegmund's eyes:

Siegmund found himself in an abbey. He looked up the nave of the night, where the sky came down on the sealike arches, and he watched the stars catch fire. At least it was all sacred, whatever the God might be. Helena herself, the bitter bread, was stuff of the ceremony, which he touched with his lips as part of the service. [p. 85]

Siegmund has reverted to a sorrowful vision which through its Christian imagery implies a loss of the pantheistic joy in nature we witnessed earlier. In face of the failure of love, nature takes on a sterner aspect, yielding a notion of fate similar in its melancholy to that in *The White Peacock*. But in this book such melancholy, though excessive on Siegmund's part, finds a greater justification in Lawrence's rendering of natural forces. The parts of nature which Helena's repulsive fairies overlooked become more significant as the book moves toward its tragic ending.

Deprived, for whatever reasons, of the hope of achieving completeness either of himself or of his world through Helena, Siegmund is thrown back upon his only other resource, nature. But, as we have seen, to make of this communion a coherent whole, Siegmund needs Helena. Without her nature wears a dual aspect which Siegmund's moments of joy sometimes overlook and of which, particularly when he is most exhilarated, he needs to be reminded. In an early scene he swims into a cove of white sand which appears to him "like Helena." But upon digging in it he finds "under all . . . [a] deep mass of cold, that the softness and warmth merely floated upon" (p. 47). A bit later he watches Helena paddling in the water with pink toes, "absurdly, childishly happy." "Her child-like indifference to consequences touched him with a sense of the distance between them. He himself might

7. Lawrence was so caught up in this scene that he expressed its substance in a poem as well. See Pinto and Roberts, *Complete Poems of Lawrence,* pp. 870-71.

play with the delicious warm surface of life, but always he recked of the relentless mass of cold beneath—the mass of life which has no sympathy with the individual, no cognizance of him" (p. 52). This relentless mass of cold appears at regular intervals throughout the book, even in the fear Helena has of Siegmund's heartbeat. Hampson at one point speaks of death beneath the surface of life, and Siegmund himself receives both cuts and bruises from the sea whenever he tends to regard it as a fanciful playmate, as Helena does. Lawrence's consistent point seems to be that nature, though a source of real joy and an expression of a greater, incomprehensible cosmic order, is fundamentally impersonal and potentially brutal as well. To a man who desperately needs both comfort and an order for impulses increasingly chaotic in their intensity, this grimmer aspect of nature amounts to a fatal rejection. That the "dark cold mass" should be symbolically coupled with Helena is of course no accident either, for her concern for her own self-preservation is a similar rejection.[8]

Faced with such bleak prospects Siegmund resorts more and more to self-pity, creating a gloomy cloud through which he continues to try to make sense of his life. He casts about for ways to escape his double failure in passion and in responsibility to his family. The two aspects of nature, with which he could live successfully as long as joy was available, become increasingly disparate and painful to regard.[9] So he continues to look toward the unknown for faith. He tends increasingly to identify the "dark cold mass" which lies at the bottom of both Helena and nature as "death."

8. Helena, who is rarely described in natural metaphors, is several times likened to the sea in her "reserve" and "self-sufficiency." See pp. 13, 15, 34.

9. At one point he seeks escape by a sudden yearning to be a farmer, which harks back to the pastoral life of the Saxon family in *The White Peacock*. "I think every man has a passion for farming at the bottom of his blood. It would be fine to be plain-minded, to see no further than the end of one's nose, and to own cattle and land" (p. 75). Coming from a musician who has shown no sign whatever of being acquainted with the life of a farm, this yearning strikes us as surprising. And, as in *The White Peacock*, the pastoral life is no solution.

> For me, quivering in the interspaces of the atmosphere, is the darkness the same that fills my soul. I can see death urging itself into life, the shadow supporting the substance. For my life is burning an invisible flame. The glare of the light of myself, as I burn on the fuel of death, is not enough to hide from me the source and the issue. For what is a life but a flame that bursts off the surface of the darkness, and tapers into the darkness again? But that death that issues differs from the death that was the source. At least, I shall enrich death with a potent shadow, if I do not enrich life. [p. 115]

This does very little to clear up the ultimate mysteries with which Siegmund is becoming obsessed, but it vaguely foreshadows Lawrence's series of essays, "The Crown," in which darkness and death become sources of life through a dialectic process. Siegmund is still trying to relate himself to the cosmos, and he will apparently be satisfied with nothing less than ontological insights, which, as this passage illustrates, are never sufficiently coherent to give form to his yearnings.

As he nears the home whose security he has violated, these yearnings become mixed with guilt, and Siegmund resorts to half-desperate assertions that his needs are meaningfully related to his pleasures. As usual, the vehicle for such assertions is found in nature: his need for a mother becomes a somewhat cloying love for mother earth. While riding homeward on the train,

> as Siegmund, looking backward, saw the northern slopes of the downs swooping smoothly, in a great, broad bosom of a sward, down to the body of the land, he warmed with sudden love for the earth; there the great downs were, naked like a breast, leaning kindly to him. The earth is always kind; it loves us, and would foster us like a nurse. The downs were big and tender and simple. [p. 120]

Since this seems to provide very limited comfort, Siegmund turns to an assertion of vitality in face of the void and compares himself to a bee:

Well, the day will swarm in golden again, with colour on the
wings of every bee, and humming in each activity. The gold and
the colour and sweet smell and the sound of life, they exist,
even if there is no bee; it only happens we see the iridescence
on the wings of a bee. It exists whether or not, bee or no bee.
Since the iridescence and the humming of life *are* always, and
since it was they who made me, then I am not lost. [p. 122] [10]

Unable to cope, Siegmund is attempting to discover the ontological base which he so desperately needs in the life of the senses
itself. He gets off the train with a newly acute "sense of wonder."
"He went forward to the Embankment, with a feeling of elation
in his heart. This purple and gold-grey world, with fluttering
flame-warmth of soldiers and the quick brightness of women, like
lights that clip sharply in a draught, was a revelation to him" (p.
125).

Despite their notable lack of success in really answering Siegmund's needs, these escapes are not really foolish. If we ignore
the element of self-pity, the pleasures are real, and they are of the
same order as those he experienced on the seashore. That these
aesthetic modes of response, however intense, will not provide
the final order for which both Siegmund and his author yearn is a
lesson which appears repeatedly in Lawrence's later work as well.
But the immediate value of the responses themselves remains intact both here and later; the success of Lawrence's descriptive
writing is strongly dependent upon his continued ability to maintain a similarly direct response to sensuous detail.

Just before Siegmund actually carries out his suicide he makes
one last pathetic attempt to put together the two aspects of life,
which have become impossibly disparate.

10. This is not the first time Siegmund has made this comparison. Earlier
he reflects on a bee which flies out to sea: "I am out of my depth. Like the
bee, I was mad with the sight of so much joy, such a blue space, and now I
shall find no footing to alight on. I have flown out into life beyond my
strength to get back" (p. 103). The difference between this and the passage
quoted above neatly illustrates Siegmund's shift toward a more immediate
source of meaning.

Siegmund had always inwardly held faith that the heart of life beat kindly towards him. When he was cynical and sulky he knew that in reality it was only a waywardness of his.

The heart of life is implacable in its kindness. It may not be moved to fluttering of pity; it swings on uninterrupted by cries of anguish or of hate.

Siegmund was thankful for this unfaltering sternness of life. There was no futile hesitation between doom and pity. Therefore, he could submit and have faith.[p. 159]

These two notions of life (which has, of course, consistently appeared as nature)—as kind and a source of pleasure and as stern, indifferent, or even brutal—are simply yoked by desperation; life is implacable in its kindness. We are told almost immediately, however, that "Siegmund forgot all his speculations on a divine benevolence. The discord of his immediate situation overcame every harmony" (p. 160). Siegmund's attempt to take comfort from the very impersonality of nature is his final failure.

The discord on which Siegmund's search for unity ends remains to an uncomfortable extent the discord of *The Trespasser* as a whole. For Lawrence, like Siegmund, shows himself incapable of putting together the two aspects of life or nature which are threaded through all the passionate interchanges in the book. Yet at the same time certain advances in Lawrence's search for a principle of coherence remain clear, especially in the light of his later work. It is evident, for example, that Lawrence, despite his exploration of society in *The White Peacock,* is moving away from the novel of manners toward a concentration upon what seems to him most intense and vital in human existence. It is also evident that this intensity will not be realized without ontological pronouncement; the two areas through which he moves toward such pronouncement in this book—response to natural phenomena and sexual response—remain, in fact, central to all his writing. And despite the clumsiness of some of his attempts to press the immediate interchange between man and nature into religious insight, Lawrence has already displayed a firm insistence that whatever nature means, it cannot be regarded as a personal presence devoted merely to the interests of man. In this conviction he of course follows Hardy, but the difference from Hardy which we noted in *The White Peacock* continues here even more obviously. For every remark or passage implying nature's sternness and indifference, there are others insisting upon its ability to provide joy and lead toward religious insight, even though that insight is not yet available in coherent form. Finally, this book shows much more clearly than *The White Peacock* that for Lawrence the man has the stronger impulse toward unifying religious experience and woman offers at once both a means and an obstacle to satisfying it. A resentment of female spirituality, which clearly implies sexual inadequacy, has definitely emerged, even though it brings with it a host of problems. Before we go on to Lawrence's next book, where such spirituality is further explored, it is necessary to examine a bit more closely this book's treatment of the problem of women.

If *The Trespasser* is much less concerned than *The White Peacock* with woman's role as a bearer of culture, it gives more weight to her role as a moral force and finally points to some of Lawrence's problems with morality in general. We have already noticed that Helena's sexual failure is followed by an attack of conscience, which, because it leads to a rejection of Siegmund, launches him on his downhill slide. His decline is in turn haunted by guilt about his family. Ford Madox Ford's impression of an earlier manuscript attributes even the sexual raptures to an "inverted puritanism":

And then one day he brought me half the ms. of *The Trespassers*—and that was the end. It was a *Trespassers* much—oh, but much!—more phallic than is the book as it stands and much more moral in the inverted-puritanic sense. That last was inevitable in that day, and Lawrence had come under the subterranean-fashionable influences that made for Free Love as a social and moral arcanum. So that the whole effect was the rather dreary one of a schoolboy larking among placket holes,

dialoguing with a Wesleyan minister who has been converted to
Ibsen . . . it had the making of a thoroughly bad hybrid book
and I told him so.[11]

Though this is facile, especially in its analysis of Lawrence's influences, and though it refers to a different version than the one
with which we are dealing, it does point to an important problem,
both in *The Trespasser* and in *Sons and Lovers*. Lawrence's search
for a coherent view of human relations has a strong moral dimension which in this book seems to exist in two versions, one an
inversion of the other. The most definite version is that we have
depicted in Helena; at one point Lawrence characterizes this as
Wesleyan, but it is generalized to represent the attitude of stern
moral judgment itself. On their trip back from the island Siegmund and Helena witness a near-disaster—a launch nearly collides
with a steamer—and Helena quickly blames the sailor of the
launch for being "abominably careless."

> Siegmund looked at her. She seemed very hard in judgment,
> very blind. Sometimes his soul surged against her in hatred.
> "Do you think the man *wanted* to drown the boat?" he
> asked.
> "He nearly succeeded," she replied.
> There was antagonism between them. Siegmund recognised in
> Helena the world sitting in judgment, and he hated it. [p. 115]

Of course, Siegmund hates an attitude of judgment because he
comes off poorly when it is directed to him, and both Helena and
his wife Beatrice are more rigidly caught up in such ways of
thinking than he is. But his agonized self-castigation and his im-
potence before his family, which is largely due to real guilt about
leaving them for a mistress, amply testify that such attitudes are
also his own. They extend, in somewhat inverted form, to his
whole attempt to put himself and his world together. This is most
obvious when he feels himself doomed.

11. Nehls, *Lawrence: A Composite Biography*, 1:121.

"Now I must get clarity and courage to follow out the theme. I don't want to botch and bungle even damnation."

But he needed to know what was right, what was the proper sequence of his acts. Staring at the darkness, he seemed to feel his course, though he could not see it. He bowed in obedience. The stars seemed to swing softly in token of submission. [p. 86]

This is not the narrow morality of the two women but a belief, or at least a yearning to believe, in a larger moral order. This order, though it appears hostile elsewhere, is at least capable of providing him with meaning for his action. Siegmund's whole series of intense plunges into passionate experience, both with Helena and with nature, may be seen as part of a search for such meaning. Lawrence's later work strongly supports the implication that religious experience must also entail ethical directives; Siegmund cannot be satisfied without discovering patterns by which to live. It is in this sense that one can speak of a nature morality in this book, even though it lacks the clarity of doctrine.

At this stage in Lawrence's career this "higher" morality is still in active conflict with the more conventional kind, which dominates Siegmund's household and adds to the power of women. The higher morality dictates that Siegmund somehow convert or even force Helena from her fairies and dreams and thereby allow passion release; he should take pride in his body and joyfully commune with nature, as long as he realizes that the deepest levels at which he and nature are alike have nothing personal about them. But because of Siegmund's own weakness and lack of confidence, none of this is possible. He in fact follows the dictates of conventional morality, returning to his wife and children with such opprobrium upon him that he cannot bear to live any longer. It is the combination of reproach from both moralities (he has rejected the natural and passionate and is rejected by the conventional and Christian) which finally makes him hang himself.

Lawrence himself does not clearly espouse either of these two possible moralities, nor does he provide evidence which points to a way to reconcile them. Although in the passage we examined above in which Helena sits in the world's judgment he is clearly on Siegmund's side, Siegmund's conflict is to some extent his as well. There is nothing in the book to condone unconditionally Siegmund's temporary escape from the home, and in the chapters describing Siegmund's homecoming his guilt in creating a rift between himself and his family is both real and deserved. Beatrice is shrewish and generally unpleasant, but her complaints are to some extent justified. The moral order of the home does provide an apparently necessary security for those who live in it and is perfectly capable of harboring and fostering love, as Siegmund's relation to his youngest child particularly demonstrates. Here, then, is another unresolved opposition, related to women but certainly entailing issues which reach quite beyond the sexual. The same difficulty was present in subdued form in the rift between the natural and the cultural that we examined in *The White Peacock*, but there the two groups of values did not come into moral conflict. Here they do, and it will take another entire book before there is any sign of resolution.

That book is of course *Sons and Lovers*. In it Lawrence lays aside his fervent attempt to find a key to ultimate unity through passion and pursues instead a thorough exploration of how the two moralities relate to one another. He seems to realize that the excesses of *The Trespasser* result from efforts to reach beyond his own experience to solve problems inevitably arising from it, especially the problems related to women.[12] Therefore he returns to that experience directly, to see what sort of sense he can make of it in its own terms. The tendency to mystical evaporation gives way to a consistently realistic narrative mode which reminds us of *The White Peacock* in its ability to capture vivid detail but which is also foreshadowed by a striking shift in *The Trespasser* itself. Siegmund's return to domestic morality is accompanied by a change from the internal monologues and conversations which

12. Even while writing the book Lawrence expressed more doubts about it than about any of his others. See, e.g., *LM,* pp. 93, 94, 97.

dominate the island chapters to a detailed and naturalistic account of his family life and final steps toward suicide. Not only is Siegmund's last "night of agony and sweat"[13] impressive in its psychological realism, but Lawrence also renders Siegmund's view of his favorite child with a thorough and accurate detail which looks forward to *Sons and Lovers* and especially to Anna Brangwen's childhood in *The Rainbow.*

> Her arms were bare to the shoulder. She wore a bodiced petticoat of pink flannelette, which hardly reached her knees. Siegmund felt slightly amused to see her stout little calves planted so firmly close together. She carefully sponged her cheeks, her pursed-up mouth, and her neck, soaping her hair, but not her ears. Then, very deliberately, she squeezed out the sponge and proceeded to wipe away the soap.
>
> For some reason or other she glanced round. Her startled eyes met his. She, too, had beautiful dark blue eyes. She stood, with the sponge at her neck, looking full at him. Siegmund felt himself shrinking. The child's look was steady, calm, inscrutable.
>
> "Hello!" said her father. "Are you here!" [pp. 133-34]

This and many similarly thorough and controlled descriptions of appearance and action in *The White Peacock*[14] testify that Lawrence could write highly effective realistic scenes from the beginning of his career as a writer. That in much of his first two novels he did not choose to do so further indicates that his ambitions were never confined to the tradition of Flaubert. We shall have to be careful, then, how we interpret the apparent predominance of such realistic writing in *Sons and Lovers.*

---

13. Ford, *Double Measure,* p. 74.

14. The scenes describing the gamekeeper's swarming family are particularly vivid, in a manner reminiscent of Dickens. But more effective still is the sequence which describes Cyril following his son into the quarry and discovering the dead gamekeeper. This is as objective as one could wish, presenting only those details which further the action. See *The White Peacock,* pp. 151-54.

3: SONS AND LOVERS

Sons and Lovers is the first of Lawrence's novels which has any claim to greatness. Lawrence's letters indicate that he was himself the first to realize this. They display a striking new confidence, all the more obvious in contrast to his cries of frustration over *The Trespasser:* "The *Paul Morel* book—to be called, I think, *Sons and Lovers,* is being got ready for the printer—I'm resting a bit after having delivered it. It's quite a great work. I only hope the English nation won't rend me for having given them anything so good."[1] Although not everyone agrees with Lawrence's estimate, virtually no one would deny that he has grounds for enthusiasm. *Sons and Lovers* is certainly far superior to the first two novels.[2]

There are several ways to account for this superiority. I have already implied that in *Sons and Lovers* Lawrence turned directly to his own experience; there is no doubt that this autobiographical approach provided him with material which he could handle better than either the fervent passion of *The Trespasser* or the uncertain narrator and culture of *The White Peacock.* And the concomitant return to "real-

1. *LM,* p. 164.
2. Some still consider it the best of all his novels, notably E. M. Forster. See C. H. Rolph, *The Trial of Lady Chatterley* (Baltimore, 1961), p. 112.

ism"[3] surely helped him to avoid the obtrusive personal elements, the uncertain generalities about sex, and the vagueness about fate which mar the first two books. But to say this much will not account for the continued presence, still not fully resolved, of the problems we have been examining. How does a return to realism provide a successful presentation of the ambivalence about the role of the female, or of the persistent tension between the natural and the moral? Some critics—most, in fact—think it does not, or at least not quite.[4] I think it does, and what follows is mainly designed to show how.[5]

What Lawrence's return to realism allows is an experiment in objectivity. The inconsistencies in value and attitude which we noticed in the first two novels are put into a dialectic opposition in which their relative force in the lives of the characters is explored. The overall impression is that these values are being lived through and even to some extent worked out. Almost all the critics have commented on this book's immediacy, its closeness to experience.[6] This immediacy is a direct result of Lawrence's testing of the uncertainties which emerged in the first two novels through modes which stay so close to his remembered experience as to cause repeated criticism that he was merely reproducing that experience blindly, without sufficient control. But I shall argue

3. Hough says "naturalism" (*The Dark Sun,* p. 41). I pursue no fine distinctions here; either word will serve my purposes. What this "realism" entails should emerge from the discussion.

4. Mark Schorer has been the most influential critic to emphasize uncertainties in the author's attitude toward his characters and themes. For Schorer these uncertainties are serious faults in the novel. See his essay "Technique as Discovery" in *The Hudson Review* (Spring, 1948); it is reprinted in various critical anthologies. Eliseo Vivas, in *D. H. Lawrence: The Failure and Triumph of His Art* (Bloomington, Ind., 1964), reiterates Schorer's condemnation of *Sons and Lovers* for formal inadequacy. But Vivas is even more emphatic; he uses Lawrence's book to illustrate his own aesthetic theory, which is strongly formalistic and insistently against notions of art as "imitation of life."

5. Barbara Hardy, in *The Appropriate Form* (London, 1964), offers an impressive refutation of Schorer and provides the strongest corroboration of my own view. Ford more casually endorses it as well (see *Double Measure,* esp. p. 41).

6. See especially Hardy, chap. 6; and Hough *The Dark Sun,* pp. 41-47.

that such control exists in his very methods, and the lack of thematic resolution with which he has been charged is not so much an aesthetic failing as an impressive and coherent presentation of problems which yield no easy resolutions.

The clearest example of Lawrence's new manner of dealing with both his unresolved attitudes and the aesthetic problems they present lies in the relationship of Walter Morel and his wife. Both Schorer and Vivas have pointed out that Lawrence favored his mother, upon whom the character of Mrs. Morel was based, and disliked his father, who served as the model for Walter Morel. In the book this results in unfair treatment of the father, which is evident in judgments condemning him and approving of the mother. But inconsistency is present in dramatic evidence favoring the father's vitality over the mother's moral restrictions. We can already see in this relationship another rendering of the conflict between the two moralities which roughly emerge in *The Trespasser,* a conflict that is central to Lawrence's career. There is double reason, then, to examine how Lawrence deals with it.

The difficulty between Morel and his wife is outlined in the first ten pages of the novel, and in the next ten the entire progress of their marriage is made explicit. Mrs. Morel's initial attraction to "the golden softness of this man's sensuous flame of life" (p. 10) is gravely disrupted by his irresponsibility with money. She soon discovers that he has not paid the household bills and has lied about possession of the house itself.

He had no grit, she said bitterly to herself. What he felt just at the minute, that was all to him. He could not abide by anything. There was nothing at the back of all his show.

There began a battle between the husband and the wife—a fearful, bloody battle that ended only with the death of one. She fought to make him undertake his own responsibilities, to make him fulfil his obligations. But he was too different from her. His nature was purely sensuous, and she strove to make him moral, religious. She tried to make him face things. He could not endure it—it drove him out of his mind. [p. 14]

If this is not clear enough, the situation is reiterated two pages later: "The pity was, she was too much his opposite. She could not be content with the little he might be; she would have him the much that he ought to be. So, in seeking to make him nobler than he could be, she destroyed him. She injured and hurt and scarred herself, but she lost none of her worth. She also had the children" (p. 16).

This is not a misleading interpretation of what happens both to Morel and his wife. The passages emphasize not that Morel is despicable and his wife good but that they are irreconcilably different. Morel becomes "bad" only if we share Mrs. Morel's point of view, and it cannot be emphasized too strongly that her point of view is not identical with that of Lawrence. Two types of values, or at least two modes of being with which we can be sympathetic, have been presented; no clear choice has been made between Morel's vitality and his wife's moral strength. She destroys him because his sensuous flame is more vulnerable than her moral consistency. Not only does Morel lack the ability to buttress his faults with rationalizations, but the very nature of his existence depends blindly upon the quality of his intimate personal relations. Through her consistency and intense motherly attention she controls the children's love, and resentment makes her stingy with her own. In effect she starves his vitality and forces him to brutality. But the brutality would not be so serious, or perhaps would not have appeared at all, had Morel ever outgrown his childish failure to comprehend the importance of consistency in human relationships.

If we are to insist, then, on moral judgment, these early passages imply that it falls upon both husband and wife for their respective failures to adjust. The degree to which such judgments are called for remains, however, somewhat in question. The book has curiously little moral judgment by the author. Even if the rhetoric here seems fairly heavily weighted on a moral scale ("in seeking to make him nobler than he could be, she destroyed him"), many of the scenes that follow are free of any such commentary. And it is its absence that has invited so much critical contention. Instead of firmly placing the Morels' failures on a consistent and dominant moral scale, Lawrence makes our sympathies shift from one to the other.

Before the end of the first chapter, Morel's ugliness when drunk is portrayed in a quarrel which results in his thrusting his pregnant wife out of doors and locking her out.

> He entered just as Mrs. Morel was pouring the infusion of herbs out of the saucepan. Swaying slightly, he lurched against the table. The boiling liquor pitched. Mrs. Morel started back.
>
> "Good gracious," she cried. "Coming home in his drunkenness!"
>
> "Comin' home in his what?" he snarled, his hat over his eye.
>
> Suddenly her blood rose in a jet.
>
> "Say you're not drunk!" she flashed.
>
> She had put down her saucepan, and was stirring the sugar into the beer. He dropped his two hands heavily on the table, and thrust his face forwards at her.
>
> " 'Say you're not drunk!' " he repeated. "Why, nobody but a nasty little bitch like you 'ud have such a thought." [pp. 21-22]

There is not much doubt where our sympathy lies here. On another occasion Morel flings a drawer at his wife and cuts open her head (pp. 38-39). His children hate him and exclude him, and his eldest son stands up to fight him in defense of his mother, who prevents the fight by stepping between them. At moments he seems repulsive indeed.

> Paul hated his father so. The collier's small, mean head, with its black hair slightly soiled with grey, lay on the bare arms, and the face, dirty and inflamed, with a fleshy nose and thin, paltry brows, was turned sideways, asleep with beer and weariness and nasty temper. If anyone entered suddenly, or a noise were made, the man looked up and shouted:
>
> "I'll lay my fist about thy y'ead, I'm tellin' thee, if tha doesna stop that clatter! Dost hear?" [p. 62]

And the authorial comment made shortly after this passage contains what seems to be the overriding judgment on Morel: "He was an outsider. He had denied the God in him" (p. 63).

Yet these scenes are interspersed with other views of Morel, which not only qualify but even contradict his ugliness. His wife does not always hate him. In a scene following—at least in presentation—a passage in which we are told she despises him:

> His wife lay listening to him tinkering away in the garden, his whistling ringing out as he sawed and hammered away. It always gave her a sense of warmth and peace to hear him thus as she lay in bed, the children not yet awake, in the bright early morning, happy in his man's fashion. [p. 18]

After Morel locks her out in the night, "he realised how hard it was for his wife to drag about at her work, and, his sympathy quickened by penitence, hastened forward with his help" (p. 26). We are then shown a brief but compelling scene of intimacy, in which Morel brings her tea and enjoys her affectionate grumbling.

This see-saw of sympathy which takes place in the presentation of Morel exemplifies Lawrence's method of presenting everyone—and perhaps everything—in the book. The sudden shifts of focus, like that from the scene of violence with the flung drawer to Morel's real intimacy with his children, are not accidental. Although Lawrence himself has made statements which imply that he was making no conscious attempt to be fair to his own father,[7] both the existence of these sympathetic views and their tendency to appear in positions contrasting with unsympathetic views strongly imply that Lawrence the writer was being fairer than Lawrence the man realized. If moral judgments of Morel are present, so are moral judgments of Mrs. Morel, and we shall encounter more of them later. These are not, in any case, the judgments directing this book. In Lawrence's view such judgments are

7. See Earl and Achsah Brewster, *D. H. Lawrence: Reminiscences and Correspondence* (London, 1934), p. 254; also Frieda Lawrence, *Not I But the Wind* (London, 1934), p. 56.

part of living and consequently of writing; they are necessary, as in Shakespearean tragedy, to understand what the characters do and feel. But they in no way provide reliable categories into which all life can fit. We need a view more inclusive than the claim that this novel is "psychological rather than moral," or that Lawrence's sympathy was too thorough to be dominated by morality. The tendency of these evaluations, which are true as far as they go, is to claim that the moral judgments are either irrelevant or cancel each other out. The problem of their relevance is more complicated. The key to its aesthetic resolution seems to lie in the principle of balance which the dialectic presentation we have just examined implies. As we shall see, this principle works in more ways than the simple see-saw of sympathy between Mrs. Morel and her husband.

Following a similar analysis of Lawrence's shifts in sympathy, Barbara Hardy offers a justification of his moral inconsistency by appealing to experience. Her formulation is helpful in its explanation of what Lawrence's immediacy entails.

The so-called contradictions in *Sons and Lovers* come out of a special kind of fidelity to individual truths. What was true does not remain true, what is recognized by the eye and mind is not always recognized by the heart. Lawrence super-imposes several restricted and changing truths upon each other in a way which may well disturb conventional moral and narrative expectations. This novel may not give a faithful record of events and people, but it gives a faithful record of feeling.[8]

8. Hardy, *Appropriate Form*, p. 146. Mrs. Hardy also invokes several of Lawrence's later statements against "static forms" (p. 135). Lawrence emphasized the continual change in which all life is involved, and he argued that such change precludes definition: "My tears of tomorrow will have nothing to do with my tears of a year ago. . . . In all this change, I maintain a certain integrity. But woe betide me if I try to put my finger on it" ("Why the Novel Matters," *Phoenix,* pp. 536-37). This is a statement against, specifically, the notion of ego, which became for Lawrence a restricting idea. As Mrs. Hardy points out, it indeed emphasizes his distrust of systems. But it does not extend to the claim that neither life nor art has

This is certainly my own view, but it leaves some difficulties unresolved. While Mrs. Hardy's essay provides the best answer to Schorer yet available, it makes little attempt to present distinctions between experience and art, and this is precisely where Schorer finds Lawrence at fault. Mrs. Hardy's account of the form of this novel is captured in the phrase "categorical form blurred by truthfulness," by which she means that moral categories are qualified by fidelity to individual truths. Again, this is true as far as it goes, but it is necessary to insist as well that the qualification is not haphazard or confused; even experience must be selected, and selection must occur according to some kind of pattern. If the charges of Schorer and Vivas are to be answered fully, something more must be said about the patterns which emerge through Lawrence's writing. Only by pointing to such patterns can we substantiate a claim that *Sons and Lovers* is not an incoherent work, a presentation of raw experience or experience inadequately assimilated.

Lawrence's fidelity to individual truths, then, is certainly worth a closer look. Here is a passage from "The Young Life of Paul":

> She spat on the iron, and a little ball of spit bounded, raced off the dark, glossy surface. Then, kneeling, she rubbed the iron on the sack lining of the hearth-rug vigorously. She was warm in the ruddy firelight. Paul loved the way she crouched and put her head on one side. Her movements were light and quick. It was always a pleasure to watch her. Nothing she ever did, no movement she ever made, could have been found fault with by her children. The room was warm and full of the scent of hot linen. Later on the clergyman came and talked softly with her.
>
> Paul was laid up with an attack of bronchitis. He did not mind much. What happened happened, and it was no good kicking against the pricks. He loved the evenings, after eight

---

order; it implies merely that such order cannot be defined as a system which leaves no room for change. We shall have repeated occasion to note the force of Lawrence's insistence on vital flux, but to claim that this in any way prevents a dynamic order in his art is to simplify and exaggerate.

o'clock, when the light was put out, and he could watch the fire-flames spring over the darkness of the walls and ceiling; could watch huge shadows waving and tossing, till the room seemed full of men who battled silently.

On retiring to bed, the father would come into the sickroom. He was always very gentle if anyone were ill. But he disturbed the atmosphere for the boy. [p. 66]

What is most impressive about this passage is its extraordinary richness. Its subject, of course, is the feeling of Paul, through whose eyes the scenes are presented. The unity of this feeling is so strong that one almost misses the shifts in the type of information Lawrence presents. We begin with something like a camera movement, from a ball of spit racing on an iron to a woman working in a circle of warmth and ruddy light—a quick but smooth movement of expansion. We then realize that we are looking through Paul's eyes; we enter his mind and discover an intense and sensitive love for the figure before the hearth, an unqualified love that stands for the relation of all the children to the mother. This last point must come from the author and not from Paul, but there is no sense of authorial intrusion, because the simple declarative sentences give us no sense of the boundary of Paul's mind. Lawrence's characteristic mode for presenting emotions deliberately blurs these boundaries. The strength of our impression that Paul's mind is indeed mediating everything lies in the devices which keep the tone consistent—here mainly the visual focus on the mother with the accompanying values of warmth, pleasure, light. We have a suggestion of plenitude through the scent of the hot linen, as another sense of the child is added to his response. And the paragraph ends, a bit curiously, with one sentence devoted to the visit of a clergyman whose soft talking folds into Paul's atmosphere. Without breaking the tone, mention of the clergyman also carries a reminder of the conflict in the Morel household, for he has already been presented as one of the expressions of that conflict.

In this paragraph, then, Lawrence manages to convey the quality of the child's attachment to his mother, even while he hints, through the child's unqualified acceptance, at the broader significance of his position in the family conflict. The next paragraph, in which Paul's illness is seen to prolong his ability to maintain the passive, receptive attitude already developed, shows us his ability to make a satisfying world out of the warm domestic security associated with his mother. The imaginative response to the firelight underlines our sense of the exclusiveness of this world and prepares us to understand the force of the father's well-meaning intrusion and the impossibility of the child's responding adequately to his father's awkward but real tenderness.

This sequence is characteristic in its ability to convey the quality of the book's dominant relationship (that of Paul and his mother) while unobtrusively embodying contradictory material. It is no accident that Morel enters and fails to find a place in Paul's exclusive world, nor is it an accident that our sympathies throughout the painful conversation between father and son (pp. 66-67) lie with the father. Even though there is no moral commentary by the narrator to help us weigh the child's intimacy with his mother against his estrangement from his father, the situation could scarcely be more clearly portrayed.

The boy's point of view, then, despite its strong predominance throughout this chapter, is never allowed to become exclusively ours or Lawrence's. There are innumerable qualifying phrases or even whole scenes. It is this to which Mrs. Hardy refers when she speaks of the superimposition of "restricted and changing truths"; what remains to be emphasized is that the restricting and superimposing itself constitutes a kind of rhetoric. The principle of dialectical balance discussed earlier here influences the selection of detail in Lawrence's apparently direct rendering of experience. The coherent tone rests upon the implicit relation of different sensual data to one another, but this very coherence contains references to activities which must destroy it, thereby implying that the order created by the boy and his mother is not sufficiently inclusive.

The rhetoric of superimposed truths must finally be contained by a more inclusive truth. This larger truth tends to accumulate by a process of antithesis. For example, the passages we have recently been examining suggest something like this: Paul and his mother have a wonderful, intimate relationship, characterized by simple domestic activities. The relationship is excessive, however, in the child's uncritical adulation of his mother. Paul's imagination abets his intimacy with his mother but tends to exclude his father. This is unfair to the father, for the father is sincerely tender. But the father also displays a simplicity and awkwardness that, if pathetic, is almost stupidly incomprehending of his son.

It is in this manner that the material of Lawrence's book coheres; neither of the first two books can make a similar claim to interrelationship of episode. The family tension is, as Mrs. Hardy points out, the center of the book, for it is the continuing element in all shifts of perspective. Since we are aware of the tension from the very beginning, virtually everything that passes has its implications for the moral problems raised, the problems of responsibility for failure in human relationships. Yet the failure to come to clear moral conclusions is deliberate and necessary to Lawrence's overriding concern, which seems to be a desire not simply for inclusiveness or fidelity to feeling but for presentation of that feeling as a coherent force influencing the direction of life and our apprehension of value, both moral and vital. At this stage in his career Lawrence could best make these complex forces and values felt by working in the antithetical mode we have just examined, through which each episode of coherent feeling, with its attendant moral implications, implies and often directly yields to another equally coherent response which qualifies or even contradicts the first. We can indeed claim that "life is this way" in its continual fluctuation; but neither life as experienced nor life as remembered is quite so firm in its emphasis, coherent in its tone, or definite in its implication for value and meaning, however temporary that value or meaning may be.

Behind this dialectical narrative, which not only presents opposing perspectives in alternation but integrates hints of one set of values in the presentation of another, is of course a directing narrator, whose presence and control are evident in other devices as well. He is never a personality in the sense that Cyril is, nor does he appear to make larger generalizations in the manner of George Eliot's narrators. But in so far as the rhetoric of super-imposed truths is present, we must suppose that the narrator is creating it to enlarge our consciousness by contrast and to insist that none of the individual judgments are to be regarded as final. If we conceive of him in this way—as a selecting presence governed by a dialectical approach to the book's problems of value—the force of the narrator is felt throughout. It appears not only in the account of a boy's intimate feelings toward his parents but in much more dramatic scenes, where one might suppose that re-membered patterns of action and speech would objectify the nar-rator beyond detection. In a brilliantly realistic account of the small boy's terror at confronting adults who have no sympathy for his self-consciousness, Lawrence presents a scene apparently directed only by the remembered sequence of events. It is done from the boy's point of view, and both the brief passages of narrative analysis and the larger pattern of the scene are designed exclusively to portray the boy's agonies. Paul has come to collect his father's pay at the company office, and the cashier is calling out the names.

"Bower—John Bower."

A boy stepped to the counter. Mr. Braithwaite, large and irascible, glowered at him over his spectacles.

"John Bower!" he repeated.

"It's me," said the boy.

"Why, you used to 'ave a different nose than that," said glossy Mr. Winterbottom, peering over the counter. The people tittered, thinking of John Bower senior.

"How is it your father's not come!" said Mr. Braithwaite, in a large and magisterial voice.

"He's badly," piped the boy.

"You should tell him to keep off the drink," pronounced the mocking voice from behind.

All the men laughed. The large and important cashier looked down at his next sheet.

"Fred Pilkington!" he called, quite indifferent.

Mr. Braithwaite was an important shareholder in the firm.

Paul knew his turn was next but one, and his heart began to beat. He was pushed against the chimney-piece. His calves were burning. But he did not hope to get through the wall of men.

"Walter Morel!" came the ringing voice.

"Here!" piped Paul, small and inadequate.

"Morel—Walter Morel!" the cashier repeated, his finger and thumb on the invoice, ready to pass on.

Paul was suffering convulsions of self-consciousness, and could not or would not shout. The backs of the men obliterated him. Then Mr. Winterbottom came to the rescue.

"He's here. Where is he? Morel's lad?"

The fat, red, bald little man peered round with keen eyes. He pointed at the fireplace. The colliers looked round, moved aside, and disclosed the boy.

"Here he is!" said Mr. Winterbottom.

Paul went to the counter.

"Seventeen pounds eleven and fivepence. Why don't you shout up when you're called?" said Mr. Braithwaite. He banged on to the invoice a five-pound bag of silver, then in a delicate and pretty movement, picked up a little ten-pound column of gold, and plumped it beside the silver. The gold slid in a bright stream over the paper. The cashier finished counting off the money; the boy dragged the whole down the counter to Mr. Winterbottom, to whom the stoppages for rent and tools must be paid. Here he suffered again.

"Sixteen an' six," said Mr. Winterbottom.

The lad was too much upset to count. He pushed forward some loose silver and half a sovereign.

"How much do you think you've given me?" asked Mr. Winterbottom.

The boy looked at him, but said nothing. He had not the faintest notion.

"Haven't you got a tongue in your head?"

Paul bit his lip, and pushed forward some more silver.

"Don't they teach you to count at the Boardschool?" he asked.

"Nowt but algibbra an' French," said a collier.

"An' cheek and impidence," said another.

Paul was keeping someone waiting. With trembling fingers he got his money into the bag and slid out. He suffered the tortures of the damned on these occasions. [pp. 70-71]

As a record of the boy's acute sensitivity to the rough yet jovial behavior of the men, this passage is perfect. Although he notices both Winterbottom's glossiness and Braithwaite's self-importance, Paul is also in awe of the adult power and control these men possess. Obliterated by the crowd of coarse and powerful colliers, he is reduced to incompetence and must pay for it by abuse of his education and nonexistent "impidence." But he is functioning well enough to notice the delicate beauty of the cashier's movement and the brightness of the gold. And though we realize that the colliers and officials are not cruel (this is made clear by giving us their conversation), we could hardly be shown more clearly how they can unwittingly make a small boy suffer. Yet as we follow Paul's trip home and witness the subsequent conversation with his mother, we can see that beneath the unifying presence of the boy's mind a principle of thematic relevance is also at work. Some of the details of this scene, like the clergyman in the earlier scene, serve to emphasize and make richer the broader conflicts of the book. "The boy went near the wall, self-consciously. He knew many of the men, but could not recognise them in their dirt. And this was a new torture to him" (p. 71). It begins to appear that the gruffness of the colliers functions like their dirt to hide something important. Within a paragraph or two the difficulty emerges more clearly. Paul has to take the money to the bar, where his father will pass out the shares of his fellow workers.

Paul sat down on the edge of the bench in the bar. Some colliers were "reckoning"—sharing out their money—in a corner; others came in. They all glanced at the boy without speaking. At last Morel came; brisk, and with something of an air, even in his blackness.

"Hello!" he said rather tenderly to his son. "Have you bested me? Shall you have a drink of something?"

Paul and all the children were bred up fierce anti-alcoholists, and he would have suffered more in drinking a lemonade before all the men than in having a tooth drawn.

The landlady looked at him *de haut en bas,* rather pitying, and at the same time, resenting his clear, fierce morality. [p. 72]

Here Paul's clear, fierce morality is opposed to his father's air beneath his blackness, and that air becomes the same deep tenderness we noticed in contrast to Mrs. Morel's moral sternness. We begin to see, then, that Paul's smallness and inadequacy in the company office were heightened by his difficulty in relating the fierce morality derived from his mother to the rougher, "dirty" behavior of the colliers. The conversation with his mother which immediately follows further clarifies the nature of the boy's morality. Upon reaching home Paul insists "in a fury" that he will not go to the office again, and to justify his fury he offers these explanations: "They're hateful, and common, and hateful, they are, and I'm not going any more. Mr. Braithwaite drops his 'h's', an' Mr. Winterbottom says 'You was' " (p. 72). Although this is more rationalization than reason, it indicates an unusual degree of snobbery in a small boy growing up in a colliery town. When we remember that Mrs. Morel speaks perfect English and Morel speaks dialect, its larger meaning is quite obvious. In his child's fashion Paul has simplified and intensified the snobbery implicit in his mother's pride, which is not altogether distinguishable from her moral consistency. We can now understand more clearly why the boy should be so sensitive to the remarks about his schooling. That those remarks are unjustified is soon pointed out, for Paul has no difficulty giving his mother the accounting which he failed to do in the office.

> "What was the cheque?" she asked.
> "Seventeen pounds eleven and fivepence, and sixteen and six stoppages," replied the boy. "It's a good week; and only five shillings stoppages for my father."
> So she was able to calculate how much her husband had earned, and could call him to account if he gave her short money. Morel always kept to himself the secret of the week's amount. [p. 73]

Paul's response to the money was not entirely aesthetic.

In this apparently descriptive scene, then, the major oppositions of the book unfold; they are, in fact, implicit in the detail of the description itself. Without changing his focus on the boy and his responses, the narrator provides an increasingly thorough explanation of both, and that explanation takes into account the main conflicts of value in the book. Like the women in Lawrence's first two novels, Mrs. Morel embodies both moral and cultural values, and for her maintenance of these values both her husband and her child must pay. The sensitive child is particularly affected; he is largely blind to the fact that the colliers, and especially his father, are warm and vital, for his mother has taught him to look first at their dirt. But before we make Mrs. Morel into a prude we should note that this scene also refers to her habit of putting aside a fresh bun for her young son, and that the overall purpose of her remarks is to soothe him and show him that his complaints about Braithwaite and Winterbottom border on hysteria. Once again a principle of balance seems to be operating.

That thematic considerations are, in fact, directing the narrative is further evident in the absence of transitional or background material, which would normally be present in an autobiography.

> The landlady looked at him *de haut en bas,* rather pitying, and at the same time, resenting his clear, fierce morality. Paul went home, glowering. He entered the house silently. Friday

was baking day, and there was usually a hot bun. His mother
put it before him.

Suddenly he turned on her in a fury, his eyes flashing. [p.
72]

Since Paul has nothing significant to do on the way home, he
gets there in one sentence. Sometimes there is no transition at
all, but simply a change of time and focus without warning:

Nevertheless, the load of anxiety scarcely ever left her heart,
lest William should do the wrong thing by himself.

Presently, Paul was bidden call upon Thomas Jordan, Manu-
facturer of Surgical Appliances, at 21, Spaniel Row, Nottingham. Mrs. Morel was all joy. [p. 91]

As the *presently* implies, the time scheme of the book is vague,
though its large movement follows Paul's development from
childhood to young manhood. This development, though it
helps to give form to the book as a whole, is never Lawrence's
main concern—at least not in the sense that it is, say, in *Ma-
dame Bovary* or *Death of a Salesman. Sons and Lovers* is not a
chronicle of a young man's progress so much as an exploration
of the values which have shaped his life, however imperfectly.
And the only way these values can be explored is by making
the characters live through them in all their contradictions. The
very abruptness of the narrator's shifts in time or point of view
or both is an expression of his involvement with these contradictions.

Thus Lawrence's presentation of the Morels is anything but
haphazard. Despite its autobiographical nature, the narrative is
by no means an attempt to render experience in its undifferentiated entirety. Once we take the trouble to notice it, the
relevance of all his detail to his larger themes is so thorough as
to account in itself for the great superiority of this book over
the first two. And these larger themes are governed by the desire not to blame any of the characters but to come to an understanding of the conflicts that disrupted the earlier novels.

The new firmness of Lawrence's sense of relevance is further evident in his treatment of natural description. Neither the personal intrusions of Cyril in *The White Peacock* nor the too-fervent strainings toward ontology in *The Trespasser* appear in this book. A strong sense of nature's vitality remains and even undergoes further definition, as we shall see shortly, but the forces of nature are almost never explored for their own sake, as they are repeatedly in *The White Peacock.* Nor are they forced, as in *The Trespasser,* to yield glimpses of a unity about which the author is uncertain. Descriptions of landscape, flora, or sky are not only much rarer in *Sons and Lovers* than in the first two novels, but when they do appear their relevance to the emotional state of the characters present is usually clear: it is almost always possible to read such passages as symbolic expressions of the characters' feelings or predicaments. The natural and the human are no longer painfully separate, as they were earlier; instead, the former tends consistently to inform or define the latter, avoiding a vague collapse into fate. Throughout *Sons and Lovers* there appears a much stronger sense that the two are fundamentally related, but the temptation to speculate loosely is resisted. Instead the narrator is consistently objective about the problem.

The Bottoms succeeded to "Hell Row." Hell Row was a block of thatched, bulging cottages that stood by the brookside on Greenhill Lane. There lived the colliers who worked in the little gin-pits two fields away. The brook ran under the alder trees, scarcely soiled by these small mines, whose coal was drawn to the surface by donkeys that plodded wearily in a circle round a gin. And all over the countryside were these same pits, some of which had been worked in the time of Charles II, the few colliers and the donkeys burrowing down like ants into the earth, making queer mounds and little black places among the corn-fields and meadows. And the cottages of these coal-miners, in blocks and pairs here and there, together with odd farms and homes of the stockingers, strayed over the parish, formed the village of Best-wood. [p. 1]

This view of man and nature is almost unique in Lawrence's novels. In his next book collieries come to signify a sense of outrage at what man has done to nature and especially to himself, but here no such tone is present. The pits change the landscape, but they do not seem to deface it; the narrator's attitude is merely that man's diggings are curious but not evil. The brook is scarcely soiled, and only queer mounds and little black places appear among the corn-fields and meadows. The verbs and participial phrases consistently avoid charging the scene with any emotion implying either strong approval or disapproval; they emphasize instead the scattered and limited nature of man's activities on the landscape, which have apparently gone on long enough to be assimilated.

Man's activities, then, need not deface nature or even create disharmony. In his masterful evocation of the mining world in which he grew up, Lawrence sympathetically tolerates not only the class from which he sprang but the whole industrial world against which he was soon to turn. At moments he is even enthusiastic about it, and the pits and nature seem animated by the same vital forces.

On the fallow land the young wheat shone silkily. Minton pit waved its plumes of white steam, coughed, and rattled hoarsely.

"Now look at that!" said Mrs. Morel. Mother and son stood on the road to watch. Along the ridge of the great pit-hill crawled a little group in silhouette against the sky, a horse, a small truck, and a man. They climbed the incline against the heavens. At the end the man tipped the wagon. There was an undue rattle as the waste fell down the sheer slope of the enormous bank.

"You sit a minute, mother," he said, and she took a seat on a bank, whilst he sketched rapidly. She was silent whilst he worked, looking round at the afternoon, the red cottages shining among their greenness.

"The world is a wonderful place," she said, "and wonderfully beautiful."

"And so's the pit," he said. "Look how it heaps together, like something alive almost—a big creature that you don't know."

"Yes," she said. "Perhaps!"

"And all the trucks standing waiting, like a string of beasts to be fed," he said.

"And very thankful I am they *are* standing," she said, "for that means they'll turn middling time this week."

"But I like the feel of *men* on things, while they're alive. There's a feel of men about trucks, because they've been handled with men's hands, all of them."

"Yes," said Mrs. Morel. [p. 123]

This takes place during an outing in the country; it is flanked by short but effective appreciations of the natural beauty upon which Mrs. Morel remarks here. That there is no obvious shift in attitude from the description of the pits to that of ponds, birds, and meadows indicates that the narrator is willing to regard them in the same way. Indeed, the description of the pit and its carts by an animal metaphor enforces our sense that they both embody the vitality which is present in Paul and his mother.[9]

This attitude, in which both natural and human activity are regarded as parts of a meaningful whole, extends even to a defense of the town. When Paul and Clara Dawes look out over the countryside from Nottingham Castle, they see the town dwellings as "poisonous herbage."

"It is comforting," said Mrs. Dawes, "to think the town goes no farther. It is only a *little* sore upon the country yet."

9. In the significance attached to "men's hands" there is also a firm Protestant belief in the value of work, which Lawrence held all his life. In the autobiographic reminiscence "Nottingham and Mining Countryside," in *Phoenix,* Lawrence, now forty-four, firmly couples this belief with his vitalism, arguing that the "intuitional contact between men" was very "highly developed" in the pit, allowing the miners to appreciate beauty, especially natural beauty, when they came up. See also "Autobiographical Fragment," in *Phoenix.*

"A little scab," Paul said.

She shivered. She loathed the town. Looking drearily across at the country which was forbidden her, her impassive face, pale and hostile, she reminded Paul of one of the bitter, re-morseful angels.

"But the town's all right," he said; "it's only temporary. This is the crude, clumsy makeshift we've practised on, till we find out what the idea is. The town will come all right." [p. 271]

This expresses a faith in man which Lawrence never again dis-plays. From *The Rainbow* on there is little optimism and no comparable belief that "the town will come all right."[10] Even here no programs are presented to indicate how this will be achieved. But the willingness to think well of man's efforts is definitely present, and it can best be explained as part of Law-rence's determined return to the fundamental values of his child-hood, values which this book is devoted to exploring and evoking once more. A significant part of its coherence depends upon Law-rence's willingness to attempt to "see life whole" as a child is able to see it, even while he knows as an adult that this wholeness is no simple matter. And in this willingness lies the basis for the claim that the book is the best depiction of working-class life in print.[11]

There is evidence, in fact, that Lawrence thought of the vitality present in both nature and man as a property of the lower rather than the middle classes:

"You know," he [Paul] said to his mother, "I don't want to belong to the well-to-do middle class. I like my common people best. I belong to the common people."

"But if anyone else said so, my son, wouldn't you be in a tear. *You* know you consider yourself equal to any gentleman."

10. The ending to *The Rainbow* may be considered an exception. See pp. 183-85 below.

11. Several critics would be willing to make this claim. See esp. Hough, *The Dark Sun,* pp. 41-42; and Moynahan, *Deed of Life,* pp. 19-23.

"In myself," he answered, "not in my class or my education or my manners. But in myself I am."

"Very well, then. Then why talk about the common people?"

"Because—the difference between people isn't in their class, but in themselves. Only from the middle classes one gets ideas, and from the common people—life itself, warmth. You feel their hates and loves."

"It's all very well, my boy. But, then, why don't you go and talk to your father's pals?"

"But they's rather different."

"Not at all. They're the common people. After all, whom do you mix with now—among the common people? Those that exchange ideas, like the middle classes. The rest don't interest you." [p. 256]

Significantly, this argument is inconclusive; it formulates again the difficulty Lawrence had with "coming to consciousness" in *The White Peacock*. Both Paul and his mother are right, judging from Lawrence's later writings as well as from this novel. Ideas remain as important to Lawrence as common warmth, even though he sometimes speaks as if warmth were all-important. And even though Lawrence continued to associate vital warmth with the common people and ideas with the establishment, his novels yield no such simple division. Paul's unstable position in the argument quoted above is one indication that these polarities are not dogma, and his tendency to fall back on what people are in themselves significantly points toward the only sort of resolution Lawrence was able to give to the vital-intellectual dilemma: he sought a more fundamental realm which could be expressed by both natural and cultural activity. And although the conflict between the elder Morels shows that such a resolution was not found here, there are strong hints that beneath their opposition to one another is a shared vitality, analogous to that between the works of man and nature.

Mrs. Morel, of course, is the most middle-class character in the book, and some critics make much of this in explaining her opposition to the lower-class Morel.[12] It has also been argued that Mrs. Morel, because she stands for ideas, "wants death"; whereas her husband, embodying "the natural life-directed condition of the human animal," is the only character to "preserve the germ of self-hood intact."[13] But we have already seen evidence which implies that this is a simplification of the qualities of Lawrence's writing and, consequently, a distortion of the values he presents. The Morels differ not so much in their capacity to embody "life forces" as in the manner in which they shape, accommodate, and direct them. Even Mrs. Morel's restrictive morality, which is presented as the main cause of her husband's destruction, significantly accommodates the vital needs of her children. Though Paul's attachment to his mother is so dominant as to cripple his adult life, its real childhood intensity is made possible by her moral consistency, which is further informed by real love. And both Morels respond to nature: Morel loves his morning walk to the mines and takes grass into the pit to keep his mouth moist; Mrs. Morel finds nature wonderful and beautiful. The intensity of Paul's sexual conflicts is a function of this shared vitality.

The relation of this vitality to the natural world is further developed in Lawrence's symbolic scenes, where he attempts both to formulate vital pressures through natural metaphors and to evoke the very quality of the vitality which man and nature share. This is particularly evident in a scene in the Morels' garden, where Mrs. Morel, thrown outside by her drunken husband, stumbles about in delirium, helpless and pregnant.

The moon was high and magnificent in the August night. Mrs. Morel, seared with passion, shivered to find herself out there in a great white light, that fell cold on her, and gave a shock to her inflamed soul. She stood for a few moments helplessly staring at the glistening great rhubarb leaves near the door. Then she

12. Mary Freeman, *D. H. Lawrence: A Basic Study of His Ideas* (New York, 1955), chap. 2.
13. See Dorothy Van Ghent, *The English Novel* (New York 1961), pp. 245-61.

got the air into her breast. She walked down the garden path, trembling in every limb, while the child boiled within her. For a while she could not control her consciousness. . . . She must have been half an hour in this delirious condition. Then the presence of the night came again to her. She glanced round in fear. . . . She hurried out of the side garden to the front, where she could stand as if in an immense gulf of white light, the moon streaming high in face of her, the moonlight standing up from the hills in front, and filling the valley where the Bottoms crouched, almost blindingly. There, panting and half weeping in reaction from the stress, she murmured to herself over and over again: "The nuisance! the nuisance!"

She became aware of something about her. With an effort she roused herself to see what it was that penetrated her consciousness. The tall white lilies were reeling in the moonlight, and the air was charged with their perfume, as with a presence. Mrs. Morel gasped in fear. She touched the big, pallid flowers on their petals, then shivered. They seemed to be stretching in the moonlight. She put her hand into one white bin: the gold scarcely showed on her fingers by moonlight. She bent down to look at the binful of yellow pollen; but it only appeared dusky. Then she drank a deep draught of the scent. It almost made her dizzy.

Mrs. Morel leaned on the garden gate, looking out, and she lost herself awhile. She did not know what she thought. Except for a slight feeling of sickness, and her consciousness in the child, herself melted out like scent into the shiny, pale air. After a time the child, too, melted with her in the mixing-pot of moonlight, and she rested with the hills and lilies and houses, all swam together in a kind of swoon. [pp. 23-24]

Dorothy Van Ghent has pointed out that the imagery of the moonlight "equates not only with that phallic power of which Mrs. Morel is the rebellious vessel but with the greater and universal demiurge that was anciently called Eros—the power spring-

ing in plants and hurling the planets."[14] She goes on to describe
the passage as "a typifying instance of the spontaneous identification Lawrence constantly found between image and meaning, between real things and what they symbolize." This it certainly is,
and we are indebted to Mrs. Van Ghent for pointing it out. But I
wonder just how rebellious a vessel Mrs. Morel is. It is true that
she does not want the baby; once she has it she feels guilty about
not having wanted it and she vows "to make up to it for having
brought it into the world unloved" (p. 37). She is obviously not
in joyful ecstasy over "the mysterious out-of-doors" and does not
quite come to terms with the universal demiurge which the moonlight magnificently captures. Yet together with her fear is a strong
fascination: she leaves the darkness at the side of the house to
seek the moonlight; her gasp of fear at the presence of the lilies
does not prevent her from making herself dizzy on the scent and
reaching in for pollen; she falls into a swoon where everything
becomes mixed together—child, lilies, houses—and emerges to
take a more quiet sensual pleasure from the roses. And when she
finally enters the house she smiles at the image of her face in the
mirror, "all smeared with the yellow dust of lilies." Mrs. Van
Ghent calls this a "grossly humorous irony," but I interpret the
scene somewhat differently.

What Lawrence seems to do here is to use the imagery of moonlight and the flowers of the garden to convey the life-force which
Mrs. Van Ghent describes as well as Mrs. Morel's complex relation
to it, and this relation gains in significance as we notice that the
causes of her immediate turmoil stem from her unresolved attitudes toward her husband. That is, the natural imagery is (1) a
symbol of a magnificent, compelling life-force which through her
pregnancy Mrs. Morel shares with the plants, (2) a descriptive
embodiment of the force, and (3) a vehicle for emotional turmoil
which has a separate, domestic cause. In blending these three
functions Lawrence also presents something in the nature of a
lesson in Mrs. Morel's vitality: she is not so much rebellious as

14. Ibid., pp. 248-49.

hesitant and fearful of the mystery she confronts, and her fear is heightened by the horrible fight she has had with her husband. In their unalloyed, inhuman power, the forces she confronts in the garden are too much for her, just as her husband in his rage is too much for her. But this is not something for which she is simply to be blamed according to a nature morality; no such morality dominates this book.[15] Morel himself certainly does not embody it, any more than Annable did in *The White Peacock*. It is questionable, in fact, whether anyone could accept the presence of the lilies unconditionally; that would amount to giving up one's humanity entirely, as Morel does only in his drunken fits. Mrs. Morel may be culpable for excessive fear, heightened perhaps by an inability to understand her "loss of self"; but her smile at the pollen dust is a small irony, not a gross one, for in it we can see her accepting the presence of the lilies and reducing it to domestic proportions.

In scenes like this Lawrence manages to express most directly the relation between man and nature upon which his earlier novels tended to flounder. Here there is no sense that he himself is confused or uncertain; both Mrs. Morel's limitations and her vital capacities are captured, and the garden and the moonlight also embody the vital forces in a more elemental form than any Mrs. Morel can ever know. There is a tension between her inhibition and the magnificent powers in the garden, but we already know enough to understand how she is inhibited, and we also know that she is capable of a good deal more than issuing moral directives. In short, Lawrence has provided a social and psychological context that itself explains the details of the symbolic scene, even though he implies the presence of more fundamental forces beneath it which inform his psychology but do not constitute it.[16]

15. Mrs. Van Ghent argues that it does, but here I think she relies too much on Lawrence's later writings.

16. Julian Moynahan has forcefully argued that the formal inadequacies of the book are a direct result of precisely this difference between a "vitalistic" and "deterministic" psychology. See below, pp. 88 ff., for a discussion of his argument.

As *The Trespasser* gives us reason to expect, the most thorough evocation of these forces appears in descriptions of sexual passion. Here the natural and the human find their most fundamental likeness, realizing a momentary harmony like that which Mrs. Morel found in her swoon, but accompanied more by joy than by fear. Paul finds such a harmony through Clara, and Lawrence is now able to evoke it much more firmly than he did in *The Trespasser*.

As a rule, when he started lovemaking, the emotion was strong enough to carry with it everything—reason, soul, blood—in a great sweep, like the Trent carries bodily its back swirls and intertwinings, noiselessly. Gradually the little criticisms, the little sensations, were lost, thought also went, everything borne along in one flood. He became, not a man with a mind, but a great instinct. His hands were like creatures, living; his limbs, his body, were all life and consciousness, subject to no will of his, but living in themselves. Just as he was, so it seemed the vigorous, wintry stars were strong also with life. He and they struck with the same pulse of fire, and the same joy of strength which held the bracken-frond stiff near his eyes held his own body firm. It was as if he, and the stars, and the dark herbage, and Clara were licked up in an immense tongue of flame, which tore onwards and upwards. Everything rushed along in living beside him; everything was still, perfect in itself, along with him. This wonderful stillness in each thing in itself, while it was being borne along in a very ecstasy of living, seemed the highest point of bliss. [pp. 363-64]

Instead of inserting a mysterious God, shedding flowers of passion upon all mankind, Lawrence stays close to the actual pattern of sensation, linking it by deliberate comparison (his hands were like, it seemed, it was as if) to the elemental world and never making the ontological leap which was to become characteristic in his next two novels. Yet the pattern for such a leap is clearly present: Paul's feeling of identity is to become actual identity with the life of the stars, and the wonderful stillness of each thing in itself becomes finally an insistence upon a pluralistic meta-physic, in which everything vital (and Lawrence was quite willing to include inanimate objects in this category)[17] is irrevocably individual as well. Although here *seem* is not yet *be,* and the entire passage may consequently be read as an expression of what Paul is experiencing without insisting upon real connections with nature, those connections are strongly implied. One might say they are affectively present if not metaphysically proclaimed.[18]

Beneath his portrayal of these several variations on the relation of man to nature, then, Lawrence seems to be affirming their fundamental relatedness through vitality. This affirmation is—somewhat paradoxically, perhaps—all the more convincing for its subordination to a thorough social and psychological realism, which never allows us to forget that the book is concerned with man as well as nature. There is little sense of conflict or divorce; only in the garden scene might this be felt. Taken alone this "flame-like" quality clearly embodies a positive value, and from it a vitalistic philosophy will grow. But at the time Lawrence wrote this book such a philosophy had not yet emerged, and it consequently has little impact here. In its place remain the problems of how this fundamental vitality can be embodied or released, what will restrict its growth, and what will encourage self-realization. In his struggle with these problems Lawrence explored the forms which had dominated his young life, notably those embodied in his mother. The result has been called an independent discovery of the oedipal com-

17. See above p. 32 n.16.
18. I have found one passage where they almost are metaphysically proclaimed. Again it is a scene of passion, again with Clara. "What was she? A strong, strange, wild life, that breathed with his in the darkness through this hour. It was all so much bigger than themselves that he was hushed. They had met, and included in their meeting the thrust of the manifold grass stems, the cry of the peewit, the wheel of the stars" (p. 353). But here too there is no insistence that the lovers have "fallen" into another realm of being, even though the description might, in the light of Lawrence's later writings, be taken to imply as much.

plex.[19] I prefer to regard it as another stage in the dialectical process discussed earlier. For the oedipal pattern, though unmistakably present, is not satisfactory in revealing either the complexity of the relationships involved or Lawrence's methods for presenting them coherently.

Lawrence has conveniently provided us with an analysis of his novel, emphasizing the relation between mother and son. It was written after he became acquainted with Freud, but this would not have been necessary to his analysis; the novel was almost complete before Freud could have had any influence upon him, and his analysis describes the novel.[20]

It follows this idea: a woman of character and refinement goes into the lower class, and has no satisfaction in her own life. She has had a passion for her husband, so the children are born of passion, and have heaps of vitality. But as her sons grow up she selects them as lovers—first the eldest, then the second. These sons are *urged* into life by their reciprocal love of their mother—urged on and on. But when they come into manhood, they can't love, because their mother is the strongest power in their lives, and holds them. It's rather like Goethe and his mother and Frau von Stein and Christiana—As soon as the young men come into contact with women, there's a split. William gives his sex to a fribble, and his mother holds his soul. But the split kills him, because he doesn't know where he is. The next son gets a woman who fights for his soul—fights his mother. The son loves the mother—all the sons hate and are jealous of the father. The battle goes on between the mother and the girl, with the son as

19. See Harry Moore, *The Life and Works of D. H. Lawrence* (New York, 1951), p. 94. The most insistently oedipal interpretation of Lawrence is to be found in Murry's *Son of Woman*. Daniel Weiss's *Oedipus in Nottingham* (Seattle, 1962) is more sophisticated.

20. See Frederick J. Hoffman, "Lawrence's Quarrel with Freud," in *The Achievement of D. H. Lawrence,* ed. Frederick J. Hoffman and Harry Moore (Norman, Okla., 1953), pp. 106-27. Moynahan tends to emphasize Lawrence's early Freudianism more than Hoffman does (*Deed of Life,* pp. 23-31). Cf. also Hough, *The Dark Sun,* pp. 39-40.

object. The mother gradually proves stronger, because of the tie
of blood. The son decides to leave his soul in his mother's
hands, and, like his elder brother go for passion. He gets passion. Then the split begins to tell again. But, almost uncon-
sciously, the mother realises what is the matter, and begins to
die. The son casts off his mistress, attends to his mother dying.
He is left in the end naked of everything, with the drift towards
death.[21]

The pattern described here is as oedipal as one could wish, but
the logic behind it does not seem altogether scientific. The sons'
vitality is regarded as the result of sexual passion between parents; William dies of a split between mother and lover; Mrs. Morel
dies of a realization that she is smothering her son. Freud would
swallow none of this, and the book in fact gives other causes for
death: erysipelas in the son, cancer in the mother. It is not that
Lawrence is guilty of distortion, but that his own account falls
into a vital or symbolic pattern quite as easily as it uses sound
psychology ("the mother is the strongest power in their lives").
One might even draw from it the notion that Lawrence was not
sure what sort of causality he believed in.[22] But if so, his book
does not adversely reflect his confusion, for both sorts of causality are successfully used and in fact usually played off against one
another.

Julian Moynahan has impressively defined "three formal orders" in *Sons and Lovers,* the autobiographical, the psychological
(or psychoanalytic) and the vital.[23] The last two are those we
just discovered in Lawrence's account of his book. All three influence the portrayal of the major characters, especially Paul.
According to the psychological pattern, Paul is fixated and
trapped into a pattern of "repetition compulsion" through attachment to his mother; the final "drift toward death" is really

21. *LM,* pp. 160-61.
22. This seems to be Moynahan's notion (*Deed of Life,* p. 27).
23. Ibid., pp. 13-18.

the last word on him. According to the vital pattern, which constitutes Lawrence's main emphasis in the later novels, Paul shows significant signs of freedom to break out of the Freudian trap and has "a better than even chance of maintaining himself whole and alive in the midst of life as the novel ends." Moynahan argues that the presence of both patterns amounts to formal confusion and ambiguities in presentation of character.[24]

Moynahan is surely right in his claim that the two "systems of interpretation" do not coincide. But are systems of interpretation equivalent to patterns in the novel? Although Moynahan presents convincing analyses of various passages according to one or the other system, he does not convince me that the systems conflict to mar the novel. What is the evidence that Lawrence used the Freudian axiom which Moynahan mentions in such a way that it confuses the reader about Paul's freedom? Moynahan himself does not seem confused about this: "The ending of *Sons and Lovers* shows that Paul Morel's nature does contain an intact core of vitality which is his freedom, that while his responses to his family and mistresses have been 'over-determined' by neu-

24. Moynahan's argument is easily the most convincing criticism of *Sons and Lovers* as a confused novel:

The conflict, with its attendant ambiguities which confuse the presentation of Miriam and Clara as well as Paul, is real but ought not to be exaggerated, as it has been by critics whose notions of formal coherence are narrowly based. Psychoanalysis and Lawrence's kind of vitalism have many points in common as readings of experience. There is a sense in which the "drift toward death" means as much in passional as in neurotic terms. But the two systems of interpretation finally do not coincide. The Freudian system is weighted toward determinism. Paul, given his conditioning and the axiom that unconscious processes cannot become conscious and therefore modifiable without a therapist's aid, is doomed. The vital context is a fluid system that is fully indeterminate. Short of death there is no occasion in experience when the individual cannot make the correct, life-enhancing choice. Even an old wreck like Morel *could* at least look at his dead wife—the possibility is implied by the very strictness with which his refusal to do so is judged. The issues of life and death are fully worked into the very texture of events, and the road to salvation runs along the edge of the abyss where Paul stands after his mother's death and his double rejection of Clara and Miriam. [ibid., pp. 18-19]

roticism, his fate remains indeterminate *au fond.*"[25] The relative emphasis of the two systems is here nicely discriminated;
the vital system is at bottom more fundamental than the pattern of fixation which Moynahan cogently spells out.[26] To me
this does not amount to formal confusion. I see no necessity to
assume that all the patterns which one can abstract from a novel have to coincide at every point, especially if their copresence
can be otherwise explained. For such an explanation we can again
use the dialectical principle discussed earlier.

Although hardly conceived in the same terms, Paul's relationship with Miriam is largely governed by the same sort of changing
focus we noticed in the elder Morels. Miriam in many ways embodies qualities which are present in Mrs. Morel, and some of
these qualities (her possessiveness and moral idealism) function to
restrict Paul, just as Mrs. Morel restricts her husband. Throughout
the relationship we are clearly shown inadequacies in both Miriam
and Paul which explain in large part their failure to marry, just as
we are shown inadequacies in the elder Morels which account for
their failure in marriage. But the whole pattern of Paul's relationship with Miriam becomes much more complicated, because Mrs.
Morel is always a presence in it. Paul seeks Miriam out not only
because she has qualities similar to his mother's but because she
also offers, or at least seems to offer, a way to pass beyond his
mother's influence. In Moynahan's terms, he goes to Miriam both
because of a "determined" need to repeat patterns by which he
has lived and because of a "vital" need to enlarge or even break
those patterns. In the novel these two needs are often indistinguishable, as indeed they would be in life; any action or feeling
which has significance must contain both elements which seem
determined and elements which seem fresh. Paul's struggle is to
find out which are which; to convey this struggle Lawrence alternately focuses upon his frustration, which tends to express

25. Ibid., p. 29.
26. This point was of course implicit in the evidence for a fundamental
wholeness that we just examined.

itself in cruelty to Miriam with accompanying guilt, or upon his exultation that he is "getting somewhere," which usually proves too optimistic. Throughout the novel Paul's strivings presuppose a vital commitment to self-realization, which entitles him, as Moynahan points out, to be labeled Lawrence's first vital hero.

Early in Paul's relationship with Miriam, before his sexual needs bring the conflict between her and his mother into the open, his links with the two women are comfortably seen as part of the same vital fulfillment.

> He was studying for his painting. He loved to sit at home, alone with his mother, at night, working and working. She sewed or read. Then, looking up from his task, he would rest his eyes for a moment on her face, that was bright with living warmth, and he returned gladly to his work.
>
> "I can do my best things when you sit there in your rocking-chair, mother," he said.
>
> ... he, with all his soul's intensity directing his pencil, could feel her warmth inside him like strength. They were both very happy so, and both unconscious of it. These times, that meant so much, and which were real living, they almost ignored.
>
> He was conscious only when stimulated. A sketch finished, he always wanted to take it to Miriam. Then he was stimulated into knowledge of the work he had produced unconsciously. In contact with Miriam he gained insight; his vision went deeper. From his mother he drew the life-warmth, the strength to produce; Miriam urged this warmth into intensity like a white light. [p. 158]

This not only emphasizes strongly the creative possibility in Paul's relation to his mother, which critics tend to ignore,[27] but it points toward an intimate connection between Miriam and Paul's "coming to consciousness." Here Miriam is regarded mainly as an influence extending Mrs. Morel's life-warmth, which is to

27. Lawrence himself stressed this possibility. Notice how strongly he expressed his idea that the mother *"urged* [the sons] into life" in the letter quoted on p. 87 above.

some extent inseparable from her cultural aspirations for her son.
Miriam most directly fosters these aspirations by becoming Paul's
student and urging him to consciousness through teaching.[28] No
rift is present here between the vital and intellectual, as there was
in *The White Peacock;* nor are the moral and intellectual forms
which Mrs. Morel maintains exposed as inadequate. Unfortunately for Paul, however, his new consciousness soon begins to reveal
inadequacies both in Miriam and in himself. They arise particularly in the different attitudes through which the young lovers interpret nature.

If Miriam extends Paul's vision, she does not always do so in a
direction he finds fruitful. For example, "She wanted to show
him a certain wild-rose bush she had discovered. She knew it was
wonderful. And yet, till he had seen it, she felt it had not come
into her soul. Only he could make it her own, immortal. She was
dissatisfied" (p. 159). Miriam requires that Paul mediate her own
natural responses, but he is not altogether comfortable in this
role. "Paul looked into Miriam's eyes. She was pale and expectant
with wonder, her lips were parted, and her dark eyes lay open to
him. His look seemed to travel down into her. Her soul quivered.
It was the communion she wanted. He turned aside, as if pained.
He turned to the bush" (p. 160). Miriam's need of Paul obviously
extends beyond that of a student for a teacher. Her response is
sexual, but, like her own mother, she conceives it in religious
terms.[29] Her quivering soul contains a mixture of adolescent
yearning and ignorance which Paul feels as a threat. On the same
page Mrs. Morel conveniently provides an explanation for Paul's
uneasiness:

Always when he went with Miriam, and it grew rather late, he

28. A good example occurs on p. 152, where Paul, trying to explain to
Miriam why she likes his painting, produces Lawrence's own aesthetic
theory in embryo.

29. This is explained at the beginning of Paul's visits. "Her great companion was her mother. They were both brown-eyed, and inclined to be
mystical, such women as treasure religion inside them, breathe it in their
nostrils, and see the whole of life in a mist thereof" (p. 142).

knew his mother was fretting and getting angry about him. . . .
She could feel Paul being drawn away by this girl. And she did
not care for Miriam. "She is one of those who will want to suck
a man's soul out till he has none of his own left," she said to
herself; "and he is just such a baby as to let himself be absorbed. She will never let him become a man; she never will."
[p. 160]

The question which immediately arises is whether this is an expression of Mrs. Morel's possessiveness, of an inadequacy in Miriam, or of an inadequacy in Paul. Or if it is all these things, as
seems likely, how are we to distinguish the degree of each?

The only way, of course, is to note whatever evidence Lawrence
provides for explaining the conflict which is emerging. The tone
of Mrs. Morel's remarks is indeed one of irritation, and strongly
implies that her judgment of Miriam is unduly harsh. This harshness is of course part of the psychological pattern outlined by
Moynahan; she fears Miriam's soul-sucking because she is in danger of losing her own control over Paul's soul. Yet Miriam also
makes a kind of "religious" demand upon Paul which his mother
does not make; this demand is in turn related to the pattern of
fearful withdrawal from the more brutal parts of existence that
her mother has fostered in her. So Miriam, too, is to some extent
caught in a psychological problem, which is complicated by her
adolescent intensity. Paul himself is clearly confused; he not only
shares with Miriam ignorance about the sexual bond which is
growing between them, but he is pained by the communion she
seeks through nature. This cannot be adequately explained as a
competitive attempt for his soul, as Mrs. Morel claims. The most
obvious reason for Paul's growing irritation is that Miriam's religiosity puts a "mist" between Paul and his most vital urges,
which include not only sex but the entire pattern of his response
to natural phenomena. By the same token, Miriam's creation of
that mist is not simply an extension of her mother's timidity but
a function of her vital response to Paul, a response whose sexual
nature she never fully admits to herself. Both the vital and psy-

choanalytic patterns, then, are functioning through these passages, not as alternative explanations for the same phenomena but as parts of the whole truth. That they do not coincide does not create confusion; it provides instead the dramatic tension which is at the core of the relationship between Paul and Miriam.

As young lovers both Paul and Miriam embody a vitality whose direction is toward self-realization and whose fulfillment presupposes freedom. In the intensity of their responses to one another this vitality shimmers, however inadequately it finds expression. At the same time they are both caught in persistent patterns of thought and behavior, of which the strongest by far is Paul's need for his mother's approval. Until adolescence his mother's forms—the fierce morality, the consistent behavior according to comprehensible rules, the assurance and dignity of a house put, however willfully, in order—were able to accommodate the intense and vital bond which the mother and child shared. But with sexual awakening comes intellectual and religious hunger, which Mrs. Morel's forms can no longer accommodate, just as she cannot accommodate sexual hunger itself. So Paul must go to other women in search of satisfaction for his persistent vitality. Because he never fully understands his reliance upon his mother's order and love, he never fully understands his difficulty in finding these qualities elsewhere. But as he grows he experiments continually with ideas and attitudes which both increase his understanding of his problem and point toward possible solutions, even though the solutions are possible only after his mother's death. Throughout this experimentation, which comprises the last half of the novel, Paul's halting, clumsy, and occasionally backward progression is conveyed by scenes which demonstrate his trial and error. The vital is repeatedly opposed to the determined. Lawrence's whole method seems designed precisely to capture this straining for freedom.

As the difficulties between Paul and Miriam come more into the open, Paul gropes his way toward an articulation of his trouble. "Their common feeling for something in nature," which "started" their love (p. 148), is increasingly used to define the strain which is becoming critical.

> She looked up at him full of pain, then continued slowly to stroke her lips against a ruffled flower. Their scent, as she smelled it, was so much kinder than he; it almost made her cry.
>
> "You wheedle the soul out of things," he said. I would never wheedle—at any rate, I'd go straight."
>
> He scarcely knew what he was saying. These things came from him mechanically. She looked at him. His body seemed one weapon, firm and hard against her.
>
> "You're always begging things to love you," he said, "as if you were a beggar for love. Even the flowers, you have to fawn on them—"
>
> Rhythmically, Miriam was swaying and stroking the flower with her mouth, inhaling the scent which ever after made her shudder as it came to her nostrils.
>
> "You don't want to love—your eternal and abnormal craving is to be loved. You aren't positive, you're negative. You absorb, absorb, as if you must fill yourself up with love, because you've got a shortage somewhere." [p. 218]

Mrs. Van Ghent has described Miriam's attitude in this scene as one of "blasphemous possessorship," interpreting Paul's accusation that Miriam wants only to absorb as Lawrence's accusation as well.[30] There is certainly some force to this view, especially when we remember that, whatever his difficulties, Lawrence resisted through his first two novels attitudes regarding nature as a possession. Miriam's lavish fondling, her fervent kisses, her swaying and stroking are all a bit disgusting, and this heavy quality, reminiscent of Helena and strongly foreshadowing Hermione in *Women in Love,* cannot be altogether dismissed as an expression of Paul's point of view; the scene is not consistently presented from his point of view. But at the same time his responses are excessive and petulant, and we are told that his "fretted soul" has

30. Van Ghent, *English Novel,* p. 256.

caused him to speak without "the faintest notion of what he was saying." Although here that fretting is ascribed to "thwarted passion," the next few pages concentrate on Paul's inadequacies: his need for tenderness and love and his admitted ability to offer Miriam only friendship. He wants to break off, and Miriam senses another influence at work—which turns out to be, of course, his mother.

As in several scenes between the elder Morels, one set of responses, with its own explanation of a prevalent tension, yields to another set with another explanation. According to Mrs. Van Ghent, this scene is a symbolic lesson in Miriam's diminished vitality, which threatens Paul because she seeks a parasitic relationship. But we are immediately and clearly shown that, if truth, this is not the whole truth. After vowing to give Miriam up, Paul returns to his mother with "the satisfaction of self-sacrifice."

> She loved him first; he loved her first. And yet it was not enough. His new young life, so strong and imperious, was urged toward something else. It made him mad with restlessness. She saw this, and wished bitterly that Miriam had been a woman who could take this new life of his, and leave her the roots. He fought against his mother almost as he fought against Miriam. [pp. 222-23]

Mrs. Morel refuses to realize that her demand for roots also encroaches on Paul's new life. Here, then, is an oedipal explanation for Paul's abuse of Miriam, which might itself account for his chanting about "absorption." But we need not choose between explanations. Lawrence's very wording in the passage just quoted, which points out the blind force of Paul's young life straining forward to something else, implies what we have been assuming all along—that the oedipal pattern is merely one sort of restrictive form for the vital forces which inhabit all the major characters. It never has the determining force which Moynahan's analysis emphasizes, though it is surely the most powerful restriction in the book.

Miriam's possessiveness is another restriction, but we have reason to believe that it is much less rigid. For all her religiosity, Miriam has more potential for fulfilling Paul's growing needs than his mother does, if only because she is younger and more flexible. Paul's ambivalence clearly forces what flexibility Miriam has into rigid postures. He has a tendency to engineer his own failure by abusing Miriam's lack of self-assurance. For example, he directly fosters in her the religiosity about which he complains.

> He talked to her endlessly about his love of horizontals: how they, the great levels of the sky and land in Lincolnshire, meant to him the eternality of the will, just as the bowed Norman arches of the church, repeating themselves, meant the dogged leaping forward of the persistent human soul, on and on, nobody knows where; in contradiction to the perpendicular lines and to the Gothic arch, which, he said, leapt up at heaven and touched the ecstasy and lost itself in the divine. Himself, he said, was Norman, Miriam was Gothic. She bowed in consent even to that. [p. 177]

Again, this sort of argument is in one sense caused by his mother, but the eternality of the will and the persistent human soul are not mere romantic abstractions. They refer directly to whatever it is in Paul that pushes him forward and sustains him in the end. Even at this comparatively early point in their relationship Paul cannot successfully relate such persistent yearnings to Miriam—not simply because his mother prevents him, but because Miriam tends to diffuse them in her religious-romantic haze, even while she awakens them in Paul.

It appears, then, that the pressures on Paul tend increasingly to resist consistent analysis by any single scheme, whichever psychology one chooses to apply. What is consistent is the relevance of everything that happens to Paul's vital struggle, which when viewed broadly is also Lawrence's struggle to make sense of the rifts between the civilized and the vital, man and nature, and man and woman which we noticed in his first two novels. And he does make much more sense of them. This is obvious not only in the clear recognition of what lies beneath the woman problem in his portrayal of Paul and his mother, but in his very ability to present thoroughly and coherently the human tensions which are this book's subject. We have no right to expect ready solutions to the problems which these tensions involve. We cannot have the elder Morels discovering complete happiness in marriage, nor can we have Paul and Miriam suddenly overcoming their inhibitions and inadequacies, without violating the patterns upon which their struggles for life depend. But this does not mean that some form of progress is not present, especially in Paul's struggles for freedom. Miriam's fight for Paul's soul is not an utter failure; Paul does not stupidly and compulsively repeat his mistakes without learning from them. And this learning indicates both the degree to which Lawrence has come to terms with the gloomy overcast of his first two novels and the direction he will take in the books which follow.

In attending to the more determined aspects of the relationship between Paul and Miriam, we have somewhat neglected the degree of energy and hope it contains. One way Lawrence presents this hope is by drawing contrasts between the two women in Paul's life:

"I *do* like to talk to her—I never said I didn't. But I *don't* love her."

"Is there nobody else to talk to?"

"Not about the things we talk of. There's a lot of things that you're not interested in, that—"

"What things?"

Mrs. Morel was so intense that Paul began to pant.

"Why—painting—and books. *You* don't care about Herbert Spencer."

"No," was the sad reply. "And *you* won't at my age."

"Well, but I do now—and Miriam does—"

"And how do you know," Mrs. Morel flashed defiantly, "that *I* shouldn't. Do you ever try me!"

"But you don't, mother, you know you don't care whether a

picture's decorative or not; you don't care what *manner* it is in."

"How do you know I don't care? Do you ever try me? Do you ever talk to me about these things, to try?"

"But it's not that that matters to you, mother, You know t's not."

"What is it, then—what is it, then, that matters to me?" she flashed. He knitted his brows with pain.

"You're old, mother, and we're young."

He only meant that the interests of *her* age were not the interests of his. But he realised the moment he had spoken that he had said the wrong thing. [p. 212]

Although as usual Mrs. Morel wins this argument (Paul is again forced to realize that she is "the only supreme thing" for him), Paul's unwitting cruelty is plain and painful truth. His new passion, the fierce vitality of his adolescence, finds articulation in the culturally oriented intercourse with Miriam; the patterns of his mother's world, though they were filled with warmth in his childhood, are no longer adequate. The resulting perspective on Mrs. Morel is considerably more poignant than mere insistence upon her possessiveness will allow. In this brief scene Lawrence depicts the almost tragic quality of the inevitable disparity between youth and age, a disparity which neither Paul nor his mother can accept.[31] And in presenting it Lawrence strongly implies an equally inevitable possibility in youth, which the early stages of Paul's intercourse with Miriam forcefully capture. The patterns of those early scenes remind us of the two earlier novels: the essential sexual attraction of the lovers tends to find both articulation and obstacle in cultural endeavors. But in *Sons and Lovers* the danger signals of the earlier books are largely absent. Unlike Lettie and Helena, Miriam is not in a dominant position; she displays no strength with which to take advantage of a corresponding

31. The trip to Lincoln cathedral (p. 240 ff.) poignantly depicts Paul's rage at his mother's age: Why can't a man have a young mother? What is she old for?

weakness in Paul. This is itself a hopeful sign, for if any simple failure can be ascribed to both George and Siegmund, it is failure to wield a firm hand when needed. And Paul, like them, displays a desire to get beneath the cultural endeavors to something more essential, only his superior ability to articulate makes his chance of finding it better from the first. And, again like George and Siegmund, he looks for it in sexual passion. If he joins them in not finding it there—that is, not finding self-realization there, in any full sense—both he and Lawrence gain considerable understanding of why he does not.

The accounts of Paul's failures with women which emphasize Mrs. Morel's determining power tend to overlook the degree to which those failures are also a function of ignorance on the part of both parties. Paul and Miriam are too deeply in accord about her spirituality, which though a common enough attitude of adolescent females toward love and nature, is perpetuated by Paul's insistence and Miriam's acquiescence. There is clear evidence that Miriam, at least before Mrs. Morel begins to exert all her powers to keep her away, has a capacity for sensuality that need not end in frigidity.

He lighted the hurricane lamp, took off his coat, turned up the bicycle, and set speedily to work. Miriam came with the bowl of water and stood close to him, watching. She loved to see his hands doing things. He was slim and vigorous, with a kind of easiness even in his most hasty movements. And busy at his work he seemed to forget her. She loved him absorbedly. She wanted to run her hands down his sides. She always wanted to embrace him, so long as he did not want her.

"There!" he said, rising suddenly. "Now, could you have done it quicker?"

"No!" she laughed.

He straightened himself. His back was towards her. She put her two hands on his sides, and ran them quickly down.

"You are so *fine!*" she said.

He laughed, hating her voice, but his blood roused to a wave

of flame by her hands. She did not seem to realise *him* in all
this. He might have been an object. She never realised the male
he was. [p. 189]

This last judgment is Paul's, and it is obviously inadequate to
explain the quality of her response and action. Although she is
obviously fearful of his sexual demands, she certainly responds to
him as a male, not merely as an object. Because he is impulsive
and demanding, he confirms rather than releases her fear and
self-mistrust; because he is tortured by the conflict with his
mother, he can never find the patience and gentleness which are
obviously necessary if she is ever to be brought around. But this,
of course, is precisely what neither of them realizes, for the simple reason that they have had no experience and therefore no
knowledge of sexual love. By the time they try to learn they
cannot see over their own obstacles. If the compulsive element in
Paul's insistence is due to pressure from his mother, this pressure
does not completely explain the failures which result. Miriam and
Paul are both free to make mistakes on their own; the possibility
that they might have done better were they wiser is always present, though of course there is no guarantee that if they should try
again in ten years they would succeed.

The presence of this possibility is one of the many indications
that Lawrence understood fully the complexity of the conflicts
he was depicting. No references to the "storm of life" are needed
here to account for failure to direct vitality, nor must any other
form of fatalism (like psychological determinism) be required to
account for everything. References to the "relentlessness of life"
are very few indeed, and when they do appear Lawrence's perspective on them seems firm.[32]

They went down to the warren. On the middle path they
passed a trap, a narrow horseshoe hedge of small fir-boughs,

32. The phrase itself is used in the Lincoln cathedral scene to refer
merely to Mrs. Morel's mortality. It is not expanded to any broader notion
of fate.

baited with the guts of a rabbit. Paul glanced at it frowning. She caught his eye.

"Isn't it dreadful?" she asked.

"I don't know! Is it worse than a weasel with its teeth in a rabbit's throat? One weasel or many rabbits? One or the other must go!"

He was taking the bitterness of life badly. She was rather sorry for him. [p. 219]

Here Miriam clearly recognizes the hysterical quality in Paul's insistence upon harsh reality. This is certainly not Lawrence's or even Paul's prevalent view of nature, for their view stresses nature's vitality as a source of joy—without, of course, insisting on human involvement or possession.

Paul's bitter response here, like his love-hate fluctuation with Miriam and indeed most of his behavior throughout the book, is evidence that his vital progress is not going well. But again Lawrence refuses to destroy possibility, even in Paul's sexual failure with Miriam. Paul's conflicts aside, it is quite unlikely that, given both his and Miriam's insistence on her vital inadequacy, she would suddenly become a satisfactory sexual partner on demand. So when Paul finally bullies her into accepting him, he experiences a sense of failure and a "reaching-out to death" afterward. Undoubtedly these "death-urges" are also influenced by his mother's demands, just as his cruelty to Miriam has been all along.[33] That he does not realize how much he has caused his own failure is both part of his neurosis (avoidance of painful responsibility) and sheer ignorance. But however we explain it, it does lead to the important decision to leave Miriam—a decision which, given Paul's ignorance and his needs, is the only vital choice possible. Without some change in attitude and understanding, the relationship is more than likely to get steadily worse, even with Mrs. Morel out of the way. So Paul, simplifying his problems immensely, but simplifying them in the only way

33. Moynahan calls attention to these "death-urges" as part of his exposition of the Freudian pattern. See *Deed of Life,* p. 26.

that is not self-defeating, looks for passion elsewhere. His decision
to do so is conveyed in a garden scene which, like the earlier one
we witnessed, emphasizes that a vital process is taking place.

> A corncrake in the hay-close called insistently. The moon slid
> quite quickly downwards, growing more flushed. Behind him
> the great flowers leaned as if they were calling. And then, like a
> shock, he caught another perfume, something raw and coarse.
> Hunting round, he found the purple iris, touched their fleshy
> throats and their dark, grasping hands. At any rate, he had
> found something. They stood stiff in the darkness. Their scent
> was brutal. The moon was melting down upon the crest of the
> hill. It was gone; all was dark. The corncrake called still.
> Breaking off a pink, he suddenly went indoors.
> "Come, my boy," said his mother. "I'm sure it's time you
> went to bed."
> He stood with the pink against his lips.
> "I shall break off with Miriam, mother," he answered calmly.
> [p. 294]

Repeating his new determination to himself, Paul chews up the
blossom "unthinking" and spits it into the fire.

This is clearly an affirmation of his masculinity in all its vital
force, even to the point of brutality. The mention of brutality,
the phallic qualities of the lilies, the munching of the petals all
point up the degree to which his decision is an almost feral rejection of the demands for gentleness and understanding which
Miriam makes and he, as we have seen, cannot fulfill. As such his
decision is not only a simplification but an escape from full manhood. But at least it is a vital escape ("at any rate, he had found
something"), and it leads to the most convincing scenes of wholeness in the book, those of his sexual consummation with Clara.
That even this does not satisfy him is a further indication that he
has over simplified his problems—that the whole range of intellectual, artistic, and generally civilized activity he had shared with
Miriam, soulful or not, is somehow necessary as well. Even after
the devastating release of his mother's death, which causes Paul to

realize that Clara's sexual competence alone does not make marriage to her feasible,[34] he shows strong signs of ability to make something of his failures. Miriam returns and offers marriage, but with the same self-defeating timidity that has put Paul off before.

> If she could rise, take him, put her arms round him, and say, "You are mine," then he would leave himself to her. But dare she? She could easily sacrifice herself. But dare she assert herself? She was aware of his dark-clothed, slender body, that seemed one stroke of life, sprawled in the chair close to her. But no; she dared not put her arms around it, take it up, and say, "It is mine, this body. Leave it to me." And she wanted to. It called to all her woman's instinct. But she crouched, and dared not. . . . Her impotence before him, before the strong demand of some unknown thing in him, was her extremity. [p. 417]

There is no way of telling exactly how helpless Miriam is before this stroke of life, this unknown thing; but the clear implication is that she should at least have dared to assert herself, to release the woman's instinct which had never been allowed to emerge from behind her sacrificial attitudes. And in implying blame Lawrence implies possibility. Paul, largely overcome with despair over his mother's death, cannot afford the energy to take a chance on this possibility; what he sees is Miriam's all-too-familiar indecision, and upon this he acts rationally and decisively. "He felt that, in

34. Clara's reconciliation with Baxter Dawes, which Paul brings about, has been interpreted as the acting out of oedipal fantasy: Dawes and Clara symbolize Paul's parents, whose conflict he has internalized and is obsessively trying to heal by bringing Dawes and Clara together. Such an interpretation, of course, emphasizes the determined element in Paul's behavior and as such does not seem adequate. One can also argue that Paul, who has awakened Clara to womanhood at the cost of almost destroying her husband, chooses to fulfill his responsibility by giving Dawes back a better wife than he had in the first place. Paul has come to recognize that he could not marry her anyway. There is no reason why both readings cannot be used, but I think the second is more fundamental, more in keeping with Lawrence's emerging emphasis on responsibility for life. See Frank O'Connor, *The Mirror in the Roadway* (New York, 1956), pp. 276-78; also Moynahan, p. 25.

leaving her, he was defrauding her of life. But he knew that, in staying, stifling the inner, desperate man, he was denying his own life. And he did not hope to give life to her by denying his own" (p. 148). Even though Paul may be exaggerating the inevitability of Miriam's tendencies to stifle him, his decision is again the only one consistent with self-preservation. It is certainly not acceptance of defeat but an attempt to rescue all he can of the stroke of life that Miriam clearly recognizes even in his battered state.

This rescue is not, especially in the face of his past failures, fraught with optimism. The final passages of the book present Paul's vitality as a "tiny spark" threatened by extinction, still yearning for the dead mother and even for the death which has taken her. "She was the only thing that held him up, himself, amid all this. And she was gone, intermingled herself" (p. 420). But the stubborn, insistent will with which he resisted his mother's attempts to keep him at home, Miriam's attempts to appropriate him for her own security, and Clara's attempts to have him as a "mate" (another sort of "possession") allows him to resist the impulse toward death as well. "He would not give in"; he walks toward "the faintly humming, glowing town, quickly" (p. 420). This is a bare and minimal sort of hope, but it is real, and all the "vital" evidence we have noted supports it.[35] We shall see in Lawrence's next two books a continuing experimentation with precisely the vital forms associated with Miriam and

35. In the "oedipal" letter quoted above (p. 87), Lawrence calls his book a "tragedy," because Paul is left only with "the drift toward death." Obviously this is not my view, nor that of a number of others (Spilka, Hough, and Moynahan, to name a few). One need not conclude, however, that Lawrence did not sense the vital possibilities in his own book. That letter was written to convince Edward Garnett that the book "has form," and its insistence is partly a response to Garnett's opposition. This is partly why the Freudian cast is so strong. I think Lawrence may have used the word *tragedy* as an overstatement to enforce this insistence on form. As David Gordon has convincingly shown, Lawrence became increasingly hostile to tragedy, either as a literary form or an attitude toward life, as he grew older. See Gordon, *D. H. Lawrence as a Literary Critic* (New Haven, 1966), pp. 75-96.

Clara—sexual love, response to nature, artistic and **intellectual** endeavor—as keys to a more articulate expression of wholeness, the quest for which has been implicit in the first three.

We need finally to take a broader view of *Sons and Lovers'* position in Lawrence's own development as a novelist. In the novel he reexamines the ideas and problems of his first two novels, and it is helpful to summarize the most tangible results. First and most obvious, here the somewhat shadowy conflict between woman as lover and woman as mother in the first two novels emerges fully, and, though not resolved, it is presented with a thoroughness that presupposes understanding. In that presentation a few conclusions are implicit. Paul's struggles strongly suggest that female demands upon masculine vitality must not be maternally possessive; none of his women is quite willing to allow him freedom for separate self-development, and in this sense each mothers him. This novel leaves no doubt that such maternal behavior is to be resisted. Also implicit in Paul's split between body and soul is a concept of the whole man, which, though it emphasizes sheer vitality, includes the entire traditional range of human endeavor as well. This range extends from the brutally physical to the most refinedly civilized, though at either extreme failure is inevitable. Sexual activity seems to offer the most direct method of experiencing this wholeness, but in itself it is not sufficient, for the need for articulation is equally human. It is this need, in fact, which seems to have driven Lawrence to the realistic methods we have been examining, for the articulation of the vague problems which flaw the first two novels is precisely what has been accomplished in *Sons and Lovers*.

More technically, Lawrence's new realism is directed by dialectical presentation of the natural-moral conflict, which has allowed thorough exploration of the values associated with each. Neither Morel's sensuous flame nor his wife's moral consistency is presented as adequate for achieving the wholeness which both Paul and Lawrence seem to seek: implicit in Morel's failures is a need for order and control of vital urges; implicit in his wife's, the need for freedom. Although no clear compromise between these two modes of behavior emerges as an ideal, the criticisms raised by their portrayal imply some principle of balance between rational, articulated forms and unconscious energies. This balance is also suggested by the dialectical presentation of the two modes. When the book proceeds to consider Paul's oedipal problems, both its method and its values become considerably more complicated but not confused. In his portrayal of Paul's split and his unsatisfactory attempts at healing it, Lawrence consistently weighs the restrictive influences which reside in the women against Paul's pressing vitality; he also manages to convey that the patterns which the women offer can accommodate as well as restrict that vitality. All three of the major female characters are portrayed with a sympathy and fullness quite absent from the first two novels, and this is itself a significant advance. *Sons and Lovers* is not a book against women but one trying to discover precisely how an intense young man can bind himself to them without drastic loss. Throughout the portion of the book concerning Paul's split with Miriam, the polarity between the vital and the moral is being redefined as a direction and form for vital pressures. In place of the more obvious dialectic between Morel's vitality and his wife's moral consistency we find an intricate pattern of pressures and restrictions. Again the method itself captures these pressures and restrictions by presenting alternately or simultaneously "free" and "determined" patterns of behavior in Paul and Miriam.

Finally, beneath all this straining for freedom lies a strong sense of its possibility, which Lawrence captures through his consistent willingness to connect man and nature and through his symbolic scenes, which strongly imply the possibility of significant vital choice. We shall see these methods gain considerably in significance in *The Rainbow,* where the possibility they embody expands beyond the "human" to the "ultimate" realm, in which both human and natural vitality are rooted.

4: THE RAINBOW

Tom Brangwen

Lawrence's early letters about the manuscript which became his next two books dramatically reveal the changes he and his art underwent after *Sons and Lovers*. Putting aside two hundred pages of an "analytical" but "improper" novel,[1] he began a "potboiler." By the time he had written a hundred pages of this second attempt, which seems to have begun as an escape from the first, he found that it had "developed into an earnest and painful work—God help it and me." Lawrence apparently did not much like the thought that a potboiler should be earnest and painful. Subsequent letters reveal that he maintained his effort to regard it as a secondary venture.

> I have written 180 pages of my newest novel *The Sisters*. It is a queer novel, which seems to have come by itself. I will send it to you. You may dislike it—it hasn't got hard outlines—. . . . But I am finishing *The Sisters*. It will only have 300 pages. It was meant to be for the *jeunes filles*, but already it has fallen

1. These phrases, written in April 1913, refer to *The Lost Girl,* then called "The Insurrection of Miss Houghton." Ford has cleared up what was a prevalent confusion about which manuscript is which. Cf. Ford, *Double Measure,* p. 41; and esp. *LM,* pp. 183, 193, 197, 200. This last letter, read in the context of the others, leaves no reasonable doubt that Ford is right.

from grace. I can only write what I feel pretty strongly about: and that, at present, is the relation between men and women. After all, it is *the* problem of today, the establishment of a new relation, or the readjustment of the old one, between men and women.—In a month *The Sisters* will be finished. (D.V.)[2]

That month was extended to almost two years. He "finished" it at least once during that time[3] and wrote some eight drafts in all.[4] Earnest and painful it remained in spite of his resistance, which only lasted for the first month or two.

Throughout its writing Lawrence seems to have alternated between puzzlement and wonder about what he was producing: he considered it "like a novel in a foreign language," with "a new basis altogether" (*LM,* p. 223), "weird" (*LM,* p. 224), "so different from anything I have yet written, that I do nothing but wonder what it is like" (*LM,* p. 230). But he also appears to have had a firm grasp of his theme, which is stated at the outset: "In *The Sisters* was the germ of this novel: woman becoming individual, self-responsible, taking her own initiative" (*LM,* p. 273). "And I am so sure that only through a readjustment between men and women, and a making free and healthy of this sex, will she get out of her present atrophy" (*LM,* p. 204).

Lawrence's wonder over his new creation has to a large extent been shared by his readers. Everyone agrees that *The Rainbow* strikes out in new directions. The difficulty, of course, is to define what these directions are. The remarks which I have quoted are only part of Lawrence's descriptions of the novel, and prob-

2. 18 April(?). There is evidence in a letter postmarked 26 April implying that it was written before this one. In the letter ostensibly written on 26 April, Lawrence refers to his completion of 145 pages of *The Sisters;* in the letter provisionally dated 18 April, he claims 180 pages. See *LM,* pp. 200, 203.

3. See *LM,* p. 276.

4. See Moore, *Life and Works,* p. 129; and especially Mark Kinkead-Weekes, "The Marble and the Statue," in *Imagined Worlds,* ed. Maynard Mack and Ian Gregor (London, 1968), pp. 371-418. Kinkead-Weekes offers the most detailed examination of the complicated order of composition yet published.

ably not the most important part. A well-known letter is generally taken as a more accurate statement of what the novel accom-
plishes. In it Lawrence considers *The Rainbow* in relation to Mari-
netti's pronouncements about futurism and claims that "somehow—that which is psychic—non-human, in humanity, is more
interesting to me than the old-fashioned human element—which
causes one to conceive a character in a certain moral scheme and
make him consistent." Lawrence's development of these ideas is
worth the lengthy quotation it often receives:

> I don't care so much what the woman *feels*—in the ordinary
> usage of the word. That presumes an *ego* to feel with. I only
> care about what the woman *is*—what she IS—inhumanly, physi-
> ologically, materially—according to the use of the word: but for
> me, what she *is* as a phenomenon (or as representing some
> greater, inhuman will), instead of what she feels according to
> the human conception. . . . You mustn't look in my novel for
> the old stable *ego*—of the character. There is another *ego*,
> according to whose action the individual is unrecognisable, and
> passes through, as it were, allotropic states which it needs a
> deeper sense than any we've been used to exercise, to discover
> are states of the same single radically unchanged element. (Like
> as a diamond and coal are the same pure single element of
> carbon. The ordinary novel would trace the history of the
> diamond—but I say, "Diamond, what! This is carbon." And
> my diamond might be coal or soot, and my theme is carbon.)
> You must not say my novel is shaky—it is not perfect, be-
> cause I am not expert in what I want to do. But it is the real
> thing, say what you like. And I shall get my reception, if not
> now, then before long. Again I say, don't look for the de-
> velopment of the novel to follow the lines of certain characters:
> the characters fall into the form of some other rhythmic form,
> as when one draws a fiddle-bow across a fine tray delicately
> sanded, the same takes lines unknown.[5]

5. *LM*, p. 282.

This letter was written later than the group quoted above, and for that reason alone it would seem to be closer to what Lawrence actually did, since by the time he wrote it he was well into the later drafts of the novel. Some critics, notable Mark Schorer, have taken the letter as a key to Lawrence's art.[6] Others speak and proceed as if the letter were rather fanciful, more defensive than illuminating.[7]

The differences are real. Surely it is difficult to conceive of people without egos, people who are unrecognizable as individuals and who exist as "states of the same radically unchanged single element." This fundamental unity, moreover, is perceptible only by "a deeper sense than we've been used to exercise." Most of us, if we take this seriously, will wonder whether we ought to attempt the book at all. On the other hand, Lawrence's early remarks about *The Rainbow* make no such requirement. They seem almost to contradict the letter's ontological claims. "Woman becoming individual, self-responsible, taking her own initiative," could not easily do without a stable ego.

Of course the answer to this apparent contradiction lies somewhere in the middle. Even if we assume that Lawrence was in all these instances making statements relevant to his book, the attitude with which we approach *The Rainbow* will depend on how we weigh the traditional quest for self-realization—the quest for which Mill's *On Liberty* is the most famous sanction—against the claim that the individual is reduced to a "rhythmic" form, somehow part of a larger pattern. The former set of ideas would seem to apply to the Victorian novel, or at least a novel in the realistic tradition; the latter would suggest a religious or mystical work. Perhaps Lawrence began in the first mode and gradually discovered a way of writing in the second; the order of the letters strongly implies as much. But the book itself yields

6. "*Women in Love* and Death," in *D. H. Lawrence: A Collection of Critical Essays*, ed. Mark Spilka (Englewood Cliffs, N.J., 1963), pp. 50-60.

7. Irving Howe is the only critic I know who explicitly rejects the notion that Lawrence's characters are without individuation ("Sherwood Anderson and D. H. Lawrence," *Furioso* [Fall 1950], pp. 21-33), although almost everyone avoids taking it as literally as I am doing here.

no such obvious pattern, and both concerns appear throughout.

Any attempt to understand *The Rainbow*, then, seems to demand that we remain open to both kinds of experience. What is unique about the book is, in fact, the manner in which Lawrence puts them together, the way in which the quest for self-realization becomes involved in self-abnegation. Put so abstractly, of course, there is nothing new about the process, for it is central to Christianity, or at least to the process of conversion. It is also an important theme in Romantic poetry, as when Wordsworth surrenders himself to a greater unity in order to emerge in some sense reborn; the process appears in more willful form in the self-obliteration of Carlyle's "Everlasting No." But the ease with which the parallels are drawn is precisely what must be resisted. Lawrence's particular achievement in *The Rainbow* consists in his methods—and sometimes experiments—in relating what we usually think of as stable egos, wrapped around in moral schemes, to areas of experience to which these labels cannot apply. The forward thrust of the book lies in the repeated attempts of the characters to release themselves into realms which are unembarrassedly transcendental and to return from this release somehow more whole—better possessed, one might even say, of a stable ego.

We cannot, then, expect an obliteration of "character" in the traditional sense of the word. All Lawrence's people are identifiable individuals, and even their transcendental experiences, as I shall try to show, are distinguishable from one another. Yet all are seeking the same thing—modes of experience which will make them complete. They surrender their stable egos in order to gain an ultimate unity which cannot itself be stable. For not only must man live in the world, where all things change, but in Lawrence's vision even the ontological realm into which his characters "fall" is in a state of flux. The unity which is accessible is a unity of relation, and as such it cannot persist.[8]

8. See the *Study of Thomas Hardy* and "The Crown" for Lawrence's elaborations of this metaphysical realm. The importance of these ideas as

When Lawrence talks disdainfully, then, of stable egos, his negative attitude is directed toward the notion of stability as stasis, with its attendant—indeed, for Lawrence, virtually automatic—associations of complacency, stagnancy, and finally death. Egos there most certainly are in Lawrence's book in the sense that people have predictable patterns of behavior and response. There is even a comfortable security in their predictability, a security which Lawrence does not disdain and seems at times even to admire. But for life to continue this security must never be complete; there must be an active capacity to respond to the unknown, together with the possibility that the ego may change radically. *The Rainbow* contains not so much leaps into the unknown (as Lawrence's letter seems to imply) as modes of living which will allow them to take place, modes which demand a constant awareness of the presence of the ultimate mysteries.

This awareness is sought by three generations in three different marriages or attempts at marriage. With *Sons and Lovers* behind him Lawrence is free to focus consistently on sexual love and its possible relations to the unknown, taking up again the pattern which unsuccessfully emerged in *The Trespasser*. The difference in effectiveness is tremendous. In *The Rainbow* Lawrence succeeds for the first time in relating man, woman, and nature. Instead of setting in opposition the moral and the vital, as he did in *Sons and Lovers*, here Lawrence opposes man's religious capacities and his limitations. Instead of emphasizing the human significance of opposed values and attitudes, he stresses the difficulties of extending to the more-than-human. As the book proceeds, in fact, Lawrence seems increasingly concerned with exploring the transcendent realm directly, and he must invent stylistic devices to accommodate this concern. It is to these devices and their relation to the larger patterns which they carry that we shall devote most of our attention.

---

they appear in the early novels is discussed below; see esp. pp. 188-95 and conclusion.

In another letter written before the completion of *The Rainbow*, Lawrence provides some useful hints to his method:

> I think there is the dual way of looking at things: our way, which is to say "I am all. All other things are but radiation out from me."—The other way is to try to conceive the whole, to build up a whole by means of symbolism, because symbolism avoids the I and puts aside the egotist; and, in the whole, to take our decent place. That was how man built the cathedrals. He didn't say "out of my breast springs this cathedral!" But "in this vast whole I am a small part, I move and live and have my being. . . ."[9]

There is only one character in *The Rainbow* who comes close to embodying the humble attitude Lawrence advocates here, and it is no accident that he is also the most successful in realizing the vast whole. Nor is it an accident that his search, in Lawrence's depiction, has no trace of the strain which occasionally mars the portrayal of his children and grandchildren. This character is, of course, Tom Brangwen.

If Tom has a secret of success, it lies in his receptivity. This in turn stems from his conviction that he is incomplete, that all things do not in fact radiate from him. His attitude toward the world is indeed "symbolic," as Lawrence here uses the word. Tom consistently attempts to see the world in large, nonegoistic patterns, and it is his relation to these patterns that he seeks to discover. To depict his search Lawrence develops a new narrative range which relates his emerging areas of concern: the natural, the psychological, and the ontological. To understand how they develop it is necessary to follow Tom's progress in considerable detail.

Like all the Brangwens before him (or at least the male Brangwens), Tom inherits a way of life characterized by a close association with the eternal processes of nature.

9. *LM,* p. 302.

Heaven and earth was teeming around them, and how should this cease? They felt the rush of the sap in the spring, they knew the wave which cannot halt, but every year throws forward the seed to begetting, and, falling back, leaves the young-born on the earth. They knew the intercourse between heaven and earth, sunshine drawn into the breast and bowels, the rain sucked up in the daytime, nakedness that comes under the wind in autumn, showing the birds' nests no longer worth hiding. Their life and interrelations were such; feeling the pulse and body of the soil, that opened to their furrow for the grain, and became smooth and supple after their ploughing, and to their feet with a weight that pulled like desire, lying hard and unresponsive when the crops were to be shorn away. [p. 2]

This is one of Lawrence's most impressive passages, and it is worth pausing for a moment to notice what it illustrates about the changes which have come since *Sons and Lovers.* It most closely resembles certain passages in *The White Peacock,* both in subject and lyricism. But here Lawrence has reached a firmness of utterance that is new in passages of this type, perhaps most evident in the extraordinary regularity of its rhythms, which strikingly reinforce the idea of cyclical repetition.

It is into this highly coherent world that Tom is born. But by the time he enters it, the Brangwen sensitivity and response to natural rhythms have begun to change. Before Tom's father's generation the men are characterized by their ability to respond to something beyond the satisfying pulsations of nature. "There was a look in the eyes of the Brangwens as if they were expecting something unknown, about which they were eager. They had an air of readiness for what would come to them, a kind of surety, and expectancy, the look of an inheritor" (p. 1). The something unknown seems to be symbolized by the church tower two miles away, which makes the Brangwen men aware "of something standing above them and beyond them in the distance." Apparently this awareness gradually disappears through intimate contact with natural process; the natural cycle becomes a circle of limitation:

> They lived full and surcharged, their senses full fed, their faces always turned to the heat of the blood, staring into the sun, dazed with looking towards the source of generation, unable to turn around . . . the Brangwen men faced inwards to the teeming life of creation, which poured unresolved into their veins. [p. 3]

The Brangwen women resent this fall into "blood-intimacy" and look to the world of cities and governments to enlarge their freedom. This enlargement, they decide, is mainly a question of knowledge, experience, and education. The vicar is their symbol for it; he "moved in the wonder of the beyond" with Lord William, master of "the hall."

We can recognize here the pattern of male versus female which has appeared in each of Lawrence's preceding books: the women have cultural yearnings; the men are somehow more vital, connected with the forces of life. As everybody notices, this opposition seems to indicate the fundamental tension upon which the development both of this book and its characters is founded.[10] But it is still difficult to be precise about what the opposition means. Julian Moynahan seems to put it most succinctly:

> Here two orientations towards life are described, one consisting of a mindless union with organic creation called "blood-intimacy," the other consisting of a capacity for a "higher form of being," for a career marked by individual moral effort, intelligent awareness, and spiritual power.[11]

Moynahan goes on to point out that the success or failure of Lawrence's characters can be measured by their success in integrating the two sides of this opposition. But, he also argues, these

10. Hough disagrees; see *The Dark Sun,* p. 60. Cf. Ford, *Double Measure,* pp. 118-19; F. R. Leavis, *D. H. Lawrence: Novelist* (New York, 1956) p. 113.

11. *Deed of Life,* p. 43.

successes and failures are ultimately incomprehensible by any psychological tests we can bring to them, or by any conceptual framework which Lawrence can provide for us. They are disturbingly arbitrary, and this is what is wrong with *The Rainbow.* By returning to Tom we can see, I think, that such conclusions are not completely warranted.

Tom avoids the satiation of his forebears by being his mother's favorite. Like the other Brangwen women she is yearning for an educated freedom, and she forces him to attend grammar school. The experience humbles Tom and increases his sensitivity. "His mind simply does not work," yet "in feeling he was developed, sensitive to the atmosphere around him, brutal perhaps, but at the same time delicate, very delicate" (p. 10). His sensitivity is further reflected in his response to oral poetry, especially to Tennyson and Shelley, who move him "beyond all calculation, he almost dreaded it it was so deep" (pp. 10-11). Although "too much alive" to be absolutely wretched, his low opinion of himself is continually reinforced while he is at school, and he is glad to leave it.

Tom takes well to running the farm after his father's death, but his pattern of failure at school seems to have released in him a consciousness and heightened sensitivity which keep him from settling down. He is strikingly disillusioned by an experience with a prostitute, for at the Brangwen farm the women were the guardians of conscience and "that further life which comprised religion and love and morality" (p. 13). Tom is beset by a terror that these ideals are indeed meaningless, that his experience with the prostitute is all there is to love. He has an "innate desire to find in a woman the embodiment of all his inarticulate, powerful religious impulses." Through the influence of the female side of the family, Tom has emerged from the vital cycle with a religious yearning which finds its focus in a yearning for women. Either the intensity of this yearning or its moral and cultural associations—or both—make it impossible for him to submit to the satisfactions of the blood which characterized the earlier generation.

As it turns out, however, neither Tom's cultural nor his moral predilections have any real force in his success in marriage. We hear no more about them, at least not in the terms just discussed. Tom's quest retains its religious nature, but its meaning changes through an experience with a foreigner and his mistress. The girl impresses Tom because she is neither a slut nor a "nice girl," the only two sorts he had been acquainted with. She also has, apparently, considerable sexual competence. Tom, therefore, has "a different experience" with her, and he is not plagued by guilt and repugnance afterward. The aristocratic foreigner accentuates the uniqueness of the sexual experience by demonstrating to Tom a new kind of relationship with women—he treats them "as if they were pleasing animals." The man has an "ageless face" and is capable of utter objectivity in his relations with people. Tom is in a state of wonder at his tact, reserve, control—in short, at his self-possession, which Tom obviously envies. "Of the two experiences, perhaps the meeting with the foreigner was the more significant," mainly because it helps him focus the hitherto inchoate cultural yearnings which were aroused by the Brangwen women and by school. The foreigner's attractiveness lies in his very objectivity, his existence as an other, which is for Tom fascinatingly divorced from the intimate patterns of his own life. There is no longer any need for confusion by the dreams and beliefs of the Brangwen women.[12] Tom has recognized that what he wants is something at once more alien and more simple than that for which they yearned.

The immediate result of this encounter is that Tom further resists the commonplace. He has dreams of "aristocratic subtlety and grace" as well as sexual gratification. But Tom's desire for experience leading beyond the farm finds no object, and he helplessly turns to bouts of drinking. He waits. Finally a woman capable of satisfying him appears.

Slowly turning the curve at the steepest part of the slope, his horse britching between the shafts, he saw a woman ap-

12. Tom is still, however, occasionally haunted by these dreams; this is evident in his envy of his "cultured" brother, Alfred.

proaching. But he was thinking for the moment of the horse.

Then he turned to look at her. She was dressed in black, was apparently rather small and slight, beneath her long black cloak, and she wore a black bonnet. She walked hastily, as if unseeing, her head rather forward. It was her curious, absorbed, flitting motion, as if she were passing unseen by everybody, that first arrested him. [p. 23]

As he passes her he sees her face clearly, "as if by a light in the air. He saw her face so distinctly, that he ceased to coil on himself, and was suspended. Although it is difficult to guage how much Tom's response simply reveals sexual need and how much is owing to her curious dissociation, it is intense and even final. "That's her," he says involuntarily; his suspension gives way to "a pain of joy running through him" (p. 24), and his courtship soon begins.

Through a rather curious concatenation of circumstances, then, Tom finds his "powerful religious impulses" directed toward the person most alien to his way of life—a Polish widow who, in their early encounters, seems not quite "real." This does not bother Tom, however, for "he moved within the knowledge of her, in the world that was beyond reality" (p. 24). This is the first clear indication that the otherness through or against which Tom seeks his own completion has an ontological as well as a psychological dimension. And Lydia's very alien nature, which Tom never fully understands, leads him back to the natural rhythms from which he has, in a sense, been weaned. Through Lydia he manages to reestablish a religious awareness of them and thereby also establishes a foundation strong enough to sustain the cultural shock accompanying his acquisition of an alien woman.

Once he discovers who Lydia is, Tom's initial doubts about his relationship with her largely vanish. "Brangwen felt that here was the unreality established at last. He felt also a curious certainty about her, as if she were destined to him. It was to him a profound satisfaction that she was a foreigner" (p. 26). From then on Tom accepts her as his fate. "The world was submitting to its transformation. He made no move: it would come, what would come" (p. 27). Judging by his previous awkwardness and hesitancy with women, his new confidence is amazing. Certainly there is something mysterious about it, as perhaps there always is in a profound emotional change. We have, moreover, additional reason to expect mystery, for Tom's responses obviously are meant to have a religious dimension. But to insist on this mystery to the point of calling it arbitrary, as some critics have done, seems to overlook the essential pattern of Tom's conversion.

> He was difficult for her to understand, warm, uncouth, and confident as he was, sure on his feet as if he did not know what it was to be unsure. What then was it that gave him this curious stability?
>
> She did not know. She wondered. She looked round the room he lived in. It had a close intimacy that fascinated and almost frightened her. The furniture was old and familiar as old people, the whole place seemed so kin to him, as if it partook of his being, that she was uneasy.
>
> "It is already a long time that you have lived in this house,—yes?" she asked.
>
> "I've always lived here," he said.
>
> "Yes—but your people—your family?"
>
> "We've been here above *two* hundred years," he said. Her eyes were on him all the time, wide-open and trying to grasp him. He felt that he was there for her. [pp. 31-32]

Lydia's questions are half answered through her own perceptions. Tom's encounters with her have allowed him to renew the old connections of the Brangwen family—the ties with the place and its latent vitality—without the sacrifice of experience that extends beyond it. It is only fitting, then, that his final decision to marry and the action that follows it should be given to us in scenes which emphasize this renewed connection.

As the time approaches for Tom to act, the self-confidence which he displayed in his kitchen undergoes a significant change; he half immerses himself in his work on the land and finds that

his decision arises from the same rhythms that have alway
tained the Brangwens. "As he worked alone on the land, or s
with his ewes at lambing time, the facts and material of his daily
life fell away, leaving the kernel of his purpose clean. And then it
came upon him that he would marry her and she would be his
life" (p. 35). The decision, to be sure, is his own, and it might be
"realistically" explained by invoking the clarity of mind which
pastoral settings traditionally induce. But as his state of mind is
further developed, it is suggested that his decision also happens to
him, that it is related to and perhaps even derived from his intimacy with greater, more mysterious forces.

> But during the long February nights with the ewes in labour,
> looking out from the shelter into the flashing stars, he knew he
> did not belong to himself. He must admit that he was only
> fragmentary, something incomplete and subject. There were the
> stars in the dark heaven travelling, the whole host passing by on
> some eternal voyage. So he sat small and submissive to the
> greater ordering.
> Unless she would come to him, he must remain as a nothing-
> ness. It was a hard experience. But, after her repeated oblivious-
> ness to him, after he had seen so often that he did not exist for
> her, after he had raged and tried to escape, and said he was
> good enough by himself, he was a man, and could stand alone,
> he must, in the starry multiplicity of the night humble himself,
> and admit and know that without her he was nothing. [p. 35]

This is not blood-intimacy but a reverence based upon it. Tom
has learned to humble himself as his sated forebears could not,
and because of this humility he is able to respond to what is alien,
to a strange foreign woman and to an unknown cosmic order. His
awe upon confronting the latter is precisely what allows his completion by the former: "He was nothing. But with her, he would
be real. If she were now walking across the frosty grass near the
sheep-shelter, through the fretful bleating of the ewes and lambs,
she would bring him completeness and perfection" (p. 35).
These scenes also contain suggestions about the peculiar force

of Lawrence's presentation of Tom. Tom's range of response, both through his contact with nature and his experience with Lydia, extends beyond the usual psychological context associated with the stable ego. These are forms of religious experience; they make Tom a creature of two worlds, which it is both Lawrence's literary responsibility and doctrinal concern to relate. To accomplish this he presents Tom's responses in such a way that they seem to have a double causation. They are comprehensible from a psychological point of view, presupposing only standard commonsense knowledge of sexual attraction and human need, and in terms of Lawrence's religious or ontological concerns. In short, with Tom Lawrence largely succeeds in presenting both a stable ego and what might be called an ontological self, a self defined by reference to inhuman, mysterious forces. We can better understand Lawrence's method by examining Tom's proposal of marriage.

A month after Tom's purpose becomes clear to him, he decides—or realizes—that the time has come. "One evening in March, when the wind was roaring outside, came the moment to ask her. He had sat with his hands before him, leaning to the fire. And as he watched the fire he knew almost without thinking that he was going this evening" (p. 36). The curious "middle state" in which Tom lives is evident even in this short passage. The moment came, as if inevitable, following the "logic of the soul" mentioned in the preceding paragraph. Tom characteristically knows almost without thinking that he must go—almost, but not quite. For there is nothing necessarily implausible or mysterious about a young man in love being spurred to action by a March wind. Lawrence chooses, in fact, to emphasize for a while the everyday aspect of Tom's activities:

> "Have you got a clean shirt?" he asked Tilly.
> "You know you've got clean shirts," she said.
> "Ay,—bring me a white one." [p. 36]

We then move away from Tom's point of view entirely and accept

Tilly's. She gives us another perspective on Tom's recent changes, a perspective not at all transcendental.

> Tilly brought down one of the linen shirts he had inherited from his father, putting it before him to air at the fire. She loved him with a dumb, aching love as he sat leaning with his arms on his knees, still and absorbed, unaware of her. Lately, a quivering inclination to cry had come over her, when she did anything for him in his presence. Now her hands trembled as she spread the shirt. He was never shouting and teasing now. The deep stillness there was in the house made her tremble. [p. 36]

Tilly has always seemed to me one of Lawrence's most felicitous touches. Through her he affirms what might be called the simple humanistic context in which most of life is carried on. Her love for Tom is the unassuming but intense devotion of a middle-aged servant for a young, vital, good-natured master. As the reference to the inherited shirt hints, she has some understanding of the Brangwen family and its ties, and through her very devotion she can sense the depth of Tom's new being. She trembles before it. Of course she has no way of dealing with it, except by being helpful in household matters, as she has always been.

Then we return to Tom, who goes to wash himself. "Queer little breaks of consciousness seemed to rise and burst like bubbles out of the depths of his stillness" (p. 36)—Tom is rationalizing his action, trying to warn himself of the possibility of failure. The metaphor is particularly apt, for it recalls the double context; the fated and somewhat mysterious stillness gives rise to commonsense consciousness. The everyday patterns continue a bit further, as Tilly warns Tom against too much "shearing" of his beard. A friend meets Tom as he leaves, and Tom explains that he's off for a "Bit of courtin', like."

> And Tilly, in a great state of trepidation and excitement, let the wind whisk her over the field to the big gate, whence she could watch him go.

He went up the hill and on towards the vicarage, the wind roaring through the hedges, whilst he tried to shelter his bunch of daffodils by his side. He did not think of anything, only knew that the wind was blowing. [p. 37]

Tom's bubbles of consciousness are receding. From this point on he is strongly associated with the wind itself—so strongly, in fact, that his connection with it is more than is usually meant by the term *symbolic*. He is looking in the window of the vicarage at the Polish mother and her child.

Then he heard the low, monotonous murmur of a song in a foreign language. Then a great burst of wind, the mother seemed to have drifted away, the child's eyes were black and dilated. Brangwen looked up at the clouds which packed in great, alarming haste across the dark sky.

The wind blew, the story began, the child nestled against the mother, Brangwen waited outside, suspended, looking at the wild waving of the trees in the wind and the gathering darkness. He had his fate to follow, he lingered here at the threshold.

He did not notice the passing of time. The hand that held the daffodils was fixed and cold. [p. 38]

"I come to have a word with you," he said, striding forward to the table, laying down his hat and the flowers, which tumbled apart and lay in a loose heap. She had flinched from his advance. She had no will, no being. The wind boomed in the chimney, and he waited. He had disembarrassed his hands. Now he shut his fists.

He was aware of his standing there unknown, dread, yet related to him.

"I came up," he said, speaking curiously matter-of-fact, and level, "to ask if you'd marry me." [p. 39]

Both Dorothy Van Ghent and Francis Fergusson have called

attention to Lawrence's tendency to create images which some-how partake of the realities they reflect.[13] Something like that is achieved here. Tom is not merely like the wind, nor is the wind merely an objective correlative for his emotional state. Tom actually shares some of its impersonal, relentless force; he derives it from the same ultimate source. The mother's foreign song is drowned out by the wind, just as Tom strips her of her foreign-ness by causing her to be reborn. The juxtaposition of Tom's fate and the wild waving of the trees in the wind and the gathering darkness is no accident either. When he finally enters, her loss of will and being is punctuated by the wind in the chimney. Every-thing we have noted about Tom's associations with nature also come to bear here. His submission to a greater ordering is dramat-ically rewarded; he is able to draw on those irresistible forces, in some sense become them, in order to reach this alien woman. This is why he moves with such unconscious authority.

At the same time Tom remains a man, conscious enough to observe in considerable detail a woman performing bedtime rit-uals with her child, patiently waiting for the proper time—and perhaps the proper accumulation of courage—to enter and make his proposal. The daffodils which he shelters and which grow cold and finally insignificant are one reminder of his everyday self. And the moment before he enters the house Lawrence inserts a short passage which emphasizes Tom's limited, human per-spective.

13. Miss Van Ghent quotes Fergusson and comments upon him in her essay on *Sons and Lovers* in *The English Novel*. See also Francis Fergusson, "D. H. Lawrence's Sensibility," in *Critiques and Essays in Modern Fiction,* ed. John W. Aldridge (New York, 1952). Something quite similar has been defined by W. K. Wimsatt as a characteristic of English romantic poetry; see his "Romantic Nature Imagery" in *The Verbal Icon* (New York, 1958). See also Eliseo Vivas's "constitutive symbol" in *D. H. Lawrence: Failure and Triumph of His Art*. Vivas's idea is that Lawrence's symbolic descrip-tions of transcendental experience contain that experience as much as they represent it. There is, in fact, no describable referent. Lawrence's "symbol-ism" has in general this tendency to bridge the gap between the everyday and the transcendental realms. It is therefore not always relevant to try tough-minded interpretations of it; its function is often as evocative as it is representative.

When they were gone, Brangwen stirred for the first time from the place where he stood, and looked round at the night. He wished it were really as beautiful and familiar as it seemed in these few moments of release. Along with the child, he felt a curious strain on him, a suffering, like a fate. [p. 39]

The limitations of the flesh are always present.

There is another mode, perhaps even more characteristic of Lawrence, in which the same range of response is portrayed. If, as I have suggested, the success of the scenes of decision depends largely on Lawrence's skill with a natural context which he has carefully developed, the success of sexual encounters often does not. Although the overwhelming role of sex in Lawrence's writing is to allow release into and connection with what are ultimately the forces involved in Tom's "greater ordering," the imagery from nature is not so readily available to indicate these relationships. If the imagery of the wind can successfully evoke a transcendent force, full access to the realm of that force entails transcendence of nature itself. Lawrence takes up fully in *The Rainbow* the indications in his last two books that sexual ecstasy is the only direct means for such transcendence. And to convey this he must create a more direct mode of description.

A good example occurs immediately after the scene in Tom's kitchen in which we noticed his new confidence. It has been his first conversation with Lydia.

He could not think of anything. He felt he had made some invisible connection with the strange woman.

A daze had come over his mind, he had another centre of consciousness. In his breast, or in his bowels, somewhere in his body, there had started another activity. It was as if a strong light were burning there, and he was blind within it, unable to know anything, except that his transfiguration burned between him and her, connecting them, like a secret power. [p. 33]

Even if we knew nothing of Lawrence's expository writings on the other centers of consciousness,[14] the word *transfiguration*, along with what we have already noticed about Tom's religious and sexual yearnings, should make it clear that this passage, like those we have been analyzing, contains a kind of double reference. An invisible connection which gives rise to a blinding of internal light and which amounts to a transfiguration suggests that once again Tom is transcending his everyday self. At the same time the passage offers a startlingly rich account of what centuries before had been reduced to a trite formula about being shot through the eyes into the heart. Its richness—and its evocation of what, because of its detail, amounts to a unique response—is perhaps best shown by simply adding up some of the information presented here. Tom is dazed and conscious of intense activity. This activity starts deep in his body, creates a kind of blindness, and connects him with Lydia. Its nature is not only something like a burning light but like power. The activity produces a sense of drifting, which in turn entails loss of will and loss of identity; it is pregnant with ecstasy. This is a sexual response, to be sure, but it is one which entails all of Tom's being—more, it seems, than his ego, and certainly more than we are used to seeing described in previous writers.

Of course, this concentration on the emotional event entails a degree of separation from the Tom that Tilly knows—the sensitive, affable, essentially stable farmer. While the responses themselves and the implications about their ontological status are carried by the prose, the associations which arise from the farm life are temporarily cut off. If we knew nothing about the person to whom these responses belonged, we would have to agree with those who argue that character is not important to Lawrence. But to consider this a literary defect is, at least in the case of Tom, irresponsible, both because passages like these always grow from a readily comprehensible humanistic context, as we have seen, and because the point of writing this way at all is to provide a per-

14. Especially *Psychoanalysis and The Unconscious,* written, as were almost all of Lawrence's expository works, after *The Rainbow* and *Women in Love.* It was published in 1921.

spective through which that traditional context may be reevaluated. All Lawrence's attempts at conveying potentially transfiguring experience entail, if only by implication, the notion of an everyday self whose limits are being redefined (if the experience is a success) or reconfirmed (if the experience is a failure).

Although in the long run Tom's marriage is probably the most successful one in Lawrence's novels, like all the other marriages it has plenty of attendant difficulties. Both Tom and Lydia have certain inadequacies which are subject, as indeed all sexual relationships in the book are, to the sort of double interpretation I have been attempting thus far. Successes and failures in marriage are comprehensible, not only in the religious terms which many readers find unsatisfactorily vague, but in terms of common sense. Yet this is not to say that they are reducible to commonsense formulae of the type found in marriage manuals. If Lawrence insists on anything, if he is deliberately teaching anything, it is that all the acts of common sense have an ultimate foundation in mystery. By pursuing Tom's success and failure in marriage we should be able to define further not only what access marriage has to Lawrence's ultimates but also how Lawrence keeps those ultimates in touch with character and with the flesh.

The emotional conflict which Tom carries from his proposal—the "intimacy of embrace and . . . foreignness of contact"—points towards his continual problem in marriage. His wife, however, does not have quite the same problem. This is particularly evident at their wedding.

> She sat quiet, with a strange, still smile. She was not afraid. Having accepted him, she wanted to take him, she belonged altogether to the hour, now. No future, no past, only this, her hour. She did not even notice him, as she sat beside him at the head of the table. He was very near, their coming together was close at hand. What more! [p. 52]

Of course, she had been married before, which may account for her lack of fear. But her strange, still smile seems to indicate a kind of inner surety as well. It is often referred to in descriptions of her, descriptions which tend to emphasize her mysterious qualities and her unquestioning acceptance of all that causes Tom anxiety. His state of mind at the wedding is strikingly different:

> Behind her, there was so much unknown to him. When he approached her, he came to such a terrible painful unknown. How could he embrace it and fathom it? How could he close his arms round all this darkness and hold it to his breast and give himself to it? What might not happen to him? If he stretched and strained for ever he would never be able to grasp it all, and to yield himself naked out of his own hands into the unknown power! How could a man be strong enough to take her, put his arms round her and have her, and be sure he could conquer this awful unknown next his heart? What was it then that she was, to which he must also deliver himself up, and which at the same time he must embrace, contain? [p. 53]

This intense wondering cannot be accounted for merely by reference to Tom's lack of experience, or even by reference to his intense need—at least not to his sexual and religious need. Tom has in a sense remained somewhat of an inadequate schoolboy; he needs also to understand.

In his struggle to cope with his wife's foreignness, Tom (and perhaps Lawrence as well) fluctuates uncertainly between two concepts of knowledge.

> And he let himself go from past and future, was reduced to the moment with her. In which he took her and was with her and there was nothing beyond, they were together in an elemental embrace beyond their superficial foreignness. But in the morning he was uneasy again. She was still foreign and unknown to him. [p. 54]

Two meanings of unknown seem to be suggested here. On the one hand Lawrence may be referring to *the* unknown, which Tom of course cannot reach "in the morning." On the other hand, Lydia's foreignness is also her Polishness, her old-world connec-

tions and old-world objectivity, which Tom never quite comes to
know, that is, to understand or put into rational order. On the
next page these two meanings are clearly separated. While Tom is
able to bask in the satisfaction he derives from the elemental
sexual experience his wife makes available, he finds that she
appears all beautiful to him. He returns home as to "a profound,
unknown satisfaction." The details of her physical appearance are
a revelation to him, "and he knew she was his woman, he knew
her essence, that it was his to possess. . . . And he seemed to live
thus in contact with her, in contact with the unknown, the un-
accountable and incalculable" (p. 55). This, of course, is to know
in the ontological sense, a direct apprehension of Lydia's being. It
has somehow spilled over into the daylight world, precisely as it
did in the proposal scene. But, as in that scene, this deep and
essentially unthinking apprehension is not stable. Almost immediately we find Tom wondering as he did at his wedding. "He
realized with a sharp pang that she belonged to him, and he to
her. He realized that he lived by her. Did he own her? Was she
here for ever? Or might she go away? She was not really his, it
was not a real marriage, this marriage between them" (p. 55).
Tom is trying to analyze his situation, to know it in the second
sense. The direct apprehension is temporary, and Tom seeks an
analogue in the commonsense world, not quite realizing that the
stability he wants is impossible. He experiences wonder, fury, and
inarticulate rage simply trying to understand her stories of her
past, which, if he could understand them, would surely help to
calm him. Hungry for and even addicted to the elemental experience which sex brings him, Tom can find no rational perspective
from which to view it.

Most of Tom's difficulties in marriage are explicable, it seems to
me, by reference to the pattern just described. Tom is too greedy
to know in the ontological sense; he wants everything to come to
him with the directness, intensity, and apparently automatic
meaning of successful sexual ecstasy. He wants the whole world
on these terms, not realizing that for this to happen he would
have to be a god. When the ecstasy fades, therefore, he falls back

onto the more conventional sense of knowing and expects his mind to lead him back to the primary sense. But the mind can never do this in Lawrence's books, or at least it cannot provide the missing connection directly. What the mind can do is put into perspective the inevitable human limitation and therefore in some sense create a freedom, an expectancy of return to the ontological realm. Lawrence makes all this much clearer in the figure of Birkin in *Women in Love,* but the outlines are already clear enough to Tom.

To some extent Tom's difficulties are Lawrence's difficulties too. Lawrence's rhetoric sometimes seems to imply that Tom's successes with his wife have nothing to do with understanding. For example, when Tom's frustration at her "mystic dark state" of exclusion reaches an unbearable pitch, "Then, suddenly, out of nowhere, there was connection between them again. It came as he was working in the fields." (p. 57). Again Tom's natural connections are useful. The sexual meeting which results yields the rhetorical question, "What did it matter who they were, whether they knew each other or not?" (p. 58). Apparently Tom simply stopped worrying about her foreignness, stopped trying to analyze it. But this does not mean that Lawrence is flatly denying the more usual uses of the mind.

If Tom's solution to the frustration at his inadequacy at rationalizing is to deny the process altogether, it remains in question whether this is the best solution. Like any solution in Lawrence it is of course temporary, and this complicates the problem of comparison. But comparisons can be made. Here is the result of Tom's renewed connection:

> The hour passed away again, there was severance between them, and rage and misery and bereavement for her, and deposition and toiling at the mill with slaves for him. But no matter. They had had their hour, and should it chime again, they were ready for it, ready to renew the game at the point where it was left off, on the edge of the outer darkness, when the secrets within the woman are game for the man, hunted doggedly, when the

> secrets of the woman are the man's adventure, and they both
> give themselves to the adventure. [p. 58]

This is doubtless a positive step in the marriage, but at the same
time it is tenuous. "They had had their hour, and should it chime
again . . . " And the metaphor of hunting is very strongly sexual
in a sense bordering on lust. The peace and completion which is
characteristic of the full awakening into being is absent, and later
instances of successful coming together enforce the impression
that this experience is incomplete.

> Their coming together now, after two years of married life, was
> much more wonderful to them than it had been before. It was
> the entry into another circle of existence, it was the baptism to
> another life, it was the complete confirmation. Their feet trod
> strange ground of knowledge, their footsteps were lit-up with
> discovery. . . . The new world was discovered, it remained only
> to be explored. . . . She was the doorway to him, he to her. [p.
> 91]

The first rainbow appears within a page of this passage, indicating
that Tom and Lydia have reached a point of greater stability than
ever before.

How, then, is the difference between these two experiences best
explained, and what have they to do with Tom's understanding?

> He did not know her any better, any more precisely, now that
> he knew her altogether. Poland, her husband, the war—he un-
> derstood no more of this in her. He did not understand her
> foreign nature, half German, half Polish, nor her foreign speech.
> But he knew her, he knew her meaning, without understand-
> ing. . . . What did it matter, that Anna Lensky was born of
> Lydia and Paul? God was her father and her mother. He had
> passed through the married pair without fully making Himself
> known to them.
>
>   Now He was declared to Brangwen and to Lydia Brangwen, as
> they stood together. [pp. 91-92]

Again the connection seems arbitrary, and again, since transcendent experiences must contain an element of mystery, it is arbitrary indeed. But the mystery does not amount to bafflement. Like the earlier episode, this meeting ends a period of great tension, a period in which Tom becomes increasingly estranged from his wife. The release is brought on by an argument in which Lydia accuses Tom of being distant and animalistic toward her, of making love "like his cattle." She also accuses him of wanting a cultured woman like his brother's mistress, whom he has recently met. Tom is astonished at her insight, but his crucial recognition comes as a response to her question, "Why do you want to deny me?" "Suddenly, in a flash, he saw she might be lonely, isolated, unsure. She had seemed to him the utterly certain, satisfied, absolute, excluding him. Could she need anything?" (p. 89). This recognition leads to Tom's release from himself: "The reality of her who was just beyond him absorbed him." The process is painful; he wants to "save himself" but succeeds, to a degree at least, in becoming "destroyed, burnt away till he lit with her in one consummation."

What Tom seeks to destroy, of course, is his stable ego. But in order to gain access to his wife's ultimate otherness Tom must first understand that she too is a subject, "lonely, isolated, unsure." Although there is no reason to disagree with Lawrence's claim that her Polishness remains as unknown as ever, we cannot accept the statement that Tom "did not know her any better, any more precisely" without qualification. He knows her better precisely because he knows she has needs like his own, which give him access both to her and to the further experience which she represents. And this recognition is brought about not by a direct flash from above, but by an unpleasant series of accusations, an argument which demands that Tom understand both himself and his wife better than he has before. In fact, the very passage which claims that understanding is irrelevant reveals quite the opposite: "What did it matter, that Anna Lensky was born of Lydia and Paul?" This expresses Tom's recognition of the irrelevancy of some of the questions he has been asking, his new understanding of the relation between the profound experience he seeks and the everyday world he must live in most of the time.

Tom's mind, then, is instrumental in freeing him from himself. He is forced by his wife's accusations to see not only her otherness (in both its senses) but her human likeness. The transfiguration itself brings new understanding of her accessibility. Tom now realizes that his own anxiety was the main barrier to reaching her, so his fear that those ultimate realms may be denied him disappears, at least for a while. What remains unsatisfactory in the marriage seems to be caused more by Lydia's lack than by his own. She is older, and her needs are less intense. When she cannot meet Tom's vitality he turns to her daughter, who through her own marriage provides additional exploration of the relation between the everyday world and the realm beyond.

Anna and Will

Anna, like her father, is a restless child. But from the first her restlessness is accompanied by an amazing degree of self-possession, a consciousness that she is separate and potentially self-sufficient. If Tom's childhood was marked by a strong sense of inadequacy and need, Anna's seems a series of lessons in self-control. When she reaches her teens she is "at once shy and wild," unable to relate to "ordinary people" who do not live on the Brangwen farm. In fact, she never even manages to overcome contempt for Tilly, because Tilly possesses neither her mother's dignity nor her father's power. Her parent's relationship is so firmly established that the outside world seems petty by contrast. Yet after a while the very stability of the farm life begins to bother her, and she yearns for escape. There are hints of complacency in this stability, especially in Mrs. Brangwen.

> She shone and gleamed to the Mystery, whom she knew through all her senses, she glanced with strange, mystic superstitions that never found expression in the English Language, never mounted to thought in English. But so she lived, within a

potent, sensuous belief that included her family and contained her destiny.

To this she had reduced her husband. [p. 99]

Surely there is denied possibility in this reduction even though it contains "profound ecstasies and incommunicable satisfactions."

Her mother's dark muzzle and curiously insidious ways, her mother's utter surety and confidence, her strange satisfaction, even triumph, her mother's way of laughing at things and her mother's silent overriding of vexations propositions, most of all her mother's triumphant power maddened the girl. [p. 100]

Characteristically, Anna resents this domination; of course, she yearns to escape. There are two quite different manifestations of this yearning. The first has to do with religion:

She had a mother-of-pearl rosary that had been her own father's. What it meant to her she could never say. But the string of moonlight and silver, when she had it between her fingers, filled her with strange passion. [p. 99]

It was her instinct to avoid thinking, to avoid it, to save herself. [p. 100]

She avoids thinking, because the words which go with the rosary are "not the same as the pale rosary meant." Like Tom, Anna has trouble with words.

She hated to hear things expressed, put into words. Whilst the religious feelings were inside her they were passionately moving. In the mouth of the clergyman, they were false, indecent. She tried to read. But the tedium and the sense of the falsity of the spoken word put her off. [p. 101]

She seems to be following in her father's footsteps; in fact, "looming, a kind of Godhead, he embraced all manhood for her." But there are important differences. Words do not baffle her as they did him; they simply seem false. And her resistance to them is to "save herself." If she, like her father, has powerful religious impulses, she wants more to preserve than to release them. Words are not so much obstacles as corruptions.

These hints that Anna's religious yearnings are self-centered become quite important when she marries, choosing a Brangwen who has yearnings more on the scale of Tom's. Her youthful restlessness also takes another direction, one more obviously amenable to self-definition. "Sometimes Anna talked to her father. She tried to discuss people, she wanted to know what was meant. But her father became uneasy. He did not want to have things dragged into consciousness" (p. 101). It is no wonder that Tom is chary of articulating, since he has always gone through a good deal of anguish for doing it badly. Anna, however, does want "things dragged into consciousness," despite her irritation at both the inadequacy of words in religion and the falsity of books. Again this is only a hint, but before long words become for Anna the means to a power very much like her mother's; through them she reduces her own husband more thoroughly than Lydia ever reduced Tom. From what Lawrence shows us of Anna's childhood, her need to do so is already half-explained. Her quest for autonomy is every bit as strong as her religious yearnings—in the end it proves stronger. Her initial aversion to words seems mainly a result of her inability to use them as a bridge between a real religious sensitivity and an all-too-precious sense of self. As it turns out she manages to build this bridge, but only at the cost of sacrificing her sensitivity to her sense of autonomy. She then has no more use for words and she sinks into her own version of a mindless state. Her husband is a casualty of the process.

This sketch is, needless to say, a simplification. As the critics all attest, Anna's relation to Will is quite complicated and possibly even confused.[15] One obvious difficulty is that Lawrence provides no context for either Will or Anna that is as coherent as the natural context from which Tom emerged and in which he re-

15. See esp. Moynahan, *Deed of Life,* pp. 50-53. Ford (*Double Measure,* p. 140) defends Lawrence by arguing that the point of his method is to emphasize the fundamental likeness of basic human responses.

mains significantly rooted. In its absence Lawrence relies more heavily on intense and passionate interchanges to carry the meaning. Because these interchanges either plunge into or flirt with the unknown it is easy—too easy—to dismiss them as unknowable. Thus it is frequently charged that in Lawrence's most essential passages the interchanges are indistinguishable from one another and the results, which are definite enough, have no definable causes. But again the main outlines of the conflict are accessible to common sense as well as to a more symbolic sort of reading, and the use of both is necessary to make coherent, or at least to appreciate with any pretension of adequacy, what Lawrence has done.

Of the two tendencies we have noticed in the adolescent Anna, it is the religious one which allows Will to reach her.

> He was interested in churches, in church architecture. The influence of Ruskin had stimulated him to a pleasure in the medieval forms. His talk was fragmentary, he was only half articulate. But listening to him, as he spoke of church after church, of nave and chancel and transept, of rood-screen and font, of hatchet-carving and moulding and tracery, speaking always with close passion of particular things, particular places, there gathered in her heart a pregnant hush of churches, a mystery, a ponderous significance of bowed stone, a dim-coloured light through which something took place obscurely, passing into darkness: a high, delighted framework of the mystic screen, and beyond, in the furthest beyond, the altar. It was a very real experience. She was carried away. And the land seemed to be covered with a vast, mystic church, reserved in gloom, thrilled with an unknown Presence. [p. 108]

Will's words do not drag things into consciousness; Anna responds to them because they extend her religious sensibility without endangering her sense of self. And there are hints that such a response is indeed adolescent, that however effective this Ruskinizing is in extending Anna's experience, her indulgence in it—and perhaps Will's as well—is somewhat limiting. If this much is not implied by the deliberate lushness of the description, Anna's further responses reveal a certain coyness, a delight in toying with the "unknown Presence." "Almost it hurt her, to look out of the window and see the lilacs towering in the vivid sunshine. Or was this the jewelled glass?" (p. 108). Anna can hardly be said to be profoundly immersed in, or even seriously yearning for, the unknown Presence that has thrilled her. The loss of self that accompanies such experience in Lawrence's writing is absent.

In two important church scenes Lawrence defines for us both Anna's attraction to and rejection of the sort of sensibility which allows Will's Ruskinizing to fascinate her. Both take place after her marriage, and both capture the conflict from which Anna emerges "victrix." In the first scene:

> He was very strange to her, and, in this church spirit, in conceiving himself as a soul, he seemed to escape and run free of her. In a way, she envied him, this dark freedom and jubilation of the soul, some strange entity in him. It fascinated her. Again she hated it. And again, she despised him, wanted to destroy it in him. [p. 155]

This ambivalence is further emphasized a bit later, when, watching her husband respond to a lamb in a church window which she had always considered as a child considers a toy, Anna suddenly finds that her husband's mysterious connection with it is founded upon a startlingly powerful reality.

> Suddenly it gleamed to her dominant, this lamb with the flag. Suddenly she had a powerful mystic experience, the power of the tradition seized on her, she was transported to another world. And she hated it, resisted it.
>
> Instantly, it was only a silly lamb in the glass again.

In the second church scene, a visit to Lincoln cathedral which apparently took place at about the same time,[16] Anna responds

16. The chapter entitled "Cathedral," in which this visit takes place, is obviously a jump backward in time, for in narrative order it follows Anna's "victory." Why Lawrence did this has puzzled some critics, but perhaps the

in much the same way. She is overcome but silenced instead of tuned; "her soul too was carried forward to the altar, to the threshold of Eternity, in reverence and fear and joy. But ever she hung back in the transit, mistrusting the culmination of the altar" (pp. 199-200).

Both scenes illustrate that the attraction is real and powerful. Unlike her more adolescent response to Will's talk of churches, Anna's response here is given against her will and is sensed as a threat. Lawrence is careful to tell us what is threatened.

> It exasperated her beyond measure. She could not get out of the Church the satisfaction he got. The thought of her soul was intimately mixed up with the thought of her own self. Indeed, her soul and her own self were one and the same in her. Whereas he seemed simply to ignore the fact of his own self, almost to refute it. He had a soul—a dark, inhuman thing caring nothing for humanity. So she conceived it. And in the gloom and the mystery of the Church his soul lived and ran free, like some strange, underground thing, abstract. [p. 155]

It is characteristic of Anna, who likes clarity of definition, to identify her self and her soul, but her more tentative formulation is the more correct one. It is indeed a mixture. The fact that she is attracted to an experience which demands self-abnegation proves that there is something in her which extends beyond what she means by self. Her rejection of this element of soul merely indicates that her egotism is stronger than her religious sensibility and that she cannot tolerate an ambivalent position.

Churches, with their windows and magnetic alters, are easy enough to avoid; husbands must be lived with. And Anna's husband possesses a power like that of her father, a power at once related to churches and to sex. Indeed Will is accustomed to think

---

answer is simply that he wished to make clearer the nature of a battle which by its intensity and length becomes confusing. Nor is there anything strikingly unusual in departing from chronological progressions, for Lawrence does it often with shorter scenes in all his books. Here the scenes of Anna's childhood are similarly shuffled. See pp. 153-54 below.

of them together, and from what we have seen of Tom there is no
reason to doubt that religious and sexual ecstasy are aspects of
something greater. "The verity was his connection with Anna and
his connection with the Church, his real being lay in his dark
emotional experience of the Infinite, of the Absolute" (p. 155).
It is this dark power, of course, which makes the marriage, and in
it Anna's soul finds a fulfilment of sorts. But because she refuses
to give up her everyday self, she must find a form of satisfaction
which does not seem to demand such a sacrifice. If we take Tom's
self-transcendence as a model, we should expect that whatever
resolution Anna comes to would be somewhat perverse. And it is;
even though she turns to the characteristically Lawrentian outlet
of sex, she does so in a way that reduces her husband's religious
capacity as well as her own. And at the same time inadequacies
on both sides of the marriage are exposed. To understand the
varieties of religious experience that Lawrence is trying to convey, it is necessary to pursue these inadequacies further.

We have already seen enough, I think, to define the lines of the
battle that rages until Will gives in. Anna hates to lose her self-
control, and Will continually leads her into experiences which put
her in danger of losing it. She must therefore diminish his power
without destroying his ability to satisfy her sexually. Her weapon
is mockery; her target, his mystic associations with the church.
Once she recovers from her momentary communion with the
lamb in the window, she attacks Will by pressing him for its
meaning and makes him ashamed of "the ecstasy into which he
could throw himself with these symbols." She also reduces the
power of the cathedral by elaborating on its most "realistic"
elements—the "wicked, odd little faces carved in stone." She
forces Will to admit the human dimension of his "vital illusion,"
his "Absolute," and leaves him with only love for "a symbol."[17]
And, by "making it up to him" when he returns from walks taken

17. It is as if Tilly were to become dominant in the Brangwen household
and decide to attack Tom's religious sensibility because her own did not
match it. Like Tilly, Anna here affirms a "basic humanistic context" which
Will, unlike Tom, seeks to escape.

to alleviate his rage, she makes him forget even his symbols. "He was black and surly, but abated. She had broken a little of something in him. And at length he was glad to forfeit from his soul all his symbols, to have her making love to him" (p. 159.) The successes and failures of that love are among the most difficult aspects of this book. What is most in question is the quality of the resolution.

We have already noted that Anna thought Will's soul a "dark, inhuman thing" and that in this darkness resided a kind of freedom. This reminds us of Tom. But here is Tom's own view of Will, after Will has been aroused by Anna but before they have had any physical contact:

> For some weeks the youth came frequently, and was received gladly by them all. He sat amongst them, his dark face glowing, an eagerness and a touch of derisiveness on his wide mouth, something grinning and twisted, his eyes always shining like a bird's utterly without depth. There was no getting hold of the fellow, Brangwen irritably thought. He was like a grinning young tom-cat, that came when he thought he would, and without cognizance of the other person. [p. 110]

Tom senses an inadequacy which cannot be accounted for merely by his jealousy, although that is real enough. With surprising frequency Will is presented as a bird:

> Suddenly, with an incredibly quick, delicate movement, he put his arms round her and drew her to him. It was quick, cleanly done, like a bird that swoops and sinks close, closer. . . . Her eyes were dark and flowing with fire. His eyes were hard and bright with a fierce purpose and gladness, like a hawk's. She felt him flying into the dark space of her flames, like a brand, like a gleaming hawk. [p. 112]

> "I don't know," he said, looking at his uncle with his bright inhuman eyes, like a hawk's. [p. 121]

She wanted his eyes to come to hers, to know her. And they would not. They remained intent, and far, and proud, like a hawk's. So she loved him and caressed him and roused him like a hawk, till he was keen and instant, but without tenderness. He came to her fierce and hard, like a hawk striking and taking her. He was not mystic any more, she was his aim and object, his prey. And she was carried off, and he was satisfied, or satiated at last.

Then immediately she began to retaliate on him. She too was a hawk. [p. 159]

These three quotations represent three stages in Will's fall. Putting it crudely, we might say that Anna brings out his sensuality while she removes his self-respect. The hawk image is essentially a vehicle to express Will's sensual powers, which may be considered the lower end of a continuum of response.[18] The other end of this continuum, all of which is referred to by the phrases about his darkness and dark powers, is of course his churchiness. Will's power tends to evaporate in the colored glooms, which, though they afford access to a sort of mystical experience, also have cultural associations which can be partially expressed and strongly evoked by words. It is these associations which make Will's mysticism vulnerable to Anna's rationalistic attacks. By forcing him to recognize a gap between his words and the emotional realities they inadequately represent, Anna does for Will precisely what the preacher did for her. The differences between their responses to this dissociation underline the essential differences between them.

The difficulty with Will's dark freedom is shared by all Lawrence's important male characters before Tom Brangwen. They lack the means by which their deeper sensibilities can be related

18. Will is also referred to as an animal with a "blind head" (both Anna and Tom perceive this) and, as he becomes more sexually involved with Anna, as a leopard. All these images enforce the notion that his capacities for sexual experience are liable to take a form too strongly sensual and therefore reductive. See n. 19 below.

to the daylight world. If Anna's sense of self (her "stable ego," in fact) is too overbearing, Will's is very close to missing altogether. And marriages, however much they are made in bed, must also go on in the daylight world. Will's soul may have a range which Anna's justly envies, but Anna has a consistency of self-regard which makes her more deadly in battle. When Anna's religious sensibilities are corrupted by words, she effects without much difficulty the romantic escape into Ruskinizing; when those sensibilities are awakened enough to threaten her stability, she forces them into sensual channels. Her ability to control them lies entirely in her confidence that she is indeed the correct measure of all emotional matters. Such confidence is never possible for Will, nor is it for Tom. But Tom lives in a world coherent enough to provide him with the necessary strength to withstand his fears, even while he gives up his sense of self to transcendent experience. It is repeatedly pointed out that even Will's work is meaningless, except for the carving which through his defeat he loses the capacity to do. Will lives too blindly; he has no substitute for the "natural" authority of his father-in-law. Tom thinks he lacks depth and Anna's bitchy retort rings true: "Fool! I've known my own father, who could put a dozen of you in his pipe and push them down with his finger-end. Don't I know what a fool you are!" (p. 170).

If we think back for a moment to the "dual way of looking at things" which Lawrence outlined in a letter (see p. 114 above), the conflict between Will and Anna makes it increasingly clear that neither way is entirely sufficient. Anna is too close to looking at all things as radiating from herself; Will "puts aside the egotist" so much that he cannot "conceive the whole." Through her denial of the ontological realm, Anna remains caught too much in the psychological, and, because she does not have her father's connections with the natural world, she must satisfy her religious needs by a kind of short-circuit. Unwilling to admit to a greater ordering, she plunges into a loss of self, but her ego remains a center of battle. No ultimate unity is sought; the end is mastery and satiation. There are hints that this essentially lustful experience may take on the additional dimension which would give it the name of love, but that would require real submission by Anna to a greater whole—a submission which she cannot sustain, even though she achieves it once or twice by being overpowered. Until Anna reaches a bearable resolution by falling into the rhythms of childbearing, her aim seems to be to reduce her husband to a slave in sexual matters. And although she does not quite succeed in this, she manages to break him of his habit of searching for the ultimate unity and to depend instead upon the fierce sensual contact which the hawk scenes illustrate.[19]

If this analysis is correct, we ought to be in a position to examine some of the more puzzling episodes in Anna's marriage. If the main pattern of the marriage is, as I have suggested, that of a fall, the early scenes ought to contain possibilities which are lost later. Some attempt should be made not only to define these possibilities but to decide whether Lawrence has presented them effectively. The honeymoon seems the logical place to begin.

One day, he was a bachelor, living with the world. The next day, he was with her, as remote from the world as if the two of them were buried like a seed in darkness. Suddenly, like a chestnut falling out of a burr, he was shed naked and glistening on to

19. Later in the marriage this becomes intensified as an absolute in its own right. Will begins to prowl for other women, returns, and plunges into intensely sensual relations with his wife which yield for him "Absolute Beauty." This seems a striking instance of what Kierkegaard would call the acceptance of the aesthetic mode as an absolute. In Lawrence's terms it is clearly an instance of sensual reduction. Compare, e.g., the latter parts of chapter 8 of *The Rainbow* with chapters 3 and 4 of "The Crown." See also Kinkead-Weekes, "The Marble and the Statue," pp. 390-93, for an analysis similar to mine but with a rather different conclusion, identifying the "absolute beauty" as "impersonal, pursued for its own sake." I think the impersonal quality of the lust is inextricably related to all-too-personal limitations, from which it represents an imperfect escape.

A recent and important book by Colin Clarke—*River of Dissolution* (London, 1969)—stresses that in Lawrence's best work "the reductive process is a deeply ambiguous one" (p. 53). Clarke explores the demonic currents in Lawrence's writing more fully than anyone else, with impressive results. If I had seen his work sooner, I should certainly have used him more. See p. 241 n. 19 below.

a soft, fecund, earth, leaving behind him the hard rind of worldly knowledge and experience. . . . Inside, in the softness and
stillness of the room, was the naked kernel, that palpitated in
silent activity, absorbed in reality.

Inside the room was great steadiness, a core of living eternity.
Only far outside, at the rim, went on the noise and the destruction. Here at the centre the great wheel was motionless, centred
upon itself. Here was a poised, unflawed stillness that was beyond time, because it remained the same, inexhaustible, un-
changing, unexhausted.

As they lay close together, complete and beyond the touch of
time or change, it was as if they were at the very centre where
there is utter radiance, and eternal being, and the silence absorbed in praise: the steady core of all movements, the un-
awakened sleep of all wakefulness. They found themselves
there, and they lay still, in each other's arms; for their moment
they were at the heart of eternity, whilst time roared far off,
forever far off, towards the rim.

Then gradually they were passed away from the supreme
centre, down the circles of praise and joy and gladness, further
and further out, towards the noise and the friction. But their
hearts had burned and were tempered by the inner reality, they
were unalterably glad. [p. 141]

This is a bit different from anything we have seen before, although it is strongly reminiscent of Tom's new world, from which
the rainbow arch sprang. For Will, through whose mind we are
looking, a significant unity—a new reality—has certainly been
achieved. The state is idyllic, peaceful, and pointedly exclusive of
all the world beyond the bedroom. The image of the kernel suggests at once that the most essential reality has been reached and
that all further possibility lies in growth from it. This second
suggestion is not developed, however, for the image of the wheel
and references to eternity emphasize that this inner reality can
only be corrupted by the rind of worldly experience. The use of
Biblical diction (the silence absorbed in praise, the circles of

praise and joy and gladness) further enforces the impression that
this is a kind of heaven. George Ford has called attention to the
likeness between this and another scene of transcendence, and the
comparison is instructive.[20]

> His soul leapt, soared up into the great church. His body stood
> still, absorbed by the height. His soul leapt up into the gloom
> into possession, it reeled, it swooned with a great escape, it
> quivered in the womb, in the hush and the gloom of fecundity,
> like seed of procreation in ecstasy.
>
> She too was overcome. . . . Here, the twilight was the very
> essence of life, the coloured darkness was the embryo of all
> light, and the day. Here, the very first dawn was breaking, the
> very last sunset sinking, and the immemorial darkness, whereof
> life's day would blossom and fall away again, re-echoed peace
> and profound immemorial silence.
>
> Away from time, always outside of time! Between east and
> west, between dawn and sunset, the church lay like a seed in
> silence, dark before germination, silenced after death. [p. 198]

Ford points out that after each of these eternal moments Will's
painful return to the daylight world is initiated by Anna, for
whom this sort of experience is not entirely congenial. The
lesson, as Ford puts it, is "that the beautiful confined world of
the marriage bed and of the cathedral is incomplete."

I think that Ford is right, but precisely what constitutes the
incompleteness? Granting that Will cannot live in this world all
the time, and granting that the similarities in diction of the two
scenes reinforce the ultimate unity of Will's sexual and religious
responses, these experiences really seem less confined than the
world of tea parties and "realistic" faces which Anna uses to
demolish Will's trance-like satisfactions. They are certainly closer
to what Lawrence considers the ultimate realities. What is there
about the daylight world that is a needed corrective, and how
should the two realms come together in marriage? If we return to

20. Ford, *Double Measure,* pp. 127-28.

the two scenes for answers to these questions, their differences take on more importance than their similarities.

The most obvious difference is one of intensity. Despite the similarity in diction, the cathedral scene is by far the more fervent: the seed image is developed to cosmic proportions, the ultimate realities which Will yearns for are leapt at, and the cathedral embodies the whole created world and time itself. The bedroom scene is a state of beatitude; its relation to the eternal realm of which it partakes is not one of throbbing ecstasy but one of quite participation. As in some of Tom's similar experiences, the eternal realm has spilled over into the temporal, even to the point of seeming to abolish time. But the extraordinary effectiveness of this scene lies not in the imputed relation to eternity but in the use of that relation to capture the quality of the honeymoon. Whatever we may think of Lawrence's actual beliefs about transcendent realms, his language evokes the completeness and exclusiveness of a new love even while it suggests that the unalterable gladness is not, in fact, unalterable. Lawrence conveys this through realistic touches, which are subtle but important. We are always aware of the physical reality of Will's and Anna's bodies and of the room, and the description of the experience itself contains reference to the temporal world which it denies (it was as if . . . for their moment). Unlike the cathedral scene, where the pulsating rhythm and insistent diction leaves behind our sense of a man standing in a church, the bedroom scene remains firmly based in the psychological reality of two lovers in bed. The scene might, in fact, be read simply as a description of that reality, whereas the cathedral scene forces metaphysical questions upon us.

These questions are more obvious as the scene continues. Here is what follows the passage quoted earlier:

Containing birth and death, potential with all the noise and transitation of life, the cathedral remained hushed, a great, involved seed, whereof the flower would be radiant life inconceivable, but whose beginning and whose end where the circle of silence. Spanned round by the rainbow, the jewelled gloom folded music upon silence, light upon darkness, fecundity upon death, as a seed folds leaf upon leaf and silence upon the root and the flower, hushed up the secret of all between its parts, the death out of which it fell, and the life into which it has dropped, the immortality it involves, and the death it will embrace again.

Here in the church, "before" and "after" were folded together, all was contained in oneness. Brangwen came to his consummation. Out of the doors of the womb he had come, putting aside the wings of the womb, and proceeding into the light. Through daylight and day-after-day he had come, knowledge after knowledge, and experience after experience, remembering the darkness of the womb, having prescience of the darkness after death. Then between—while he had pushed open the doors of the cathedral, and entered the twilight of both darknesses, the hush of the two-fold silence, where dawn was sunset, and the beginning and the end were one. [pp. 198-99]

For Will the cathedral not only represents the beginning and the end, but it contains them, making the whole ultimate unity available to him as experience. His consummation is real, fervent, and apparently complete. The insistently effective diction, with its curious mixture of Biblical echo and sensuous detail, is as close as Lawrence has yet come to mystical experience in the Christian tradition. As such it seems to raise questions about not only that tradition but the relation of ecstasy to Anna's struggle for domination.

It is significant that Anna attacks Will's experience directly. Although she finds the cathedral awesome enough at first, she soon rebels, claiming "another right. The altar was barren, its lights gone out. God burned no more in that bush. It was dead matter lying there. She claimed the right to freedom above her, higher than the roof. She had always a sense of being roofed in" (p. 200). This criticism is by no means identical with that which led to dissolution of the honeymoon scene. There Anna simply insisted that Will was trying to prolong artificially an experience in which she fully participated; here it is the quality of the ecstasy itself which she attacks. She flatly asserts that the meaning Will finds in the cathedral is gone, that his consummation in dark silence is a sham. And her criticism also seems to contain an indictment of Christianity: "God burned no more in that bush." How is one to reconcile this denial with the dramatic force of Will's experience? For it is more "complete" than anything else available to him. A passage from "The Crown" offers a helpful gloss:

It may be there is a great inequality, disproportion, within me, that I am nearly all darkness, like the night, with a few glimmers of cold light, moonlight, like the tiger with white eyes of reflected light brindled in the flame of darkness. Then I shall return again and again to the womb of darkness, avid, never satisfied, my spirit will fall unfertile into the womb, will never be conceived there, never brought forth. I shall know the one consummation, the one direction only, into the darkness. It will be with me for ever the almost, almost, almost, of satisfaction, of fulfilment. I shall know the one eternity, the one infinite, the one immortality, I shall have partial being; but never the whole, never the full. There is an infinite which does not know me. I am always relative, always partial, always, in the last issue, unconsummate.

The barren womb can never be satisfied, if the quick of darkness be sterile within it. But neither can the unfertile loins be satisfied, if the seed of light, of the spirit, be dead within them. They will return again and again to the womb of darkness, asking, asking, and never satisfied.

Then the unconsummated soul, unsatisfied, uncreated in part, will seek to make itself whole by bringing the whole world under its own order, will seek to make itself absolute and timeless by devouring its opposite. Adhering to the one eternity of darkness, it will seek to devour the eternity of light. Realising the one infinite of the Source, it will endeavour to absorb into

its oneness the opposite infinite of the Goal. This is the infinite
with its tail in its mouth. ["The Crown," pp. 28-29]

This is not, perhaps, an exact interpretation of the cathedral
scene, but it indicates Lawrence's meaning. Will's infinite, which
contains for him both beginning and end, is indeed the most
complete satisfaction of which he is capable, but it represents an
ontological regression, "the infinite with its tail in its mouth."
That his ecstasy is embodied in a Christian cathedral is also an
indication that for Lawrence the Christian tradition, though still
of great power, had run its course.[21] Anna, then, makes a needed
and natural correction when she insists that the sky, not the
cathedral roof, is the ultimate confine. Although they go home
"both altered," it is Will's alteration that is emphasized, and it
almost seems as if Anna has indeed converted him to an attitude
which will allow more "light."

Outside the cathedral were many flying spirits that could never
be sifted through the jewelled gloom. He had lost his absolute.
He listened to the thrushes in the gardens and heard a note
which the cathedrals did not include: something free and careless and joyous . . . he was glad he was away from his shadowy
cathedral. [p. 203]

Yet in the midst of his joy and carelessness the flat statement
remains: "he had lost his absolute." And "The Crown" provides
other dicta which point up the undeniable force of this loss.
"Without God, without some sort of immortality, not necessarily
life-everlasting, but without *something* absolute, we are nothing"
("The Crown," p. 89). We have already seen Will and Anna avoid
being nothing by seeking to immortalize dark sensual experience
itself. Anna's conversion of Will, then, contains no religious dimension which can replace the absolute of the cathedral, certainly no dimension of light through which Will's darkness can

21. In "The Crown" (p. 97), Lawrence calls the Christian tradition
"stale."

find issue. What she does, in fact, is to reduce Will's already regressive religious behavior still further.

In the cathedral scene Lawrence has presented for the first time in his novels an experience whose ontological character is at once complete—that is, both satisfying and fully transcendent of the everyday world—and inadequate. This inadequacy, though it may be explained by reference to Will's escapism, is fundamentally a reflection of the nature of Lawrence's ontology itself. As such it represents a portion of Lawrence's thought which is in an experimental stage, and it raises problems with which *The Rainbow* does not attempt to cope. Anna is an able critic, but she offers no alternative to the absolute which she reduces to her own measure. Neither does Lawrence, for nowhere in this book is the balance between the ontological forces of darkness and light for which Lawrence argues in "The Crown" realized.[22] The closest he comes to such a balance is Anna's insistence on the limitations of the cathedral roof. Her own religious experiences, of which her "dance before the lord" is the most striking, are wholly involved in forces of darkness less inclusive than whose Will found in the cathedral.[23]

---

22. It can be argued as well that in "The Crown," too, Lawrence asserts a principle of balance but spends most of his efforts developing the dark rather than the light side. See chap. 5 below.

23. In earlier versions of this scene Lawrence devotes much more attention to Anna's responses. They are quite similar to Will's at first:

> There was only the awful, shadowy height, and shadowy recurrence in height. She was taken up each moment, she was lifted and consummated there in the light, in the upper shadow where the stone met and clinched. But her soul yearned after the stately mystic march of the pillars down the nave. She wanted to follow the pillars. Whither? Ah, there was no goal, and every time she was caught up and carried to the great, clinched rapture above, she was lost. [Hol. p. 304; Roberts's listing, E 331b]

As he develops this version, Lawrence makes it much clearer than in the published text that he is identifying Anna's yearnings with the goal of light described in "The Crown."

> Was this all the knowledge of God, to know the utmost, immemorial "I"? Could she not yearn forwards, forwards? Was there nothing else? whither could she follow the moving pillars, the silent, marching pillars

What the cathedral scene implies from a broader perspective is that Lawrence is moving toward a more intensive exploration of the infinities—for there are several—which underlie all of life. The traditional associations with nature (at least since the Romantics) which were so useful in the portrayal of Tom are no longer avail-

---

of shadow? Would they not lead her forward, forward, on to the threshold of the unknown, to the brink of the mystery, the altar steps, and there cast her down?

She dreamed of the angels, who went in shadow day by day, at night in flickering flames. They flickered on the outer circle of the Most High like altar flames, they quivered in flames of praise. And she knew in her dream, that beyond these were the fiery, stately archangels, and beyond these the fiercely bright circle of the Cherubim, the Innermost palpitating to the awful brightness of the Presence, absorbed in their wonder of praise. [Hol., p. 305]

This passage is a dream. Upon awakening she returns to the cathedral to seek the archangels at the altar, but they are not there. It is then that Anna turns to the "blue rotunda" of day, rejecting the experience in the cathedral as too egoistic.

Remembering the sky above the cathedral, how tiny was man's stud of ecstasy in his immortal soul, how little and partial his passion for God! Could man with his Ego occupy the whole rotunda of Day, or the dome of night? [Hol., pp. 306-07]

Once this far, Anna gropes for a new direction, without any firm result.

For her heart asked, whither, whither? And there was no reply. If she turned her round in the great, noble rotunda of the day, she could only know its completeness. And she knew her own incompleteness. Therefore whither? The blue rotunda of the day made no answer, nor the twinkling dome of night. [Hol., p. 307]

The angels she seeks are supposed to be "brightening the horizon" of day; she wants to "give herself to the pulling of the goal." The best she can do, however, is to "thrust off" from the "resistance" the stone faces provide.

In preparing this scene for publication, Lawrence cut Anna's yearnings down to a minimum and removed altogether her groping toward the goal. Perhaps his only reason was to leave room to develop more fully and dramatically Will's experience so that Anna's rejection of it could be simpler, more direct. But I think he cut Anna's groping because it was also his groping. He does not know whither she might go, and the same problem appears with Ursula. See below, pp. 173 ff.; also Kinkead-Weekes, "The Marble and the Statue," pp. 389-90, with whom I again find myself in rather close parallel. He emphasizes the gain in complexity and literary adequacy of Lawrence's revisions.

able; in fact, Lawrence has set them aside to try new directions. This new effort is in part a test of the Christian tradition, an attempt to relate it to the forces from which Lawrence thought it had been dissociated. Will's experience seems to indicate that Lawrence had already decided against this reawakening, though he was apparently just beginning to articulate this decision. Thus Will's consistent attitude toward Christianity is toward revelation as artifact, toward the physical objects it has left behind, still wrapped in mystery. Will attempts to reawaken these mysteries in a manner as far removed from the rational tradition of Augustine and Aquinas as possible. In the cathedral scene he comes close to succeeding but is limited by the physical boundaries of the cathedral itself. Will's most ultimate experience reveals in him as well as in the tradition which the cathedral symbolizes an ultimate limitation.

Through Will and Anna, Lawrence's methods of writing also undergo something of an expansion; his own conceptual patterns become more daring. His assaults on the ontological realm, which have never been entirely absent from his writing, take on greater importance. Although both Will and Anna are understandable as characters in the usual sense, it is more persistently necessary than it was with Tom and Lydia to take into account their religious experience, and this experience is beginning to have doctrinal implications of its own. What is most affected is the firm progression which, despite occasional shuffling of the time sequence, kept the relationship between Tom and Lydia clearly in the reader's mind. Realistic detail is subordinated to the characters' thoughts and feelings, which in turn have ontological implications.[24] To understand what is going on, the reader must therefore rely more heavily on the usual literary devices for portraying states of mind: images, rhythmic patterns, tone in general.

Although the cathedral scene precedes in time most of the

24. "I shan't write in the same manner of *Sons and Lovers* again, I think—in that hard, violent style of sensation and presentation" (*LM*, p. 259). Lawrence returned to a more specialized version of that style, however, in parts of *Women in Love*.

scenes of marital conflict, it actually finished Lawrence's demonstration of why those battles had to be fought. By extending his portrayal to include a view of Will's full religious capacity, and by associating that capacity with a tradition which he is himself in the act of rejecting, Lawrence sets the stage for the next generation, where a similar capacity leads to wider-ranging rejections as well as more ambitious hopes.

Ursula

The last part of *The Rainbow* is devoted to the growth to adulthood of Anna's first child, Ursula. Ursula's progress is given in more detail than that of any other character in Lawrence, and this detail has raised critical objections. Some of these objections are justified; Lawrence here displays signs of greater uncertainty of direction and purpose than is evident earlier in the book. We are almost forced to recall the early letter in which he described *The Sisters* as a book for *jeunes filles* which he expected to finish in three hundred pages. This and other letters, in fact, provide strong if inconclusive hints that the portions dealing with Ursula were written first; they tempt us to dismiss the evident uncertainties as early and tentative exploration.[25] But of course this is too easy, for it ignores Lawrence's habit of rewriting his books several times. If there are uncertainties in the second half of the book, Lawrence did not recognize them as such, and probably he had reasons for leaving the book as it is.

Lawrence's account of Ursula falls into three sections: her sexual and religious awakening, her excursion into the daylight world, and her return to the dark forces. Of these the first and third are primarily concerned with the relations between men and

25. See Harry Moore, *The Intelligent Heart* (New York, 1962), p. 242; also *LM,* pp. 263, 272. In this last letter Lawrence speaks of "The original Sisters" as if it began with "The School Inspector" (Birkin), who finally got pushed back into *Women in Love.* Ford (*Double Measure,* p. 161) offers a few interesting comments on what is left of the earlier stages of the manuscript, but the most detailed work so far is that of Kinkead-Weekes (pp. 375-79).

women; they obviously carry on the thematic emphasis of the first half of the book. The middle section[26] is concerned with Ursula's formal education and her attitudes toward society. In it her development seems to slow down; she undergoes something like a loss of innocence; and finally she rejects, sometimes with vehemence, almost all the alternatives which this larger world seems to afford. Lawrence's characteristically forceful prose, moreover, occasionally flags and descends into shrillness. Yet granting all this, we need not charge Lawrence with a major loss of direction.

We saw that both Tom and Anna had difficulties with education as well as with their relation to the outside world. Tom did not so much resolve these difficulties as dismiss them; Anna found them more difficult to ignore. Her commitment to rational argument was, despite her somewhat perverse use of it, more thorough. And the main questions left over from her marriage are precisely those regarding the relationship between this rational world and the darker one beneath. By using reason as an instrument of the ego, Anna kept her power over her husband, but her lapse into sensual and generative rhythms was essentially a denial that reason could be put to positive use. It is clear, I think, that this denial is inadequate—that her fulfillment, though real, is incomplete. And Will's failures raise the question again. We are told at one point that he "had failed to become really articulate" (p. 203). The cathedral scene, too, raises among other questions that of the adequate form, both social and personal, for the dark forces. There is reason to expect, then, that Ursula, representing a new generation and moving with the usual Brangwen force and sensitivity on her own quest, would look in precisely those places which her parents and grandparents did not explore.

We have in fact come to the place in Lawrence's career where he begins to confront directly the social and cultural problems

26. I mean by this chaps. 12 and 13, though Ursula's early education is portrayed in chap. 10. Some critics have objected to this and to other parts of the last half of the book as well. See esp. Roger Sale; "The Narrative Technique of *The Rainbow,*" *Modern Fiction Studies* 5 (1959): 29-39.

which hover on the periphery of his earlier work. Not since *The White Peacock* has he given the social structure much attention, and there his efforts amount to little more than a means of revealing his characters' weaknesses, although something like an adolescent yearning toward "society" is also present. Here Lawrence is beginning to make definite statements about those negative aspects of the outer world against which he was to fight the rest of his life. Ursula is among other things a vehicle for this definition.

But if we are to justify Ursula's rather prolonged experiences as a student and teacher, we need to emphasise not her role in Lawrence's development but the adequacy of these experiences in her own. Do they provide a perspective which helps us understand her more passionate experiences? Do they help her to relate her desires and needs to the world in which she finds herself? From questions such as these we can return to the broader concerns of Lawrence's ideas and their influence on his writing.

Like her mother, Ursula has a rainbow in her childhood. But it is a different rainbow from that under which Anna found peace and security as a child. For the adult Anna the rainbow is the hope she chooses not to pursue, the completion she willingly relinquishes to motherhood. It is Ursula who must carry on the quest. And as Anna dedicates her daughter to the future, the "shadow-door" takes on a much more intense, if equally vague, character. "The child she might hold up, she might toss the child forward into the furnace, the child might walk there, amid the burning coals and the incandescent roar of heat, as the three witnesses walked with the angel in the fire" (p. 193). The Biblical reference, though not to be taken in allegorical detail, is significant.[27] It reaffirms that the quest of the Brangwens is a religious one and that its resolution, if found, is not to be found easily or without a test of faith.

Ursula's growth is portrayed in a series of deliberate parallels

27. See Ford (*Double Measure,* p. 130) for a somewhat different view. This scene represents for him Ursula's consecration as a prophetess.

with that of her mother. Through these parallels Lawrence manages to define the essential differences between mother and
daughter and to show how Ursula takes up the quest where her
mother left it. For example, Ursula, like the child Anna, finds her
most intense bond with her father, and she too is concerned with
"asserting her own detachment." But this detachment is almost
entirely a negative response to Anna, not comparable to the need
for self-assertion which possessed Anna herself. The bond with
the father, moreover, is more intense and intimate; it leads to a
premature awakening. "She set herself towards him like a quivering needle. All her life was directed by her awareness of him, her
wakefulness to his being."

> Her father was the dawn wherein her consciousness woke up.
> But for him, she might have gone on like the other children,
> Gudrun and Theresa and Catherine, one with the flowers and
> insects and playthings, having no existence apart from the con-
> crete object of her attention. But her father came too near to
> her. The clasp of his hands and the power of his breast woke
> her up almost in pain from the transient unconsciousness of
> childhood. Wide-eyes, unseeing, she was awake before she knew
> how to see. She was wakened too soon. . . . From her the re-
> sponse had struggled dimly, vaguely into being. [p. 218]

Obviously the child is becoming more self-conscious than is usual,
more aware of the differences between herself and the rest of the
world than are her sisters. But it is clear from the preceding pages
that her responses to her father are also direct responses to his
passionate nature, as "the power of his breast" implies here. The
awakening brought on by her father is clearly a step both in
self-definition and in release of the power which underlies the
self. Both previous generations imply that ideally the two are
inseparable; Ursula goes further than either in trying to define the
relationship between them.

The parallels continue after Tom Brangwen's death in the flood.
In the first of two chapters entitled "The Widening Circle" we see
Ursula's adolescent yearnings for escape, which strongly recall

those of her mother. Like Anna, Ursula finds the outside world petty in contrast to the Brangwen dignity, and she too has romantic and spiritual yearnings. But, unlike Anna, she feels she should relate somehow to the "mob lying in wait for her." Her girlish fantasies take aristocratic form because aristocracy seems necessary for self-preservation. For much the same reason Ursula defends aristocracy in political arguments with her lover later on. But what is more significant in Lawrence's own development is her response to religion. It combines, as we might expect, her father's intensity with her mother's analytic habits.

Like all the Brangwens, Ursula has little use for the more literal and practical interpretations of Christianity. "It was the impudent suburban soul which would ask, "What would Jesus do, if he were in my shoes?" For her Christ is "beautifully remote"; "Ursula was all for the ultimate." This ultimate soon takes on a strongly sexual character. Her favorite Bible story is that of the Sons of God coming to the daughters of men; this, she felt, "was a genuine fate."

> So utterly did she desire the Sons of God should come to the daughters of men; and she believed more in her desire and its fulfilment than in the obvious facts of life. The fact that a man was a man, did not state his descent from Adam, did not exclude that he was also one of the unhistoried, unaccountable Sons of God. As yet, she was confused, but not denied. [p. 275]

To clear up her confusion she pursues Christian lessons with a persistence lacking in Anna. The saying which causes her to brood most has to do with her aristocratic leanings: "It is easier for a camel to go through the eye of a needle, than for a rich man to enter into heaven." After a disturbing analysis of her own situation she concludes, "she was *not* going to be as poor as the Wherrys, not for all the sayings on earth—the miserable squalid Wherrys. So she reverted to the non-literal application of the scriptures." Unlike her mother, Ursula uses her common sense to keep not only her sense of self but her religious impulses intact.

Already Ursula has gone further than Anna in trying to relate herself to Christianity. She has decided that religion has to do with an "Absolute World" and that this cannot be "interpreted in terms of the relative world." At times she prefers visual rather than verbal interpretations of the Absolute World, and through her father she learns to love early Italian painting. "She adored Fra Angelico's flowers and light and angels, she liked the demons and enjoyed the hell. But the representation of the encircled God, surrounded by all the angels on high, suddenly bored her. The figure of the Most High bored her, and roused her resentment" (p. 277). This resentment is not so much a girlish resistance to authority (though Ursula feels some of that as well) as a response to the sensual inadequacy of Fra Angelico's idea of God. For Ursula's concern with the ultimate, despite all its resistence to practical application, insists upon including the flesh. Christ's resurrection seems to her inadequate.

> The resurrection is to life, not to death. Shall I not see those who have risen again walk here among men perfect in body and spirit, whole and glad in the flesh, living in the flesh, loving in the flesh, begetting children in the flesh, arrived at last to wholeness, perfect without scar or blemish, healthy without fear of ill-health? [p. 280]

It is obvious, then, that Ursula has embarked on a course significantly different from that of both her parents. She has much stronger religious yearnings than her mother, a more definite sense of self than her father, and a concern to be related to the world around her, to both its social and religious forms. She is also aware at an early age that her search for relatedness must take into account her sensual nature.

These passages also give a strong impression that Lawrence is writing his own critique of Christianity. This is especially clear in the passage which concludes the chapter: "Can I not, then, walk this earth in gladness, being risen from sorrow? Can I not eat with my brother happily, and with joy kiss my beloved, after my resurrection, celebrate my marriage in the flesh with feasting, etc." (p. 280) This is the sort of realization to which Ursula but not Will can come, and it implies a more positive use of the religious impulse than either Anna or Will can achieve. Lawrence's apparent participation through the rare use of the first person strongly indicates that Ursula is somehow closer to him than were either of the preceding generations. The reason, in fact, probably lies precisely there; Ursula represents Lawrence's own generation. Perhaps this is also why he has the most trouble with her.

Lawrence's problems first appear in a need to recapitulate the thematic concerns of the book by a further series of parallels between Ursula and the previous generations. The whole chapter on "First Love" seems devoted to a theme and variations pattern, by which Ursula's needs are related to those of her predecessors. There is, of course, no reason to attack Lawrence for using this method to define Ursula's particular quest, nor even to bring together the loose ends from the first parts of the novel, but Lawrence does seem to be feeling his way more than usual. For it is precisely the problem of definition implicit in this method (what *is* most striking, most important, about Ursula?) that causes problems later.[28]

Ursula's attempt to revise Christianity eventually leads her to confusion—a function of the increasing intensity of her adolescent desires—complicated by her powerful responses to natural rhythms.

Early in the year, when the lambs came, and shelters were built of straw, and on her uncle's farm the men sat at night with a lantern and a dog, then again there swept over her this passionate confusion between the vision world and the weekday

28. Although, again, there is little reason to quibble about the relevance of passages like the following, they are unusual in Lawrence in the deliberateness of their recapitulation. Lawrence seems to be seeking a vantage point from which to view his three generations as one progressive development: "Hesitating, they continued to walk on, quivering like shadows under the ash-trees of the hill, where her grandfather had walked with his daffodils to make his proposal, and where her mother had gone with her husband, walking close upon him as Ursula was now walking upon Skrebensky" (p. 282).

world. Again she felt Jesus in the countryside. Ah, he would lift up the lambs in his arms! Ah, and she was the lamb. [p. 285]

Jesus—the vision world—the everyday world—all mixed inextricably in a confusion of pain and bliss. [p. 285]

This passage recalls the very beginning of the book and with it Tom's whole pattern of response to nature. Yet Tom lacked Ursula's adolescent intensity. She seems compelled to use traditional religious terms to account for her strong sensuous responses, and the terms do not quite fit. The image of Jesus in the countryside is indeed a confusion, not an integration. Ursula's awareness of this incongruity is also more acute than we would have expected from the earlier, less conscious Brangwens (Anna, of course, though conscious enough, lacked the religious intensity to create the problem): "And all the time she knew underneath that she was playing false, accepting the passion of Jesus for her own physical satisfaction" (pp. 285-86). When she finds a real lover, Jesus simply slides out of the picture. And part of her difficulty with her real lover is the very tendency for which she feels shame here: she accepts him mainly for her own satisfaction and creates for herself an idea of him to fit her desires.

When Anton Skrebensky arrives he brings with him another bundle of Lawrentian motifs. He is a Pole, son of a friend of Lydia Brangwen's, and has already been noticed by Anna as detached and self-possessed. Like her mother, Ursula responds to his touch of foreignness and apparent confidence. "This, she said to herself, was a gentleman, he had a nature like fate, the nature of an aristocrat. She laid hold of him at once for her dreams. Here was one such as those Sons of God who saw the daughters of men, that they were fair. He was no son of Adam. Adam was servile" (p. 290). Not only does Lawrence give us both the beginning of the love affair and its potential collapse (this idealization of Skrebensky is bound to bring disillusion), but he is obviously picking up loose ends as well. Anna's response to the Skrebensky household was to a freedom which Brangwen intimacy would not allow. Tom, to go back even further, was fascinated by the little aristocrat at the inn, and the foreignness of his wife remained for him a tantalizing mystery. Ursula, too, is seeking a counterbalance to Brangwen intimacy, but she has her own context in which to fit it. Skrebensky becomes her hope for the future, her bridge between the vision and the weekday world. And he is even less fit for such a role than either Tom or Will.

To complete the pattern of Ursula's yearnings, Skrebensky also has associations with the larger social world. "He seemed more and more to give her a sense of the vast world, a sense of distances and large masses of humanity" (p. 291). She is proud of his aristocratic descent, and her pride reaffirms her desire to move beyond Brangwen domesticity. Ursula has in fact brought together all the strands of her quest for a complete self in the figure of Skrebensky. This concentration of her desires allows him to awaken fully her adolescent sexuality, but the exposure of the inadequacies of this sexuality is also an exposure of his own inadequacy in being. Lawrence, by insisting on these inadequacies, sets the stage for Ursula's long and rather painful apprenticeship in the everyday world.

As the affair develops, it tends to be described as an "adventure" and a "game." Lawrence tells us quite early in the relationship that it is bound to go wrong, for they are both seeking "self-assertion." "And after all, what could either of them get from such a passion but a sense of his or of her own maximum self, in contradistinction to all the rest of life? Wherein was something finite and sad, for the human soul at its maximum wants a sense of the infinite" (p. 301). What follows is largely a dramatization of this lesson. It is clear that both Ursula and Skrebensky are too egotistic to meet as Tom and Lydia met. But it is not the familiar lesson about egotism that is important here; the exploratory variations on this theme, which the scenes of contact provide, convey, or attempt to convey, Ursula's particular search for completion. For even though she can be justly charged with an adolescent's narcissism, a tendency to demand that she be sensually gratified at whatever cost, she also wants to move beyond the "something finite and sad" which is in Lawrence's world a necessary adjunct of religious failure. This cannot be said of Skrebensky, for Lawrence makes it increasingly clear that Skrebensky's apparent self-possession and confidence is a sham. The best we can say for him is that he has a capacity for sexual response and is physically beautiful, both of which qualities keep Ursula attached to him even when it is clear, at least to us, that fulfillment will not result.

The intense and repeated sexual encounters between Ursula and Skrebensky therefore constitute another problem, especially since they occur in two parts, one before and one after Ursula's experiences in "the man's world." If the point is merely to expose Skrebensky's inadequacies, there is surely unnecessary repetition. The more important intention must be to teach Ursula—and us, of course—something about the nature and possibility of her quest. The fact that Lawrence has two tries at Skrebensky seems to indicate that the quest is difficult for him to define. The first encounter brings negative results, so he sends Ursula to school in the world which Skrebensky so complacently defends. It is here that his uncertainties become most evident.

As if to find a way of defining more precisely Ursula's needs for self-assertion, Lawrence devotes a hundred pages to a prolonged exploration of her efforts to extend herself beyond the unthinking patterns of her home. In doing so he not only emphasizes her more thorough need to understand but emerges for the first time as a social critic. This part of the book emphasizes "woman becoming individual, self-responsible, taking her own initiative" (*LM,* p. 273), initiative which apparently entails confronting the man's world directly and making a place in it. Unfortunately there seems no way for Ursula to do this without putting aside and almost sacrificing altogether her religious needs. This sacrifice is not, of course, obvious to her—and perhaps not to Lawrence either—when she finds it necessary to leave home.

Her departure is by no means joyful, but it seems the only way that offers possibility.

"I shall be proud to see one of my girls win her own economical independence, which means so much more than it seems. I shall be glad indeed to know that one more of my girls has provided for herself the means of freedom to choose for herself."

It all sounded grim and desperate. Ursula rather hated it. But her mother's contempt and her father's harshness had made her raw at the quick, she knew the ignominy of being a hanger-on, she felt the festering thorn of her mother's animal estimation. [pp. 357-58].

As it turns out, it is grim and desperate, and the force of this desperation is not as clear as we might wish. The amount of energy and anguish which Ursula determinedly expends in making her place as a schoolteacher seems to yield disappointingly little either for her personal search for freedom or for the larger movement of expansion which this whole section of the book embodies. Neither of these difficulties can be altogether dismissed, but we should at least try to understand why they appear. Throughout these sections of the book Lawrence is exploring the possibility of relating the personal to the social. The uncertainties that do exist can be attributed to his own emerging attitudes about the man's world itself; Lawrence is not sure whether it offers possibility or not, and Ursula's progress reflects this uncertainty.

The manifestations of the social theme are essentially three: the mechanical world of the collieries, the brutal impersonality (also "mechanical") of the school in which Ursula struggles, and the vapid "democratic" imperialism which Skrebensky embodies and tries to defend. Lawrence criticizes these manifestations for reducing human individuality to interchangeable units, impersonal and meaningless. The criticism has considerable force, especially as it is conveyed by Ursula's excruciating attempts to teach a mob of children brought up in the system in a personal way, applying the virtues of patience, warmth, and even love—though she never quite manages love. Ursula must learn the need for sheer power of will, for only by such power, demonically intense when necessary, can such a system be upheld. Her lesson is essentially that the prevalent social forms have been emptied of human value too thoroughly for any personal rescue; success in the man's world means transforming oneself into another unit of willpower at the cost of her yearnings toward the unknown. Yet even though—or perhaps because—this lesson is so clear, its meaning either for Ursula or for the system is not so clear. Ursula's responses range from intense loathing and rejection (the colliery scenes) to a social view which comes at times curiously close to Skrebensky's too-willing acceptance of his role as "just a brick in the great social fabric, the nation, the modern humanity" (p. 326). Once she finally proves that she can dominate her students, she falls with suspicious ease into similar thinking, which we have every reason to assume that Lawrence detests: "She had her place as comrade and sharer in the work of the school, her fellow teachers had signed to her, as one of them. And she was one of all workers, she had put in her tiny brick to the fabric man was building, she had qualified herself as a co-builder" (p. 425). Of course, this does not mean that she has become like Skrebensky; taken alone it might be dismissed as simply an expression of the feeling of warmth aroused by the somewhat unexpected kind behavior of her fellow teachers as she is about to leave the school. And she *is* leaving the school, to return to college. But there is further evidence indicating that Lawrence himself was not sure that such a tiny brick is meaningless, that there is hope in the system itself. What that hope may be, and how it may relate to the violence of his rejection, is never made clear.

This difficulty is directly evident in a vagueness which keeps the meaning of Ursula's whole experience in the school unresolved. Whatever the cost, the "prison" of school "was a prison where her wild, chaotic soul became hard and independent" (p. 385). It is the value of this hardness and independence which eludes us. If she is merely learning to be tough in order to function in a brutalized world, what meaning can such functioning have? Even being a suffragette is irrelevant to Ursula's needs. "She had within

her the strange, passionate knowledge of religion and living far
transcending the limits of the automatic system that contained
the vote. But her fundamental, organic knowledge had as yet to
rise to utterance" (p. 406). The implication here is that once her
organic knowledge finds utterance, the world of petty struggles in
which she is engaged will be irrelevant. Or will it? "She wanted so
many things. She wanted to read great, beautiful books, and be
rich with them; she wanted to see beautiful things, and have the
joy of them for ever; she wanted to know big, free people; and
there remained always the want she could put no name to" (p.
406). Of course Ursula has not been able to relate her passionate
knowledge of religion to her newly hard and independent soul.
She is obsessed by the idea of freedom and does not know what
she means by it. But does Lawrence know? The immediate context gives no reason to doubt that all Ursula's wants are real, that
she wants a cultural and social as well as a religious freedom; the
fact that she is gaining victories over herself further implies that
she might achieve it. This means coming to terms with the mecha-
nistic system she hates or attempting to make some significant
change in it, a change which will allow her all these freedoms and
transcendent knowledge as well. Yet every time Lawrence attempts confrontation of the larger social forces which underlie
the constricting school he becomes violently negative and rebellious in his language,[29] or else he falls into the apparent acceptance of progress which was evident in Ursula's last scene at the

29. For example, Ursula's uncle Tom, who was in earlier scenes viewed
sympathetically as a mysterious figure in intense conflict (see pp. 248-49),
becomes a mere symbolic representative of the loathsome system. He suddenly has a "strange, repellent grossness . . . a commonness which revealed
itself in his rather fat thighs and loins." And in Ursula's violent rejection of
the world Tom represents, Lawrence makes another of his rare entries in
the first person. "No more would she subscribe to the great colliery, to the
great machine which has taken us all captives" (p. 349). Lawrence's personal resentment seems if anything too clear. Its violence is not earned by a
full portrayal of the evils of the colliery. In his next book he takes up this
evil once again and, though he is no less set against it, thoroughly explains
it, dramatizes it, and relates it to everything else in the book, leaving no
room for objections like those I am advancing here.

school. It is as if he were trying to find a viable social mode of fulfillment but keeps being overcome by a repulsion to everything beyond the personal and religious searching of the first two generations of this book. His next book develops a position more consistently negative.

Lawrence's uncertainty about Ursula's yearnings is also part of a larger pattern, which is not so much confused as incomplete. Her trouble in relating the personal, with its possibilities of confronting ultimate mystery, to the social, with its ruling principle of willful domination, is the problem of modern man as Lawrence saw it. Ursula's attitude toward this is summed up in a scene with a train.

> Below she saw the villages and the woods of the weald, and the train running bravely, a gallant little thing, running with all the importance of the world over the water meadows and into the gap of the downs, waving its white steam, yet all the while so little. So little, yet its courage carried it from end to end of the earth, till there was no place where it did not go. Yet the downs, in magnificent indifference, bearing limbs and body to the sun, drinking sunshine and sea-wind and sea-wet cloud into its golden skin, with superb stillness and calm of being, was not the downs still more wonderful? The blind, pathetic, energetic courage of the train as it steamed tinily away through the patterned leaves to the sea's dimness, so fast and so energetic, made her weep. Where was it going? It was going nowhere, it was just going. So blind, so without goal or aim, yet so hasty! She sat on an old prehistoric earth-work and cried, and the tears ran down her face. The train had tunnelled all the earth, blindly, and uglily. [p. 463]

This is her view as she becomes increasingly disenchanted with Skrebensky toward the end of their engagement. "She wished she could become a strong mound, smooth under the sky" (p. 463); the train and the villages seem shortsighted and petty. Ursula has returned from her cultural yearnings to the more fundamental yearning for nature and eternal rhythms which have dominated

her family. But her attitude toward the train is neither disdain
nor indifference; it is pity at the apparent futility of materialistic,
willed progress. And even though her tears spring partially from
self-pity, Lawrence seems to share her view. The pathos presupposes sympathy and real concern over man's blindness, not a
violent rejection or an uncritical acceptance. In this concern both
Ursula and Lawrence carry the Brangwen quest considerably beyond the personal; they are searching with some fervency for a
way to relate civilization to man's religious needs. The ending of
this book strongly attests to the hope that still remains in such a
search.

In the last section of the novel Lawrence returns to the more
intimate aspects of Ursula's quest, her need for sexual as well as
intellectual maturity. Here she once again explores her yearning
for the unknown, through both the familiar sexual darkness of
her predecessors and a new, somewhat puzzling, leap apparently
beyond this darkness. And again her partner is Skrebensky.

Skrebensky returns just as Ursula is reaching her last stage of
disillusionment with the system. College has lost its initial interest
and now appears a "little, slovenly laboratory for the factory."
Ursula begins again to yearn for something beyond "the lightened
area, lit up by man's completest consciousness." She becomes
aware of a darkness similar to the darkness of Will and Anna,
populated by strange animal shapes and gleams.

> The darkness wheeled round about, with grey shadow-shapes
> of wild beasts, and also with dark shadow-shapes of angels,
> whom the light fenced out, as it fenced out the more familiar
> beasts of darkness. And some, having for a moment seen the
> darkness, saw it bristling with the tufts of the hyaena and the
> wolf; and some, having given up their vanity of the light,
> having died in their own conceit, saw the gleam in the eyes of
> the wolf and the hyaena, that it was the flash of the sword of
> angels, flashing at the door to come in, that the angels in the

darkness were lordly and terrible and not to be denied, like the flash of fangs. [p. 438]

The light referred to here is the light of consciousness, which says "there *is* no darkness." After lying dormant for a long time, subjected to the will which relies entirely upon this sort of light, Ursula's deeper sensibilities are once again awakening. What lies beneath the falsity of the university is the denial of eternal mysteries of unexplained powers and irrational forces. The more familiar beasts of darkness—the wolves and hyaenas—have been associated with sensuality throughout the book. Will was seen as a hawk and a leopard; now, in a series of tempting and powerful animal figures, the theme appears again. (Anthony Schofield is the main example so far.[30]) The angels of the darkness, available only to those who have lost their conceit (their egotism), give off their own sort of flash, the flash of the sword. This hints that Lawrence's ontological realm is more than sensual darkness alone. But only by giving oneself up wholly to the darkness can this flash be seen. Skrebensky, for all his inadequacies, is well able to help Ursula release herself into darkness; but he cannot go so far as to see the flash of angels, and he finally has cause to mourn that they cannot be denied.

The awakening which these scenes imply very soon reaches an epiphany which follows a pattern we noticed in Tom.[31] Irritated by a female physics professor's insistence that life is simply chemical and physical activity, Ursula begins to muse, "But the purpose, what was the purpose?" She wonders about soul, and will, and self, and she looks at a "plant-animal."

It intended to be itself. But what self? Suddenly in her mind the world gleamed strangely, with an intense light, like the nucleus of the creature under the microscope. Suddenly she had

30. See Moynahan (*Deed of Life,* pp. 59-63) for a good discussion of these "symbolic figures."
31. See above, pp. 132 ff.

> passed away into an intensely-gleaming light of knowledge. She
> could not understand what it all was. She only knew that it was
> not limited mechanical energy, nor mere purpose of self-preser-
> vation and self-assertion. It was a consummation, a being in-
> finite. Self was a oneness with the infinite. To be oneself was a
> supreme, gleaming triumph of infinity. [p. 441]

Like Tom, Ursula has by intense questioning managed to clear
away some of the doubt that stood in the way of her religious
impulses. Tom's insight was much more homely—an instance of
compassion, the realization of another's need. Ursula's is significantly the result of a place of learning, a context much more
deliberately metaphysical. Perhaps there is some connection between the light of knowledge and the flash of the angel's sword
after all. And the paradox itself, which Lawrence has hinted at
before but never made this explicit, is central to an understanding
of his metaphysics: the triumph of infinity is somehow also the
triumph of individuation.[32] Tom and Lydia, who have achieved
the most successful movement into the infinite which this book
affords, managed it at least partially by their separate status as
individuals. Will and Anna have both failed (in complementary
ways) to maintain individuality. Skrebensky is at bottom a cipher
in the social masses. Ursula is beginning to understand what full
individuality entails.

Ursula's intensely gleaming knowledge is perhaps the most definite instance in Lawrence of a direct movement from rational
endeavor to ontological knowledge. And the result, it should be
noted, is, like the result of Tom's transfiguration, an advance in
understanding. If Ursula were willing to face up to the implications of this moment before the microscope, she would be able to
realize that Skrebensky is not her man. If anyone is concerned
with mere self-preservation, Skrebensky is. But Ursula has again
focused her yearnings on an idealized Skrebensky, and this stops
her from readily admitting his weakness. "She was in dread of the

32. The importance of this paradox is explored below. See the section
on the *Study of Thomas Hardy* in chap. 5 below.

material world, and in dread of her own transfiguration. She wanted to run to meet Skrebensky—a new life, the reality." When she meets him she is frightened by his "self-effacing diffidence," but "she would not admit to herself the chill like a sunshine of frost that came over her. This was he, the key, the nucleus to the new world."

And in a sense he is, for Ursula must get to know the familiar beasts of darkness better. This far Skrebensky can certainly take her; he now has exotic African experience with which to tantalize.

> Then in a low, vibrating voice he told her about Africa, the strange darkness, the strange, blood fear.
>
> "I am not afraid of the darkness in England," he said. "It is soft, and natural to me, it is my medium, especially when you are here. But in Africa it seems massive and fluid with terror— not fear of anything—just fear. One breathes it, like a smell of blood. The blacks know it. They worship it, really, the darkness. One almost likes it—the fear—something sensual."
>
> She thrilled again to him. He was to her a voice out of the darkness. [p. 446]

The implications of this passage remain to be taken up in *Women in Love*. Here the passage yields only an overpowering sense of fecundity, which deprives Ursula of the will for which she has been struggling during Skrebensky's absence. "The lighted vessel vibrated, and broke in her soul, the light fell, struggled, and went dark. She was all dark, will-less, having only the receptive will" (pp. 446-47). She begins to walk about with "her eyes dilated and shining like the eyes of a wild animal" and mocks the "pale citizens" who are "primeval darkness falsified to a social mechanism" (pp. 447-48).

Skrebensky, too, has a sensual awakening which makes his usual social ties irrelevant. "He had an amused pleasure in everything, a great sense of voluptuous richness in himself, and of the fecundity of the universal night he inhabited." Finally they reach a consummation, which is rendered entirely from Ursula's point of view.

> She was caught up, entangled in the powerful vibration of the night. The man, what was he?—a dark, powerful vibration that encompassed her. She passed away as on a dark wind, far, far away, into the pristine darkness of paradise, into the original immortality. She entered the dark fields of immortality. [p. 451]

This makes her soul "sure and indifferent of the opinion of the world of artificial light." She is "implicated with Skrebensky—not the young man of the world, but the undifferentiated man he was." "She had never been more herself." And Skrebensky himself seems to have come further than we have had reason to expect he could. "They were both absolute and happy and calm."

It would seem, then, that this sexual consummation is a complete, if somewhat surprising, success for both. If Ursula has indeed reached the dark fields of immortality, what more could we ask? But then all Skrebensky's negative aspects must be dealt with, aspects which have only disappeared as sensual darkness has taken over the relationship and which soon come back. The final failure after all this success has, in fact, puzzled various critics, and not without reason.[33] But I think we have seen enough of Lawrence's variations on immortality to explain the pattern, if not necessarily the dramatic force, of this relationship.

We saw that such a thing as a sensual absolute existed for Anna and Will and that a partial fulfillment could be found in it. The only additional difficulty here is that Lawrence has not included qualification within the experience itself; his rendering of it implies unmitigated success. The absence of qualification may sim-

33. This whole section of the book has stimulated a wider variety of readings than any other, a fact which tends to underline its puzzling nature. Since the best of these readings deal closely with detail, they are too complicated to summarize here. Roughly, Hough most directly attacks Lawrence for confusion (see *The Dark Sun*, pp. 69-71); Ford (*Double Measure*, pp. 151-62) and Daleski (*Forked Flame*, pp. 115-26) defend him with good arguments.

ply indicate that he wants to preserve the full force of those experiences. For Ursula this is truly a completion; perhaps it should not be qualified until she herself is far enough along to see that there is still more to be desired. We also know from previous examples that the sensual darkness into which she enters has never been adequate for true completeness in Lawrence. But these arguments do not quite erase the reader's uneasiness, because with both earlier generations Lawrence has included the necessary qualification within the experience itself. To this there is only one exception—the cathedral scene between Will and Anna. In that scene the satisfaction of Will's dark mystical experience was convincing enough to make us wonder about the qualification, and we have the same problem here. At the bottom of it lies Lawrence's continuing difficulty in deciding what he means by the forces of light, a difficulty particularly evident in the scenes of moon consummation.

These scenes are perhaps the most puzzling in the book. Through them Lawrence certainly means to convey that Ursula has vital resources quite beyond Skrebensky's, resources upon which she draws to "annihilate" him and make real marriage impossible. They expose a sexual inadequacy in Skrebensky which is surely an inadequacy in "being." But the demonstration of this inadequacy is also a demonstration of Ursula's religious capacity, and there seems to be no way to arrive at a satisfactory understanding of how her capacity differs from that of her forebears or what sort of new life it may imply for new generations of seekers. It seems that Lawrence is experimenting with his ontology through these scenes, and his experimentation does not meet the expectations his characterization has raised in the reader.

There are two scenes beneath the moon, one before and one after Ursula's trial period in the man's world. The first is the more fully developed; it takes place at the wedding of Ursula's uncle, Fred Brangwen, when Ursula is still sixteen. "A kind of flame of physical desire was gradually beating up in the Marsh," and Skrebensky, for one, wants to participate in it fully. Ursula also responds, but with her own peculiar intensity. "The darkness was passionate and breathing with immense, unperceived heaving. It was waiting to receive her in her flight. And how could she start—and how could she let go? She must leap from the known into the unknown" (p. 316). This desire takes a different form from anything we have seen before.

> She turned, and saw a great white moon looking at her over the hill. And her breast opened to it, she was cleaved like a transparent jewel to its light. She stood filled with the full moon, offering herself. Her two breasts opened to make way for it, her body opened wide like a quivering anemone, a soft, dilated invitation touched by the moon. She wanted the moon to fill in to her, she wanted more, more communion with the moon, consummation. But Skrebensky put his arm around her, and sat holding her hand, whilst the moonlight streamed above the glowing fires. [p. 317]

It is not that the moon seldom appears in Lawrence; it pervades his writing, often appearing in scenes of passion.[34] But up to now it has been a presiding genius or part of a larger context; never has

---

34. Such scenes appear in each of the earlier novels. Those which come most quickly to mind are Mrs. Morel's expulsion into the garden full of lilies and moonlight and especially the other stackyard scene in *The Rainbow,* in which Anna and Will carry out a ritual with the sheaves which results in their engagement. There are some striking similarities between this scene and the one between Ursula and Skrebensky. For example, "Her hands fluttered. Yet she broke away, and turned to the moon, which laid bare her bosom, so she felt as if her bosom were heaving and panting with moonlight" (p. 118). But it is really moonlight and not the moon itself which pervades the scene, and the rhythmic movement of the bodies of Anna and Will is continually in focus. There is descent into the sort of detail which keeps the ontological implications in check: "He wondered over the moonlight on her nose! All the moonlight upon her, all the darkness within her! All the night in his arms, darkness and shine, he possessed of it all! All the night for him now, to unfold, to venture within, all the mystery to be entered, all the discovery to be made" (p. 119). Throughout passages like this one we are conscious of the romantic young man discovering his love. The scene between Ursula and Skrebensky leaves this psychological dimension almost entirely behind and is therefore much harder to interpret.

it taken so significant a part in the action. As the scene progresses Ursula indeed manages to take from the moon a consummation of sorts, much to Skrebensky's disadvantage. For the more Ursula takes on the moon's qualities, the more she leaves Skrebensky behind.

> His will was set and straining with all its tension to encompass him and compel her. If he could only compel her. He seemed to be annihilated. She was cold and hard and compact of brilliance as the moon itself, and beyond him as the moonlight was beyond him, never to be grasped or known. If he could only set a bond round her and compel her! [p. 318]

They move into the stackyard and find a "moon-conflagration," before which Skrebensky is afraid. "His heart grew smaller, it began to fuse like a bead. He knew he would die." Ursula deliberately tempts him, "like a beam of gleaming power." She finally destroys him with a kiss, "cold as the moon and burning as a fierce salt."

Obviously Ursula has been transformed into a fierce, destructive presence. The moon is at once her lover and herself: "And she was the quarry, and she was also the hound." Throughout the scene Ursula's growing power becomes increasingly demonic; it is reminiscent of Helena's mother-ecstasy over Siegmund, only here the qualities of coldness, hardness, and impersonality replace Helena's literary gushiness. Ursula's transformation is even more clearly egotistical than Anna's dance before the Lord, for she deliberately tempts Skrebensky, intending only his destruction. Yet Lawrence also implies here, as he did in Anna's dance, that some contact with "being" has taken place. After she comes back to her everyday self, she is appalled at the stacks which had "glistened and gleamed transfigured" a moment before. "Looking away, she saw the delicate glint of oats dangling from the side of the stack, in the moonlight, something proud and royal, and quite impersonal. She had been proud with them, where they were, she had been also" (p. 321). When she returns to her room the moon seems a bridegroom, "blond" and "debonair," but she also carries a "wound of sorrow" for having hurt Skrebensky.

It is at least clear that this experience, like the hawklike marital battles of Ursula's parents and also like Anna's dance, brings neither peace nor wholeness in the sense that Tom's moments of transcendence did. Instead it is powerfully self-assertive and destructive of a lesser male.[35] In seeking an unknown that combines the qualities of coldness, light, and destructive power, Ursula seems to have made the most egotistical assertion of "being" thus far. What is not so clear is the precise weight this assertion is to have in either her own development or the development of Lawrence's book. Although Ursula is sure she has been in another realm, she is simply confused about what the experience means and remorseful because she cannot reconcile this demonic self with her everyday warmth and goodness. It would seem, moreover, that Skrebensky's utter insufficiency has now been adequately exposed. But Ursula's intense yearning for Skrebensky persists, and it is accentuated by his going off to war. When he returns she must go through an even more devastating scene of destruction, strongly echoing this one, before she can dispense with him. This scene, too, leaves open some important questions.

> There was a great whiteness confronting her, the moon was incandescent as a round furnace door, out of which came the high blast of moonlight, over the seaward half of the world, a dazzling, terrifying glare of white light. They shrank back for a moment into shadow, uttering a cry. He felt his chest laid bare, where the secret was heavily hidden. He felt himself fusing down to nothingness, like a bead that rapidly disappears in an incandescent flame.
>
> "How wonderful!" cried Ursula, in low, calling tones. "How wonderful!"
>
> And she went forward, plunging into it. He followed behind.

35. The self-assertion, once remorse dies down, does have a rejuvenating effect; Ursula is exhilarated the next morning.

She too seemed to melt into the glare, towards the moon. [p. 478]

Again Skrebensky fuses like a bead. We have also seen Ursula tossed into a furnace before, in the dedication scene which Anna imagined. And again Skrebensky's darkness must be exposed by a scene drenched with light.

> He felt as if the ordeal of proof was upon him, for life or death. He led her to a dark hollow.
>
> "No, here," she said, going out to the slope full under the moonshine. She lay motionless, with wide-open eyes looking at the moon. He came direct to her, without preliminaries. She held him pinned down at the chest, awful. The fight, the struggle for consummation was terrible. It lasted till it was agony to his soul, till he succumbed, till he gave way as if dead, and lay with his face buried, partly in her hair, partly in the sand, motionless, as if he would be motionless now forever, hidden away in the dark, buried, only buried, he only wanted to be buried in the goodly darkness, only that, and no more. [p. 479]

Skrebensky's sexual failure is vividly and powerfully portrayed. But the imagery of the light remains puzzling.

In both scenes Ursula's destructive power is firmly associated with the moon and its light. If in the first her self-assertion is clear, in the second even this is brought into doubt; sexually, no consummation takes place, egotistic or not. Ursula has repeatedly cried out "I want to go," and the reader, even at the scene's conclusion, still asks where. If this cold and corrosive power is intended to balance Skrebensky's sexual darkness, why is it only destructive? If it is, as one critic has called it, an "insane assertion of self,"[36] what sort of self is it supposed to assert? The ques-

36. See Daleski, *Forked Flame,* pp. 119-21. His reading is the most convincing I have seen:

The invitation is to something far removed from ordinary sexual experience; it is not even an invitation to the sort of heightened experience which Lawrence describes as the "destructive fire" of "profane love . . .

tions are surely not irrelevant, for Lawrence has created great expectations about Ursula's selfhood and its relation to transcendent experience. The new use of the light imagery implies a new direction for Ursula, or at least a failure which helps define that direction. But Lawrence himself seems unsure of what this direction is.

"The Crown" can help us focus on the possibilities. There Lawrence associates light with the male pattern of the *Study of Thomas Hardy,* which develops a set of meanings associating the will-to-motion and progressive, other-directed activity with masculinity. But Lawrence finds it difficult to maintain these associations in both expository works (see esp. pp. 197-206 below). He shows a persistent tendency to translate ostensibly male patterns of other-directed activity into a female emphasis on the flesh and on sexual darkness. In these schemes egotism is an inhibitory state, preventing vitality from progressing to male accomplishments or returning to female creative and sensual (including sexual) darkness. As the dialectic would have it, these two directions are supposed to have equal value; the ideal result is a consummatory meeting of male outgoing vitality and female receptive vitality. In trying to describe what can go wrong with this ideal meeting, Lawrence uses images somewhat like those associated with Ursula's power.

---

the only fire that will purify us into singleness, fuse us from the chaos into our own unique gem-like separateness of being." It is an invitation to a battle in which the aim is to conquer and kill, to remain destructively *apart* in the act of intercourse in an insane assertion of self; for Ursula, who has given "her breast to the moon, her belly to the flashing, heaving water," has passed beyond relationship with him.

Ursula's tears, then, are "a tacit admission of the vanity of her victory." She "cannot be Woman, be more than Ursula Brangwen." But I doubt this last; it seems more likely her tears are signs of failure in the experience itself, owing to Skrebensky's inadequacy. Her intention seems to be to transfigure the sexual experience, and this might have been possible had Skrebensky's power of darkness matched her immersion in moonlight. Short of such a meeting she must destroy him to free herself from his influence, to keep from sharing his ultimate inadequacies. But Lawrence does not provide conclusive evidence for either my reading or Daleski's.

But here are only the angels that cleave asunder, terrible and invincible. With cold, irresistible hands they put us apart, they send like unto like, darkness unto darkness. . . . they set the cold phosphorescent flame of light flowing back to the light, and cold heavy darkness flowing back to the darkness. . . . This goes on within the rind . . . my false absolute self, my self-conscious ego. . . . The rind also, the public form, the civilization, the established consciousness of mankind disappears as well. [pp. 47-48]

There is a hint here, but only a hint, that Ursula's cold, gleaming power may have something to do with this state of regression or redirection of an ontological force. The implication would then be that Ursula, like the civilization she learns mainly to reject, is manifesting ego-bound vitality. Here is another passage containing similar hints; in it the separation described above has become a flux of corruption, for which one of Lawrence's symbols is a swan.

For the swan is one of the symbols of divine corruption . . . its beauty white and cold and terrifying, like the dead beauty of the moon, like the water-lily, the sacred lotus . . . it is for us a flame of the cold white fire of flux, the phosphorescence of corruption, the salt, cold burning of the sea which corrodes all it touches, coldly reduces every sun-built form to ash, to the original elements. . . . This cold white salty fire of infinite reduction. [pp. 76-77]

We have here a greater overlap of images. Ursula, too, has a yearning for "the salt, bitter passion of the sea" (p. 477), which has a corrosive power and is "white and cold and terrifying"—at least to Skrebensky. But if Lawrence's intentions are indeed partly reflected in these passages they certainly are not made clear in *The Rainbow*. The above passage, in fact, has more relevance to Lawrence's next novel, the more "destructive" *Women in Love* (see pp. 241-43 below).

Both passages, however, may help us understand Lawrence's

problem with Ursula. The eternal moonlight in the novel is neither the sexual darkness nor the ordinary light of day; it implies
in both scenes a transcendence of these, and of course a transcendence of the ordinary stable ego as well. "The Crown" suggests that Ursula may be acting out a male leap toward a new
mode of being, a mode associated with socially progressive and
spiritual activity and a movement away from sexual darkness. If
this movement were to follow the usual Lawrentian patterns, it
would not fail to provide Ursula with a new sense of purpose and
coherence of self. Since it does very little of either, we can assume that it somehow fails. Yet it does not seem to fail because it
insufficiently transcends the sexual but because the sexual experience itself fails to take on a new dimension. In short, Lawrence cannot seem to find an intellectually or dramatically viable
mode of transcendent experience which also transforms his sexual
paradigm. He wants Ursula's quest to broach new realms of being;
in addition, he wants to associate them with a new role for the
woman in society, based, of course, on a new, purposive self. But
the more he asserts the social role, the more he denies the sexual,
and the sexual remains the more essential. He has not found a
conception of selfhood which can integrate his desires for fulfillment on a sexual model and for newly purposive activity both
spiritual and socially significant. He therefore tends to concentrate increasingly on what is wrong, and in "The Crown" he
arrives at patterns of vital inversion which freely use sexual imagery: these are theories of ontological inhibition. Ursula's characterization does not quite turn in this destructive direction, so
the "flux of corruption" does not really fit her experience. But
the basic ambivalence toward this new dimension of light remains
in the quality of the scenes themselves and in their results. She
fully transcends her ordinary self for a new, powerful, impersonal
one, but neither she nor Lawrence knows what to do with this
mysteriously unsatisfactory leap into the unknown.

In a state of apathy apparently caused by her ultimate disillusionment with Skrebensky, Ursula shows a further confusion
which Lawrence clearly does not share. Finding that she is preg-

nant, she is tempted to accept her mother's mode of life, that fecund immersion in sexual and reproductive rhythms which marked the limit of Skrebensky's capacities. She finds a nobility in this simple mode, for she is not only becoming desperate about her pregnancy but feeling guilty about the egotism of continually striving for something better. "Her mother was simple and radically true. She had taken the life that was given. She had not, in her arrogant conceit, insisted on creating life to fit herself." At this point Ursula writes to Skrebensky to get him back, not knowing that in his escape into secure banality he has married the colonel's daughter. Writing the letter brings her a sort of peace, for she knows she has great power over him. But she cannot maintain such complacency. She is shocked out of it by a herd of horses during a lonely walk in the rain. Through this shock Lawrence purges Ursula of her apathy and prepares her for the vision which ends the book.

As Ursula walks she feels a "heaviness on her heart. It was the weight of the horses. But she would circumvent them." She finally does circumvent them, but not before they terrify her.

> She was aware of their breasts gripped, clenched narrow in a hold that never relaxed, she was aware of their red nostrils flaming with long endurance, and their haunches, so rounded, so massive, pressing, pressing, pressing to burst the grip upon their breasts, pressing forever till they went mad, running against the walls of time, and never bursting free. Their great haunches were smoothed and darkened with rain. But the darkness and the wetness of rain could not put out the hard, urgent, massive fire that was locked within these flanks, never, never.
> [p. 487]

We have seen horses before, associated with Skrebensky's sensuality.[37] The association is relevant here, for their fire is the fire

---

37. Ford (*Double Measure,* p. 159) notes that Lawrence has discussed the meaning which horses may have both in *Apocalypse* and *Fantasia of the Unconscious.* Lawrence points out that a "persistent passionate, fear-dream about horses" contains not only fear but admiration (see *Fantasia of*

of the flesh, always caught in temporality yet never extinguished because it is cyclical. Ursula is laboring under burdens of the flesh in a double sense; not only has her attempt to move beyond it into the mysterious eternity of light been a failure, but she is bound to it by pregnancy. The horses help relieve her of both burdens. Through her terror at the horses Ursula is made violently ill, but from her delirium emerges the conviction that the kernel of her individual being is intact. She also conveniently loses the baby, which continues as a nightmare all through her sickness because it would have reduced her to the cycle of the flesh which Anna welcomed. Through her encounter with the horses, then, Ursula both actually and symbolically acts out her purgation of the flesh, freeing herself for the prophetic vision which closes the book.

Ursula's vision represents Lawrence's only attempt to consolidate the social and religious themes whose separation has seemed insurmountable through this last third of the book. In the passing colliers she sees "a sort of suspense, a waiting in pain for the new liberation"; in their stiffened bodies and horrible houses, "corruption triumphant and unopposed, corruption so pure that it is hard and brittle." Then she sees a rainbow.

> The arc bended and strengthened itself till it arched indomitable, making great architecture of light and colour and the space of heaven, its pedestals luminous in the corruption of new houses on the low hill, its arch the top of heaven.
>
> And the rainbow stood on the earth. She knew that the sordid people who crept hard-scaled and separate on the face of the world's corruption were living still, that the rainbow was

---

the Unconscious, pp. 199-200). And in "St. Mawr" this admiration is brought out clearly. Here Ursula feels fear most strongly, for she is in real danger of succumbing to more trivial forms of the sort of vitality the horses represent. But I do not mean to imply that she is going to give up the flesh; she must merely be shocked into full realization of the compromise which her acquiescence implies. See also Moynahan (*Deed of Life,* pp. 67-69) for a reading which emphasizes both the threat to order which the horses represent and the essential vitality which they contain.

arched in their blood and would quiver to life in their spirit, that they would cast off their horny covering of disintegration, that new, clean, naked bodies would issue to a new germination, to a new growth, rising to the light and the wind and the clean rain of heaven. She saw in the rainbow the earth's new architecture, the old, brittle corruption of houses and factories swept away, the world built up in a living fabric of Truth, fitting to the over-arching heaven. [pp. 494-95]

F. R. Leavis and others have complained that this rainbow has no support in the book which it ends, that the theme of social regeneration makes its first appearance here, somewhat contradicting the mechanical horrors to which Ursula responded with revulsion earlier.[38] This criticism, it seems to me, is at least partially valid. There is an assertive quality to Ursula's vision, part of which derives simply from the fact that it does end the book. We tend to read it as Lawrence's answer to the social problems examined above, and seen in this way it is inadequate.

But this is Ursula's vision too, and as such it has both a dramatic and a thematic relevance to what has gone before. It is not at all out of character, for we have seen repeated attempts on Ursula's part toward some sort of religious insight. The immediate psychological basis for it is also beyond question; the emotional chaos into which Skrebensky and the horses finally led her, together with serious physical illness, make a visionary recovery plausible enough. And of course religious quests seldom—and, in Lawrence, never—have answers. Each of his books ends with unsolved problems and a degree, however slight, of hope. We can ask only that there be some direction to this hope, and only insofar as Lawrence has failed to provide this direction can be blamed.

If we look back for a moment at the patterns of Ursula's development, we can discover a series of indications that Lawrence

38. See Leavis, *D. H. Lawrence,* pp. 169-70. Leavis very strongly emphasizes Lawrence's new social awareness in the last parts of the book and, since the implications of this awareness are predominantly negative, regards the optimism as "a note wholly unprepared and unsupported."

was straining toward larger and more inclusive schemes, trying persistently to relate the ontological realm and the everyday world. Ursula's early years were designed to bring to mind virtually all the themes of self-development that the older generations of Brangwens pursued. The continuing implication was that she would move beyond them all: in conscious knowledge, social achievement, and religious experience. And she has, at least in the sense that she has opened up new and important problems which the earlier generations did not face, partly because the cultural pressures were not so great. With Ursula such pressures were inevitable; her prolonged struggles with the man's world were necessary to expose the difficulties inherent in them. This has certainly been accomplished, but at the cost of raising questions that could hardly be resolved in the remainder of the book. They are taken up, therefore, in the next novel, which was originally conceived as part of the same story.

But this does not entirely excuse Lawrence for the uncertainties which accrue, not only about the value of the social but about Ursula's self-development. While individually powerful, her destructive transfigurations do not have clear implications about the direction of her goal. The firm relation between the psychological and the ontological which Lawrence brilliantly captures in the early parts of the novel is here under less complete control. Although we know from the pattern of the Skrebensky episodes that Ursula has finally come to realize the limitations of darkness, there seems no firm way to translate what few hints we have about her need for individuation into a program for either social action or religious endeavor. And the presence of both these themes is too persistent to be denied.

But Lawrence's real achievements must not be slighted: *The Rainbow* manages to relate convincingly sexual and religious experience, and the methods it uses are strikingly original. Various modes of transcendent experience are not only distinguished but connected to common and fundamental patterns of attraction and repulsion. If, in his desire to expand these achievements to include a broader view of man and his efforts, Lawrence is not altogether successful, his difficulties should be viewed sympathetically, as part of the same search for an order at once coherent and inclusive which has been evident from the first. In his next book he comes as close as he ever would to finding it. For *Women in Love* takes up directly the loose ends of *The Rainbow* and puts them into firm relation, although the nature of that relation is not entirely predictable from *The Rainbow* itself.

5: STUDY OF THOMAS HARDY and "The Crown"

Study of Thomas Hardy

Where Lawrence's fourth novel ends with a rainbow, assuring us of a world containing possibility and even strong promise, his fifth novel ends with a hanging question. No comparable promise is evident, though possibility has not disappeared. The most obvious as well as the most compelling reasons for this diminished hope have to do with the war and with the rejection of *The Rainbow* as pornography. It is difficult to write optimistic books when civilization seems bent on destroying itself and in doing so attacks one personally. But even if we allow these reasons full weight, they do not go far in accounting for the form *Women in Love* takes in its destructiveness.[1] Nor do they clarify Lawrence's most persistent problems as a novelist.

These difficulties may, of course, also be viewed as part of the developments we have been tracing. Conceived originally as parts of the same novel, *The Rainbow* and *Women in Love* have a great deal in common, despite the startling differences in tone and method which we shall examine shortly. What is most obvious are a great many shared ideas: the conceptual apparatus by which Lawrence's continuing search for definition is carried out. It is useful to examine some of these in their own right, as they appear

1. See *LM*, p. 519.

outside the novels—for, as I indicated above, it is at this time in Lawrence's career that they do appear, especially in the *Study of Thomas Hardy* and "The Crown." These works reveal the direction of Lawrence's thought more explicitly than the novels; they also reveal certain problems, which are related both to Lawrence's difficulties and to his particular achievement as a novelist.

The movement in *The Rainbow* through three generations, from the country to the city, and from the natural to the social was, of course, intended to capture the movement of history into the present; to comprehend it Lawrence sought an ontological perspective from which it could be evaluated. This ontology arose directly from a study of character. The figure of Tom Brangwen in particular reveals an expansion from conventional psychology to a kind of metapsychology or psychology of being. The principles developed in Lawrence's portrayal of Tom became the central principles of the ontological perspective. Since they all grow from a concern for how we ought to live, and since the novel examines and tests them through the lives of its characters, it is most convenient to summarize them as ethical directives: Everyone must live out a religious quest or risk stagnation and death. The object of this quest is fulfillment, but this concept cannot be explained (and therefore dismissed) by analogies from the senses or by reference to existing dogma. Sexual consummation is one of the most important modes of achieving fulfillment, and when achieved it includes transcendence of the usual, reasonably stable conceptions of selfhood, culminating in significant self-renewal or even in radical change of personality. There is no easy set of rules, but certain kinds of behavior are more conducive than others. Closeness to nature helps; highly organized or systematized social activity hinders. Some degree of dissatisfaction with oneself is necessary; smugness, egotism, willful pride are all obstacles. These last requirements take us, of course, past Tom Brangwen into the younger generations. And their relative failures show that the departure from the land brings difficulties which threaten to be insurmountable and which contain lessons about the limitations of the ideas just summarized. Ursula has the most trouble achieving fulfillment, and depicting her is Lawrence's biggest problem, particularly when the individual's quest must be related to society and civilization itself. The clearest and most consistent presentation of the man's world is strongly unfavorable, implying rejection; yet Ursula's efforts to come to terms with it extend far beyond what is necessary to justify its dismissal, and the ending of the novel argues for acceptance.

There are several problems here which the *Study of Thomas Hardy* may clarify. They all seem to center around the relation of the individual to larger wholes, particularly society, and finally around the possibility of self-transcendence of any sort. Lawrence's long expository work is a strenuous, sometimes tortured attempt to get at the basis of this possibility.

The *Study of Thomas Hardy* is Lawrence's first concerted attempt to bring the vitalism which has been directing the writing of his novels to articulate development. In what was to become the characteristic manner of his expository works, Lawrence seeks articulation by repeatedly asserting his most important ideas; the repetitions are never quite identical, and the gradual changes constitute gradual redefinition. What he attempts to define is the nature of life itself, in a manner direct enough to be called, for the first time, metaphysics. This metaphysics turns out to be pervasively dualistic. In the *Study of Thomas Hardy* its most important formulation is in terms of male and female principles, which Lawrence then uses for various applications to history, especially the history of visual art. How adequately these principles explain the art to which they are applied is often questionable; what is more interesting is the process by which Lawrence arrives at them. The very necessity for dualism is a bit puzzling, especially since it is inextricably linked to the need for unity which has emerged increasingly through the first four novels. Not only have Lawrence's protagonists been suffering from the need for a unity of self-possession, but they have been under considerable pressure to reconcile their individual desires with larger social and natural wholes. The *Study of Thomas*

Hardy seeks to define this pressure and, if not to resolve it, at least to place it in a context—social, historical, metaphysical—which will provide some coherent explanation. Viewed this way, the apparently disorderly progression of the essay can be perceived as a continuation of Ursula's quest. Like the closing chapters of *The Rainbow,* the opening chapters of the *Study of Thomas Hardy* show both an ambivalence toward community and a growing tendency to assert not only the possibility of but the necessity for indivdual fulfillment.

Lawrence's argument begins with a favorite image of natural vitality, the poppy. He is concerned with asserting a fundamental vital principle, shared by both flowers and men: "The final aim of every living thing, creature, or being is the full achievement of itself" (p. 403). But his attempt to relate this principle to social problems gets him involved in a chapter whose title is self-explanatory: "Still Introductory: About Women's Suffrage and Laws, and the War, and the Poor, with some Fanciful Moralizing." The moralizing amounts to an attempt to dismiss the man's world which bothered Ursula by criteria derived from the poppy. "What does the law matter? What does money, power, or public approval matter? All that matters is that each human being shall *be* in his own fullness" (p. 406).

The attempt to dismiss the social and communal fails, as the very length of the *Study of Thomas Hardy* testifies. The essay tries instead to relate an emerging ontology to both society and civilization. This more comprehensive effort soon focuses on the book's ostensible subject, though it does not remain there long. Lawrence argues that Hardy gave in to communal morality when he should have recognized that the natural vitality of his characters constituted a more fundamental morality. "Upon the vast, incomprehensible pattern of some primal morality greater than ever the human mind can grasp, is drawn the little, pathetic pattern of man's moral life and struggle" (p. 419). Hardy, failing to recognize this fully, wrote tragic novels; Lawrence, much more concerned with affirmation, seems on the verge of asserting that his own novels will deny man's pathetic struggles in favor of the primal morality. Fortunately, however, the rhetoric of rejection repeatedly collapses into a rhetoric of qualification; Lawrence continues to seek a bridge between Hardy's oppressive community and his own life forces. In order to build such a bridge he must further define these forces, and that definition emerges from an examination of the vital meaning of work (work is both communal and individual, repetitive and vital). A new term, very important to Lawrence's later writing, emerges—"It seems as if the great aim and purpose in human life were to bring all life into the human consciousness. And this is the final meaning of work: the extension of human consciousness. The lesser meaning of work is the achieving of self-preservation" (p. 431). Once the concept of consciousness is introduced, Lawrence worries, in characteristic fashion, about its applicability.

> But the bringing of life into human consciousness is not an aim in itself, it is only a necessary condition of the progress of life itself.
>
> It seems as though one of the conditions of life is, that life shall continually and progressively differentiate itself, almost as though this differentiation were a Purpose.
>
> Man's consciousness, that is, his mind, his knowledge, is his greater manifestation of individuality. [p. 431]

The problem of what work means has become a problem of what freedom means, and both must be understood not only in terms of communal activity but as possibilities implicit in the human being. In effect Lawrence resists a powerful temptation to allow his concern for man and his possibilities to collapse into the mindless vitalism of which he has been accused. His rhetoric repeatedly implies that communal activity is false and superficial; in his letters he argues as well that he is seeking final, "impersonal" forces.[2] Lawrence's difficulties here in defining them imper-

2. See *LM,* p. 365, where Lawrence, working on "The Crown," describes it as his "idea of the other, impersonal freedom." See also *LM,* p. 395.

sonally, or exclusively in terms of natural sensation, indicate his concern to take into account the obvious complexity of the human animal. This concern leads (not exactly directly) to the somewhat surprising equation, or at least the fundamental association, of individual consciousness and its need for articulation with life itself.

We can now begin to see the necessity for Lawrence's dualistic formulations. By the simple assertion that the life force seeks differentiation Lawrence makes room for both the differentiation of thought (articulation) and the differentiation of things (individuality). A similar argument can be used to justify novels which teach (articulately) both individual definition and the return to a primal unity. There is room, then, for the social and the personal, but there is also room to transcend them. Trying to define this transcendence, Lawrence moves on to a more directly metaphysical exploration and offers us a theory of the Creation.

> In the origin, life must have been uniform . . . a great not-being, at once a positive and negative infinity: the whole universe . . . one motionless homogeneity, a something, a nothing. And yet it can never have been utterly homogeneous: mathematically, yes; actually, no. There must always have been some reaction, infinitesimally faint, stirring somehow through the vast, homogeneous inertia. [p. 432] [3]

If life does not somehow move, how can it progress? Lawrence

3. Faced with a similar problem Henri Bergson asserts much the same thing.

> And it is that we express when we say that unity and multiplicity are categories of inert matter, that the vital impetus is neither pure unity nor pure multiplicity, and that if the matter to which it communicates itself compels it to choose . . . its choice will never be definitive: it will leap from one to the other indefinitely. The evolution of life in the double direction of individuality and association has therefore nothing accidental about it: it is due to the very nature of life. [*Creative Evolution*, trans. Arthur Mitchell (London, 1964), p. 275]

This double direction has direct bearing on the problem of novelty or potentiality. See pp. 202-03 below.

obviously wishes to assert both its ultimate stability and its creative force, however difficult it may be to reconcile the two con-
ceptually. One way to make, or at least to attempt, such a reconciliation is to think of the generating movement as a reaction
toward self-definition of the individual being. The life force then
becomes a double force (reactions need reagents), and Lawrence
has created a metaphysical foundation for his dualism.

The relation between Lawrence's vitalism and his dualism is
not, then, as illogical as it first seems. In a post-Darwinian, post-
Spencerian age, even the pantheistic unity of a Wordsworth did
not seem possible, yet the need for such a unity had not diminished, nor had its natural model altogether lost its authority.
Although Lawrence sometimes goes to ridiculous extremes with
his "science" (as in *Fantasia of the Unconscious*), denying the
necessity for empirical verification, clearly he continually attempts to make his desires and the theories they produced fit the
world as he perceived it. The primal unity must be defined in
such a way as to account not only for divisions between man and
society but for the very diversity of a world full of individual
objects. Part of this diversity is, quite naturally, the mind itself,
with its need to articulate—precisely the need which made Lawrence write philosophic essays. A merely unitary conception of
the life-force would not allow either felt oppositions or the sheer
variety of the phenomenal world, so the fundamental definition
must present the life-force as self-dividing.

But, as Lawrence was to discover and rediscover, saying that the
world is both One and Many does not make it so. If the life-force
is self-dividing, where do the divisions stop? All Lawrence's philosophical writings may be analyzed as an attempt to answer this
question; he tends to stop dividing at two, or at most three. And
he keeps the different pairs from adding up into unmanageably
long lists; when he does use a third term it usually serves as a
bridge between the other two, a reconciler of opposites. Most
fundamentally, he clings to the idea of opposition or reaction
itself and so becomes a kind of dialectician. But he does not
always use his oppositions to seek reconciliation, the usual goal of

dialectic. Often he is entranced with the drama of the conflict, and often one of the opposites appears to be much more important—not truly opposing—than the other. In his fondness for the drama we see the literary artist pushing aside the philosopher; in his failure to balance opposites, a collapse into the need for unity which started this whole process.

In fact, the very nature of Lawrence's need for a coherent world dictates obvious limits to the process of articulation and examination of values to which he is committed. Closely following his assertions of the need for consciousness is a distrust of knowledge and the word.

> We believe that only the Uttered Word can come into us and give us the impetus to our second birth. Give us a religion, give us something to believe in, cries the unsatisfied soul embedded in the womb of our times. Speak the quickening word, it cries, that will deliver us into our own being.
>
> So it searches out the Spoken Word, and finds it, or finds it not. Possibly it is not yet uttered. But all that will be uttered lies potent in life.

> We start the wrong way round: thinking, by learning what we are not, to know what we as individuals are: whereas the whole of the human consciousness contains, as we know, not a tithe of what is, and therefore it is hopeless to proceed by a method of elimination. [p. 434]

Passages like these, and especially like the second, may seem to deny the very process by which they were written, since the *Study of Thomas Hardy* is a continual effort to speak the relevant Word. But they need not lead us into attacking Lawrence for inconsistency; the first passage makes clear again what he has asserted repeatedly, that vital possibility can be embodied in words. It is merely necessary to remember that words, like any other forms, are limiting by the very fact of their completeness; if the primal reality is an ever-changing vital force, no words can capture it, not even the words Lawrence uses in his description. It should not be surprising, therefore, that this essay tends to develop as an alternating series of dualistic distinctions and vital assertions. Since the dualities are a continual threat to the vital unity which they seek to define, analytic modes tend to give way to rhapsodic passages asserting a vital unity in its own right. Of course this alternation can and does cause inconsistencies. But they, too, grow directly from the nature of Lawrence's problem, his attempt to construct a metaphysical scheme which would reflect a coherent unity without abolishing either progressive movement or the importance of the individual object—and, of course, the individual subject.

Underlying this problem is Lawrence's difficulty in deciding how dualistic his thinking really is—whether or not, in fact, his dualities exist only to be transcended. In his continual efforts at defining them, he has repeated difficulty adhering to the pattern established in passages like this one.

> So life consists in the dual form of the Will-to-Motion and the Will-to-Inertia, and everything we see and know and are is the resultant of these two Wills. But the One Will, of which they are dual forms, that is as yet unthinkable.
>
> And according as the Will-to-Motion predominates in race, or the Will-to-Inertia, so must that race's conception of the One Will enlarge the attributes which are lacking or deficient in the race.
>
> Since there is never to be found a perfect balance or accord of the two Wills, but always one triumphs over the other, in life, according to our knowledge, so must the human effort be always to recover balance, to symbolize and so to possess that which is missing. Which is the religious effort of Man. [p. 447]

According to this, the principle of balance seems all-important, and Lawrence in fact uses it with considerable consistency in his historical analyses. But as this quotation implies, the idea of balance is always qualified by the idea of struggle; indeed, in Lawrence's view the process of balancing—of opposed forces within the individual, of male and female, of historical forces conceived under the male and female principles—is always a struggle. As Lawrence works out his analytic schemes, particularly his historical ones, the idea of struggle seems to grow in importance and get out of hand until he finds it necessary to introduce the idea of balance in "consummation." It is as if his dualities, once stated, soon lead to a way of thinking dangerously Manichean in its divisions. They must therefore be brought to a resolution, if only to begin with a new set. This process is obviously compelling because of its dramatic force, its insistence on continual change and continual possibility of renewal; but it is also alarming, because the more one insists on change, the more one denies stability, consummation, and fulfillment.[4]

Another aspect of Lawrence's reconciliation of the One and the Many, then, is his attempt to reconcile the stable and the progressive, vital security and vital change. It is in these terms, in fact, that some of his historical analyses run into trouble. For example, Lawrence's analysis of the Renaissance associates the idea of abstraction with both maleness and femaleness, with asexuality, and with the timelessness of consummation. He characteristically resolves this conceptual experimentation by settling on consummation.[5] The same sort of uncertainty soon infects even the idea of perfection.

---

4. There are interesting parallels between this process and Mircea Eliade's accounts of the myth of "eternal return." According to Eliade, this myth was used by archaic societies to "cure the work of Time" and return man to a safe ontological realm, usually through some sort of ritual. By learning the origins of things, one could also learn to control them (see *Myth and Reality* [London, 1964], esp. pp. 88, 142-43). Lawrence persistently and repeatedly sought to realize such an ontological realm and, by knowing it, to place the phenomenal world in order. Unfortunately he was irremediably infected by history, and some of his most startling literary failures occur when he tries to develop his own archaic rituals—notably in *The Plumed Serpent*. In the *Study of Thomas Hardy* the difficulty of being a modern man with archaic yearnings is evident in the alternation between the stable and the progressive itself.

5. See *Study of Thomas Hardy*, esp. pp. 459, 463-64, 465.

Whenever art or any expression becomes perfect, it becomes a lie. For it is only perfect by reason of abstraction from that context by which and in which it exists as truth. [p. 475]

For in Botticelli the dual marriage is perfect, or almost perfect, body and spirit reconciled, or almost reconciled, in a perfect dual consummation. And in all art there is this testimony to the wonderful dual marriage, the true consummation. But in Raphael, the marriage in the spirit is left out so much . . . that the picture is almost a lie, almost a blasphemy. [pp. 475-76]

Perfection, like abstraction, implies both completion (consummation, fulfillment) and stasis. Lawrence wants to adopt the former but exclude the latter. I do not think that these uncertainties can be dismissed as a trivial part of Lawrence's intellectual exploration, the initial difficulty all theorists have in fitting theory to object, dualities to paintings. Lawrence is unsure not merely about the province of the various pairs of analytic notions but about the process of pairing itself. Both the nature and the desirability of even eternal stability come persistently into question.

However undefinable an ultimate state may be, it was necessary for Lawrence to at least define how it might be reached. This was largely, as we saw, the concern of *The Rainbow*. In the *Study of Thomas Hardy* he forges his dualities from material apprehended as a whole (though an unthinkable whole) and then proceeds to put them back together, explaining history and literature as he goes. Where his explanations continually run into trouble is where parts become wholes, where motion becomes stable, where struggle becomes peace. The same problems are pervasive in the novels; there we have a parallel attempt at definition of these complex relationships. All Lawrence's important characters seek some sort of vital stability but fear stasis; all of them think of their lives as open and full of possibility, but they are hardly free from the old-fashioned struggle for identity. They seek at once self-transcendence and self-definition. Lawrence, I suggest, is among other things trying to define the latter as a presupposition for the former.

If this basic pattern of ambivalence is indeed at the heart of Lawrence's thinking, it should be no surprise that a number of his most important answers to questions I have been raising can be expressed as paradoxes. For example, if we ask generally, How vital is change? How temporary is consummation? How integrated should art, writing, or the individual be? Lawrence's most consistent answers would have to be something like these: change is vital when it produces stable moments; consummation is momentary but eternal; art, writing, and the individual should be at once integrated and open to radical rearrangement. This is not to reduce Lawrence's work to a series of riddles; clumsy as these formulations may be, I think they all point toward a central issue in his development as an artist and a thinker. He cannot settle on any theory or belief which does not leave room for change, but the change remains a threat, a struggle, a fear of incoherence.

We can make more definite sense of Lawrence's need for, as well as his problems with, his dualities if we notice that he tends to favor one side—the female—more than the other.[6] This bias has, as we might expect, important bearing on Lawrentian notions of selfhood, with which the novels are of course centrally concerned. We have already noticed some of the salient associations with the female; these include the Will-to-Inertia, acceptance of the physical, the earth, stability itself. In the novels the bias is most obvious in the importance given to sexual activity; from the *Study of Thomas Hardy* on it also appears rather consistently in attacks upon certain male associations, especially the killing sort of abstract mental activity which emerges as a large target in *Women in Love*.

In terms of the patterns we have been tracing, Lawrence's bias is in favor of unity. This is easy enough to understand once we

6. Daleski's entire book *(Forked Flame)* is devoted to explaining the influence of this preference on Lawrence's successes and failures as a novelist.

notice that the transcendent terms of balance and consummation more readily imply stability (female) than motion (male)—even if one insists, as Lawrence often did, that the transcendent state is "out of time," or at least momentary in human experience. The male principle of motion does not seek its own resolution in the sense that the female principle of inertia does, so that, insofar as Lawrence's dualities are intended to seek resolution at all, their very conceptual framework leans toward the female.

This still subtle leaning has, of course, other implications. An attraction toward stability is also, it would seem, an attraction toward solidity and palpability. One more easy association leads to concreteness, which in turn leads to the definite object. But definition (of both self and object) is listed as part of the male pattern. If we look a bit more closely at the qualities associated with maleness, they reveal another variation on Lawrence's difficulties with the One and the Many, a variation which has specific relevance to novel writing.

Here are some of the meanings Lawrence variously associates with maleness:

1. motion, doing (pp. 447- 481)
2. community, public good (p. 487)
3. love, the golden rule (p. 487)
4. spirit (p. 509)
5. mind, consciousness (pp. 459, 509)
6. dissolution of form, escape from the object (p. 470)
7. distinct identity (p. 453)

Most of these notions can, at least in a rough way, be subsumed under the larger idea of the Will-to-Motion. That is, most can be conceived as part of a movement away from female stability, centrality, unity. Some, however, provide difficulties, especially if we try to relate them to a coherent idea of selfhood. If we compare items 6 and 7, an obvious problem emerges. There is surely contradiction between distinct identity and dissolution of form, even though the latter appears mainly in reference to (male) visual art and the former to (male) characters in a novel. Again, a similar but less obvious difficulty can be perceived by reflecting on the terms in items 4 and 5. In common usage the spiritual is often contrasted to the intellectual; the former refers to states beyond the dissecting powers of consciousness—if, indeed, they are to be conceived as dissecting. Lawrence's usage ranges from a defining or limiting power (as in "self-consciousness") to a transcendent leap into the eternal ("the complete consciousness . . . two in one").[7] Both pairs of terms are ambiguous about the act of definition itself: to define or not to define.

This difficulty is evident in Lawrence's attempts at a new sort of characterization in his novels. We have seen him reject, at least theoretically, traditional notions of the stable ego, and in *Women in Love* he is even willing to forego physical description of the characters who are most vitally promising (see pp. 217-19 below). There must be a vagueness about the characters' limits to make room for potentiality. But though this worked with Tom Brangwen, it did not with Ursula; her particular needs are too vague. In short, Lawrence could not make the decisions about Ursula's individuality that were necessary to make her transcendence of the stable ego satisfactorily intelligible. How distinct should a character be without closing off possibilities of creative self-transformation? There is of course no easy answer.

We can see Lawrence wrestling with this problem in his analysis of Hardy's characters, especially Angel Clare. Angel's problem with Tess is defined as a maleness that is too exclusive. "To marry her, to have a physical marriage with her, he must overcome all his ascetic revulsion, he must, in his own mind, put off his own divinity, his pure maleness, his singleness, his pure completeness, and descend to the heated welter of the flesh" (p. 484). But Lawrence does not make Angel's male singleness as convincing as Tess's female, aristocratic individuality. Although his rhetoric wavers, his rejection of Angel Clare is most clearly based upon a distaste for the asceticism and "divinity" that denies the flesh.

Who is he, that he shall be pure male, and deny the existence of

7. See p. 190 above, and pp. 215-16 below.

the female? . . . is he even the higher or supreme part of life?
Angel Clare thinks so: as Christ thought.

Yet it is not so . . . Life, that is Two-in-One, Male and Female.
Nor is either part greater than the other. [p. 485]

Lawrence's continuing argument does not depict Angel Clare as a
man who merely denies the need for balance. Rather, he is casti-
gated for denying life itself. At one point we are told that his
"body, his life, is too strong for him." And he is portrayed as a
man gone wrong in Lawrence's concluding paragraph, which
warns against male conceit:

Hardy really states his case, which is not his consciously stated
metaphysic, by any means, but a statement how man has gone
wrong and brought death on himself: how man has violated the
Law, how he has supererogated himself, gone so far in his male
conceit as to supersede the Creator, and win death as a reward.
[p. 488]

Tess is much more evidently self-sufficient. Her individuality
seems to lie in her very capacity to be "root and source" for the
male. Although Lawrence uses singleness and individuality on
both sides of his male-female dichotomies, here and elsewhere his
rhetoric reveals a preference for the female and the flesh. What is
even more apparent is the importance that notions of individuality have in Lawrence's developing thought; he demonstrates
the same ambivalence toward setting limits to ideas as he does
toward limiting his protagonists.

A good deal more is involved here than a sexual preference.
Lawrence's terms leave him room to translate abstract ideas of
separateness into ideas of corporeal distinctness, but he has less
leeway to think in the reverse direction—when he tries, he tends
to lose the very concept of distinct identity. It is in fact much
harder to conceive of separateness as spiritual or bodiless, as Lawrence requires for male separateness. If the male spirit must "dissolve the object" to achieve singleness, we are hard put to see
what this singleness could mean in a character in a novel. This is

perhaps why Lawrence's analysis of Angel Clare indicates much more forcefully what he is not than what he is. And Lawrence's own characters tend to be much more like Tess than like Angel Clare.

All this testifies to the difficulty, probably the impossibility, of having characters of "pure carbon." Any attempt to create a character without using any of the traditionally recognizable attributes of stable egos is subject to the same sort of evaporation that maleness undergoes here; there is by definition a gap between ontological forces and distinctly identifiable individuals. However much Lawrence is able to inform his characterization with the forces that lie beneath it, he cannot—and of course does not—dispense with the more old-fashioned individuating devices. One of the most important of these is simply involvement with the definite objects of this world: bodies, clothing, animals, things. His troubles in the *Study of Thomas Hardy* certainly highlight the safety and security of sticking to such things, even if they fade away in more transcendent moments.

It seems inevitable, then, that an art so determinedly devoted to rejuvenating and even reconstituting characterization should encounter difficulties at the boundaries. The bias toward the female may be regarded as an affirmation that, no matter how far into eternal realms the self may penetrate, it will not lose touch with the flesh. If an initial loss of the self is necessary for transcendent experiences of self-renewal, regaining it may be difficult; the "return" may deny, or seem to deny, the transcendent activity. But an undefined self is in danger of becoming a Shelleyan spirit;[8] although laudably open to change and renewal, such a spiritual creature has left the phenomenal world below. And Lawrence, however intense his need for comprehensive religious schemes, could not and would not have them at the expense of the real world of nature and of bodies. It should be no surprise, then, that the matter of otherness reflects conceptual confusion, being associated with both the male and female side of Law-

8. "Shelley is pure escape: the body is sublimated into sublime gas" (*Phoenix*, p. 561).

rence's dualities and tending to show greatest stress at the point where the individual seeks nonphysical definition.

This would help to explain Ursula's denial of the man's world as well as her female turn toward the flesh. Self-definition through a social system is too much other-directed activity, not self-defining but self-avoiding; if such activity is to be fruitful it presupposes more precise location of her vitality, specifically in full acceptance of her sexuality. But the final resolution remains for the moment out of her (and Lawrence's) reach. For the full acceptance of sexuality also leads to narcissism, a form of self-containment. How to avoid this without dissolving the self in communal or otherwise self-transcendent principles is the problem that the optimistic rainbow which ends the novel avoids. It is basically the problem of how distinct any self should be.

Again this is a real dilemma, not merely a question of philosophic ineptness. Philosophers are liable to encounter similar troubles if they try to define potentiality. There is an important need for definition at least of direction ("potential" must be "potential for"), but final definition is impossible.[9] Lawrence attempts to get around this problem by resorting to the formula of consummation in the *Study of Thomas Hardy* as well as in the more puzzling sexual consummations of Ursula and Skrebensky. Perhaps a more interesting way of dealing with it is indicated by some of the terms he uses to function like the term *potential,* terms which can embody, at least in fiction, new but directed possibility.

I am thinking of Lawrence's double usage of *consciousness, knowledge,* and *truth* in *The Rainbow* and the *Study of Thomas Hardy.* All these words refer in dictionaries to intellectual, rational, "male" activity; in Lawrence's writings they take on a second, ontological meaning revealed in Tom's problems of knowing

9. See Leone Vivante, *A Philosophy of Potentiality* (London, 1955). Vivante argues persistently for potentiality as a creative principle of "intrinsic purposiveness." Some revealing applications to Lawrence follow, in a section entitled "Reflections on D. H. Lawrence's Insight into the Concept of Potentiality."

Lydia and in Will's and Anna's dark knowledge of each other. We have also seen *truth* and *consciousness* acquire ontological dimensions in the *Study of Thomas Hardy,* where they refer to the eternal meeting of Lawrence's historical-metaphysical forces, the peak of man's efforts. Their double usage obviously tries to capture Lawrence's double need to articulate direction and to realize without mental mediation his own religious efforts. As such these terms are on the forefront of his developing thought, and their use in the novels helps reveal the direction in which he is going. Through them he apparently hopes to accomplish a conceptual transformation; he has borrowed the terminology of the mind for uses referring to, and especially through and beyond, the body. If we are merely conscious of ideas, we are likely to undergo a Shelleyan sort of rarefication and find our vitality abstracted. If, however, we are "blood-conscious," we can evade (or seem to evade) the Cartesian dichotomy and retain both a sense of purpose and full use of the body.[10] This is why, in the passages concerning consciousness discussed earlier (p. 190 above), Lawrence somewhat ambiguously speaks of it as a "great necessity" and then qualifies this immediately with "the bringing of life into human consciousness is not an aim in itself, it is only a necessary condition of the progress of life itself." The more he thinks of consciousness as merely mental, the more he tends to describe it as an epiphenomenon; the more he thinks of it as a nonmental apprehension of vital purpose and direction, the more central it becomes, with direct connections to his ontological forces.[11] A good deal of *Women in Love* is taken up with the struggle to define the differences between these two modes of consciousness.

10. There are interesting parallels here with modern phenomenology, especially the work of M. Merleau-Ponty; see, e.g., his *Phenomenology of Perception,* trans. Colin Smith (London, 1962), pt. 1, chaps. 4-5.
11. This finally results in even a new physiology in the two books on the unconscious. They testify, as does his "Education of the People," to his continuing effort to articulate the new notions of selfhood on which he embarked when he got involved in "The Sisters." Not only do his later novels explore these possibilities politically, his expository works develop theories of individual development which may actually be used by Law-

"The Crown"

Shortly after completing the *Study of Thomas Hardy* and *The Rainbow,* Lawrence, increasingly distressed by the war, wrote "The Crown."[12] Originally intended as lectures (to be given with his new but temporary friend, Bertrand Russell), it consists of six essays devoted to Lawrentian metaphysics, with almost no historical and literary forays. Its main effort is to summarize and further articulate Lawrence's metaphysical forces, with particular emphasis on what they reveal about the civilization actively destroying itself through war. Because of this emphasis on destruction, "The Crown" has more affinities with *Women in Love* than with *The Rainbow* and must, indeed, have helped create the new consistency with which Lawrence attacks modern civilization in *Women in Love.*

Much shorter than the *Study of Thomas Hardy,* "The Crown" seems at first totally different; it marks the emergence of a new attitude toward expository writing, an attitude which Lawrence was to employ in most of his essays thereafter. His opening sentence dispenses with the formalities of introduction: "What is it then, that they want, that they are forever rampant and unsatisfied, the king of beasts and the defender of virgins?" This is part of Lawrence's newly urgent campaign against complacency. He was in fact writing for quite a different audience from the one for which he had embarked on "a little book on Hardy's people." "I don't want the *Signature* to be a 'success,' " he wrote "I want it only to rally together just a few passionate, vital, constructive people. But they must consent first to cast away all that is of no use—all that is wrong. And we have been, we are, colossally

---

rentian parents. The political theories tend to follow (rather than precede) the Lawrentian psychology. Indeed, it can be argued (see Gordon, *D. H. Lawrence as a Literary Critic,* pp. 130-32) that Lawrence always stops short of or stays beyond the sort of theory that implies political action (his own) and the foundation of governments. See also p. 251 below.

12. It was apparently finished by October 2, 1915. See *LH,* p. 259.

wrong, so much so, we daren't face it."[13] In short, Lawrence now thought of himself as something of a reformer, or at least a vital leader. If this role was implicit in his earlier writings, it was only now emerging, not without a touch of belligerence. "I see you are rather hostile to what I say, like everybody else. But I didn't write for 'average stupidity.' And the lion and the lioness[14] are at any rate better than 'the universe consists in a duality, but there is an initial element called polarity, etc. etc.' "[15] The bristling was not without cause. Besides involving Britain in the war, "average stupidity" had just declared *The Rainbow* pornography, and before the war was over it was to deny Lawrence the right to leave England and forbid him to live on the coast for fear of his spying. "The Crown" was his way of interpreting the persecution which was to come, of explaining destructive tendencies already obvious, and finally of condemning them without resorting to nihilism or hopelessness. His rejection of a more formal, philosophic style was an integral part of his resistance to the bewildering collapse of civilization itself. He sought to avoid bewilderment by incorporating this collapse into his metaphysical schemes and in fact using it to help define these schemes. Through this "placement" of hostile forces he hoped, finally, to encourage the "new shoots of life" which would replace the "whole great form of our era."[16] The "passionate and constructive people" for whom he wrote were expected to reject the moribund philosophic forms of the era as well and to welcome the symbolic and dramatic form of "The Crown."

The crown for which the lion and the unicorn fight is the transcendent moment of balance to which Lawrence kept return-

13. *LH*, p. 293. The "Signature" was a short-lived magazine that Lawrence and John Middleton Murry put out in the fall of 1915. It went through three issues before collapsing, and these issues contained the first three chapters of "The Crown."

14. There is no lioness in "The Crown" as it was published in 1925. This may refer to a lost early draft.

15. *LH*, p. 292.

16. From the 1925 introduction to "The Crown."

ing in the *Study of Thomas Hardy*. Again the conceptual scheme
is dialectically, or at least dualistically, formulated. And again
there is a female bias, though this time it is not so much evident
in conceptual inconsistency as in strong preference for the lion's
darker activity. In a sense this preference is part of the argument;
Lawrence's second chapter is called "The Lion Beat the Unicorn
and Drove Him Out of Town." The modern era was self-indul-
gently lionlike, reducing itself through self-destructive sensualism,
of which the war was the greatest manifestation. So these essays
ought to be unbalanced in favor of darkness, the flesh, and
power; the prevalent mistakes must be exposed. This is fine, except for two things: the lion's side is not merely more present but
more convincing, and before he is through Lawrence has converted his reductive processes into processes of possible rebirth and
purgation. The war may not be all bad after all.

Throughout "The Crown" Lawrence avoids hammering out
dualities through literary and cultural investigations; he consistently asserts connections between the psychological and the
ontological realms, and this more personal mode leads directly to
his reductions. When he generalizes about modern civilization, he
uses the metaphors developed in these consummatory passages,
particularly the metaphor of the womb (the more negative forms
are "rind" and "shell"). Here is the passage which prepares the
way for his whole denunciation of modern civilization in *Women
in Love* as well as in the rest of "The Crown." It has grown
directly out of *The Rainbow* (see pp. 148-50 above).

It may be that there is a great inequality, disproportion, within
me, that I am nearly all darkness, like the night, with a few
glimmers of cold light, moonlight, like the tiger with white eyes
of reflected light brindled in the flame of darkness. Then I shall
return again and again to the womb of darkness, avid, never
satisfied, my spirit will fall unfertile into the womb, will never
be conceived there, never brought forth. I shall know the one
consummation, the one direction only, into the darkness. It will
be with me for ever the almost, almost, almost, of satisfaction,

of fulfillment. I shall know the one eternity, the one infinite, the one immortality, I shall have partial being; but never the whole, never the full. [p. 27]

This denial of fulfillment and satisfaction dramatically conveys considerable satisfaction itself. A sterile "quick" is still quick; a single immortality is still immortality, however undeserving of the ultimate label of timelessness. Lawrence is asserting the onto-logical value of the dark experience, even though he must condemn it by his "final" ontological criteria. As we have seen, this caused some trouble in *The Rainbow*;[17] it is rather more useful in *Women in Love*.

Thinking now more in terms of metaphors than principles, Lawrence can indulge more freely in psychological and natural models than he could when he was still using the language which he has since rejected ("There is a duality . . . etc."). He need be less self-conscious about philosophic categories and can more readily translate his own psychological needs into ontological patterns. His argument develops like this: We are trapped in the womb of our era, because the opposing eternal forces of flesh and spirit, darkness and light, sensual power and chastity have not achieved sufficient balance within us. Each seeks to dominate the other, as the lion seeks to devour the unicorn, and vice-versa.[18] The lion in us (will-to-power, love of the flesh, identification with the One God, the absolute monarch) is now dominant, to a large extent succeeding in encompassing the "seed" of light which would "bring us forth" into full being. The force which prevents this ultimate fulfillment is a form of the will-to-power, egoism. It hardens the shell of complacent selfhood and collectively hardens the shell of the era. This state of affairs must, apparently, get worse before it gets better. Having turned away from meeting the

17. See above pp. 149 ff., 173 ff.
18. All these oppositions are suggested but not adequately developed to function as a balancing force in the argument itself. If we ask, for instance, what meaning the opposition chastity and sensuality may have, how they might fit into the consummatory pattern, "The Crown" does not tell us.

light,[19] we can break away from our shells by indulging in darkness itself, to the extent that we obliterate ourselves in sexual ecstasy—or even in bloodlust. Now, in fact, this seems the only way. Ecstasy is only possible if vitality still exists; demonic indulgence is better than apathy. This ecstasy should therefore be encouraged, but only if it leads to the new life made possible by self-obliteration. And there is no way to tell if it will. It may just make things worse, since vital energy is expendable; the disastrous result, a mere further hardening of the womb (again of both the egoistic shell and the historical epoch), is possible. If this should happen the next step is probably actual suicide, a last attempt at the ultimate sensation. Even here some hope remains, for contact with death may at last provide vital release, if only in the instant before physical death arrives. So the war may, for some individuals who come very close to death but just escape it, constitute the means for Lawrentian salvation. But for the majority Lawrence clearly thinks it will not; it will only make things worse without making them better and is therefore abominable and blasphemous.

The whole argument depends heavily upon the psychological-ontological movement which Lawrence learned to use as a technique of characterization in *The Rainbow.* The prevalence of metaphors which imply enclosed vitality clamoring for release clearly indicates profound frustration on the part of the author, and the process by which it is expressed has a direct effect on his fiction. In "The Crown" Lawrence presents a charged version of the ancient analogy between the body and life of man and the body and life of civilization. He takes this analogy very seriously—more so, certainly, than some of the political theorists who have used it. A collective body is not merely an aggregate of individuals but an entity, in the same relation to Lawrence's vital forces as the individual. The one is no simple abstraction or extension of the other but another manifestation of forces beneath and beyond either. Both can therefore be regarded as suffering

19. This is another instance such as those discussed in n. 18 above.

from the same diseases, be described in the same metaphors, and be directly related by mutual implication. Lawrence has little tendency to set out their differences; he prefers, because of his pervasive need for coherence, to emphasize their connections. This allows him, for the time being, to avoid social criticism altogether; he is working on both a grander and more personal scale than that. His attacks on communal inhibitions in the *Study of Thomas Hardy* become, in "The Crown," attacks on civilization. In *Women in Love* Lawrence was able to use this shift in perspective to place social groupings, until manners became significant mainly or even exclusively through their relation to the eternal forces. He thereby avoided the confusion about progress which created difficulties in *The Rainbow,* and he was also able to exploit his theory of reduction to help give form to his novel.[20]

Ontologically, the reductive process is a reversal or inversion of the creative meeting which Lawrence tried to define in the *Study of Thomas Hardy.* The opposing forces move away from each other, turn back on themselves. To make room for this new direction, Lawrence's language tends in "The Crown" to expand his whole metaphysical framework. He places the ultimate realm of

20. This circumvention of social progress is at bottom a circumvention of the theory of progress itself, almost an evasion of history. Frank Kermode and others have called attention to the Romantic tendency to remake history by creating new mythologies; this is partly what Lawrence is doing here, somewhat more radically than in the *Study of Thomas Hardy.* He thereby avoids, both in "The Crown" and in *Women in Love,* the necessity to predict that he obviously felt at the end of *The Rainbow* and even at the end of the *Study of Thomas Hardy.* It is easy here to multiply paradoxes: Lawrence seeks to explain contemporary life by transcending it; he finds in damning it hope for its salvation (albeit a tentative hope); he asserts the radical ontological responsibility of the individual yet seeks to translate this responsibility into social and communal ethics (these efforts emerge most forcefully after *Women in Love*). These are finally paradoxes of the religious sensibility itself, what Mircea Eliade discusses under the rubric of the *coincidentia oppositorum* (see *The Two-in-One* [London, 1965], esp. pp. 94 f.), the attempt to unite immanence and transcendence, being in the world and out at the same time. See also Gordon's excellent short chapter on myth and history in *D. H. Lawrence as a Literary Critic.*

timeless relation beyond eternity, calling it another dimension.
"In Time and Eternity all is flux. Only in the other dimension,
which is not the time-space dimension, is there Heaven" (p. 96).
This is required, it seems, by Lawrence's need to examine experience which is fully transcendent of the merely temporal but is
not yet his ultimate. We have seen such experience in *The Rainbow* and in earlier passages of "The Crown." Now, perhaps as a
result of reading Heraclitus,[21] he places both his creative and
destructive forces in a world of flux and reserves his most ultimate realm for the "perfect relation." This has the double effect
of making eternal or immortal experience more readily available
to characters in his novels while leaving the absolute more distant.[22] Perhaps sensing this, and certainly concerned to follow
his new reductive processes to whatever conclusion they suggest,
Lawrence works his way into a new path to the absolute itself.
The first passage is more tentative than the second:

> In infinite going-apart there is revealed again the pure absolute,
> the absolute relation: this time truly as a Ghost: the ghost of
> what was. [p. 74]

> And corruption, like growth, is only divine when it is pure,
> when all is given up to it . . . the pure absolute, the Holy Ghost,
> lies also in the relationship which is made manifest by the de-
> parture, the departure *ad infinitum,* of the opposing elements.
> [p. 76]

Lawrence is in effect turning his consummatory formula upside
down. After asserting that the process of egoistic sensationalism is
a form of death and destruction, he gives it new possibility by
emphasizing that destruction, like creation, requires vital energy.
Since all vital energy is rooted in ontological forces, destruction

---

21. *LM,* pp. 351, 352. "I shall write out Herakleitos, on tablets of
bronze."

22. The merely eternal experiences are now by definition incomplete.
See not only Ursula's ontological frustrations (pp. 173-81 above) but
especially Gudrun's experiences in the mountains (pp. 277 ff. below).

or reduction is also an eternal process. Implicit in any eternal process is the possibility of ultimate release into the final realm of absolute being. But absolute being has only been possible, in previous formulations, through a consummatory meeting of the opposing forces. One more abstraction is therefore needed, the insistence that the ultimate part of the ultimate meeting consists in a relation; we need not, then, insist on meeting at all.

Philosophically, of course, this leaves something to be desired, since not even a metaphor is available to help us understand what a relation made manifest by infinite departure might be. (For meeting we at least had the rainbow.) Nor do Lawrence's later works exploit this particular formulation. Still, by thinking in this direction, Lawrence is able to set up an ontological framework for destructive vitality, and the process of reduction—the "flux of corruption"—brings with it a series of metaphors and a basis for criticizing materialism in *Women in Love.* However difficult it is to conceive of the final release presented here, the assertion that destructive, self-centered activity can contain vital possibility is clear enough. By asserting even this much Lawrence expands the possibilities of his exploration of darkness. He even makes voracious sensualism respectable, or at least potentially respectable. This gives new sanction to the more intensely sensual activities of all three generations of Brangwens, and it foreshadows the persistent quality of Gudrun's sexual responses.[23] But, as *Women in Love* overwhelmingly demonstrates, the possibilities in the destructive process are severely limited and in fact lead to disaster, not final release.

Lawrence's difficulty in formulating this final release through reduction in "The Crown" remains at the core of his fascination with demonic characters and intensely sexual experience throughout his life. Of course, this fascination has appeared before,[24] but through "The Crown" he found ways to embody it successfully in his fiction. By identifying a dying civilization with destructive

23. Even Ursula and Birkin seem to indulge in this variety of sensualism. See below, p. 288 and note.
24. See, for example pp. 39-41 above.

but still vital ontological forces, "The Crown" provided Lawrence with a vehicle for expressing the ambivalence toward community which caused difficulties in *The Rainbow*. And by enlarging the realm of transcendent but incomplete experience, it gave him room to explore more thoroughly than before a variety of modes of characterization.

One figure in particular foreshadows Lawrence's application of his newly formulated reductive processes in *Women in Love*.

I have seen a soldier at the seaside who was maimed. One leg was only a small stump, with the trouser folded back on it. He was a handsome man of about thirty, finely built. His face was sun-browned, and extraordinarily beautiful, still with a strange placidity, something like perfection, abstract, complete. He had known his consummation. It seemed he could never desire corruption or reduction again, he had had his satisfaction of death. He was become almost impersonal, a simple abstraction, all his personality loosed and undone. He was now like a babe just born, new to begin life. Yet in a sense, still-born. The newness and candour, like a flower just unloosed, curiously, into the light of death. [*Women in Love*, p. 72][25]

The soldier belongs to the family of symbolic figures which emerged in *The Rainbow:* the taxi driver, Anthony Schofield, and, to a slightly lesser extent, the bargeman. Like them he is presented as an example of a particular sort of vitality; the conventional psychological dimension is undeveloped or missing altogether. As Lawrence became increasingly involved in articulating his metaphysics, figures of this sort became increasingly important. *Women in Love* abounds with them: Loerke, Minette, the Bohemians, often Hermione, and at times all four major characters. This maimed soldier represents the result, as far as Lawrence had yet conceived it, of the reductive process. He is near perfection but not quite perfect; he is almost impersonal, almost

25. Like most of the characters in the novels, this figure is based on someone Lawrence actually saw. See *LH,* pp. 222-23.

a simple abstraction, almost beyond humanity altogether. This, clearly, is the point of release brought about by the violent experiences with natural death, a release into the light of the more crucial death of the ego-bound self. Thus the soldier is beautiful, like a flower, newborn. And he has a new power.

> The women particularly were fascinated. They could not look away from him. The strange abstraction of horror and death was so perfect in his face, like the horror of birth on a new-born infant, that they were almost hysterical ... they wanted him so badly, that they were almost beside themselves. [p. 73]

His sexual magnetism is an indication that his release is into new life. But despite the power of this life to bring on hysteria in the bound women, Lawrence is very tentative about its final possibility.

> We who live, we can only live or die. And when, like the maimed soldier ... we have come right back into life, and the wonder of death fades off our faces again, what then?
>
> Shall we go on ... waiting all our lives for the accomplished death? ... And continuing the sensational reduction process? Or shall we fade into a dry empty egoism? Which will the maimed soldier do? He cannot remain as he is, clear and peaceful.
>
> Are we really doomed, and smiling with the wonder of doom? [pp. 74-75]

The hesitation is of course related to the problem of defining, philosophically or otherwise, the ultimate separation just discussed. The questions about what "we" shall do are also questions about the direction and particularly about the character definition of *Women in Love*.

No character in the novel reaches this stage of release through death. But the sexual power of Gudrun and Gerald is portrayed, as we shall see, in terms closely related to the vitality embodied in this soldier. Gerald, in particular, seeks this sort of release,[26] and much of our interest in him derives from our asking the same sort of questions about doom as Lawrence asks here. The answers tend to be negative: there are no rainbows in *Women in Love,* no optimistic assertions about the rejuvenation of souls and societies. Instead the book demonstrates, vividly and variously, the limitations of both, and these limitations are rooted in the ontological reductions. To portray them Lawrence draws not only on the imagery of "The Crown" but on the symbolic mode implicit in the maimed soldier. Just as "The Crown" insists with new directness on the connections through ontology between the personal and the social, *Women in Love* explores characters who tend to symbolize the same connections, sometimes to the extent of making them inhuman and merely symbolic. Though Lawrence's flux of corruption opened a whole new realm for exploitation in novels, it also, through its negative direction, set stricter limits to ordinary human possibility.

26. See especially his childlike state after sexual consummation with Gudrun.

6: WOMEN IN LOVE

If we live in the mind, we must die in the mind, and in the mind we must understand death. Understanding is not necessarily mental. It is of the senses and the spirit.

But we live also in the mind. And the first great act of the living mind is to understand death in the mind. Without this there is no freedom of the mind, there is no life of the mind, since creative life is the attaining a perfect consummation with death. When in my mind there rises the idea of life, this idea must encompass the idea of death, and this encompassing is the germination of a new epoch of the mind.[1]

This passage, written at the same time as *Women in Love*,[2] may be read as a description of the impulse which made Lawrence's fifth novel significantly different from his fourth, to which it was supposed to be a sequel. Like "The Crown" (but unlike *The Rainbow*), this book was in large part written to gain an understanding of death in order that life might move beyond it. What Lawrence means to include in this understanding is further indicated by the foreword he wrote two years later:

1. "The Reality of Peace," in *Phoenix,* p. 682.
2. Although it was not published until 1920, *Women in Love* was begun with *The Rainbow* and essentially finished in 1916. "The Reality of Peace" appears to have been written immediately afterward, and it was partially published in the summer of 1917. See Ford (*Double Measure,* pp. 164-68) for interesting conjecture as to which parts of *Women in Love* were directly influenced by events dating after the beginning of the war.

Man struggles with his unborn needs and fulfilment. New un-
foldings struggle up in torment in him, as buds struggle forth
from the midst of a plant. Any man of real individuality tries to
know and to understand what is happening, even in himself, as
he goes along. This struggle for verbal consciousness should not
be left out in art. It is a very great part of life. It is not superimposition of a theory. It is a passionate struggle into conscious
being. [p. viii]

This has a familiar ring and might at first glance be a foreword to
The Rainbow as well. But now Lawrence is vigorously defending
his own struggle for verbal consciousness, which, he is careful to
point out, is not superimposition of a theory. Besides the shift in
tone and subject matter which makes *Women in Love* unmistakably different from *The Rainbow,* there is a shift in both
method and purpose at which these phrases hint. More than any
of Lawrence's other books, *Women in Love* is a struggle for consciousness, a search for definition.

The struggle, it should be noted at the outset, is in aesthetic and
even intellectual terms a success. *Women in Love* is both Lawrence's most coherent and most ambitious book; it addresses itself to a greater range of problems and puts those problems in
clearer perspective than any of his other novels. In struggling for
consciousness Lawrence becomes, to put it simply, more articulate than he has been in at least some parts of *The Rainbow;* his
meaning, therefore, is very seldom obscure in the sense that it was
with Ursula's more puzzling experiences. Perhaps even clearer
than this is the gain in consistent emphasis which Lawrence's
concentration on the idea of death brings about; it is always
easier to define failure than success, and part of Lawrence's grasp
of his material may be due to a fact as bare as this. Finally,
Lawrence's struggle for consciousness emerges with something
like a cosmology, an inclusive pattern into which he can fit most
of the loose ends of his previous book and relate them to the
ever-present concern for human need. How this pattern emerges,

and especially what force Lawrence's shift in emphasis toward understanding has in creating it, shall be my main concern.

The first chapter of *Women in Love* presents, concisely and unmistakably, virtually all the themes and characters of any importance. It is entitled "Sisters," and it is upon the conversation of sisters that we immediately intrude. They are discussing marriage, which both of them consider a remarkably unpromising alternative to their world of schoolteaching and domesticity. We are not told what is bothering them, why marriage seems likely to be "the end of experience." But as they continue to speak we are made aware of certain pregnant similarities and differences between them.

> The sisters were women, Ursula twenty-six, and Gudrun twenty-five. But both had the remote, virgin look of modern girls, sisters of Artemis rather than of Hebe. Gudrun was very beautiful, passive, soft-skinned, soft-limbed. She wore a dress of dark-blue silky stuff, with ruches of blue and green linen lace in the neck and sleeves; and she had emerald-green stockings. Her look of confidence and diffidence contrasted with Ursula's sensitive expectancy. The provincial people, intimidated by Gudrun's perfect sang-froid and exclusive bareness of manner, said of her: "She is a smart woman." She had just come back from London, where she had spent several years, working at an art-school, as a student, and living a studio life. [p. 2]

The degree of attention paid to details of clothing is not characteristic of the Lawrence of *The Rainbow*. Its significance can perhaps best be seen in another descriptive passage on the next page.

> The two sisters worked on in silence. Ursula having always that strange brightness of an essential flame that is caught, meshed, contravened. She lived a good deal by herself, working, passing on from day to day, and always thinking, trying to lay hold on

life, to grasp it in her own understanding. Her active living was suspended, but underneath, in the darkness, something was coming to pass. If only she could break through the last integuments! She seemed to try and put her hands out, like an infant in the womb, and she could not, yet. Still she had a strange prescience, and intimation of something yet to come. [p. 3]

Gudrun is presented visually; her sister cannot, in these and nearly all other passages in the book, be "seen" in the same way. Instead Ursula is presented to us in terms of her feelings, her struggles, and her potential; in place of details of clothing we are given metaphors emphasizing expectancy and possibility: the essential flame, the infant in the womb.

The differences in these two descriptions have implications not only for the differences in character between the two sisters but for Lawrence's themes and methods as well. Our impression of Gudrun, whose brilliance of dress is accompanied by hints of a sensual nature under great control (passive, soft-skinned, soft-limbed, perfect sang-froid, bareness of manner), is developed consistently throughout the book. As we shall see, she is the most limited of the four characters upon whom most of the book focuses, and her limitation is related to precisely this control over sensuality. Ursula, on the other hand, carries half of the positive thrust of the book; as the passage quoted above implies, her essential flame need only be freed from its integuments. She is not described visually because in *Women in Love* Lawrence associates more consistently than before internal states with external detail. A brilliant and self-sufficient appearance would imply a finished self as well. In this book those characters who are repeatedly presented as visually impressive, whether magnificently (like Gudrun) or disgustingly so (like Loerke), are also internally limited. The two characters who tend to elude such detailed description also tend to elude the pervasive barriers to the Lawrentian quest for being.

This correspondence between internal states and external detail may be taken as evidence for the new degree of thoroughness in

Lawrence's drive toward articulation. Yet it may also, and more importantly, be seen as a corollary to those concerns for coherence that have been predominant in his writings from the first. For if, as Lawrence assumes, the universe is fundamentally (if mysteriously) coherent, there is every reason to expect that perception will also be coherent. In literary terms this means that the novelistic devices of significant detail—in gesture, dress, speech, movement, or anything else—are always significant in *Women in Love*.[3] It is of little use to call the faith which lies at the bottom of Lawrence's insistence on coherence naïve, though it may well be. What is important is how thoroughly the book most influenced by this faith avoids the obvious trap of becoming simply allegorical or meretriciously symbolic. This is all the more remarkable since Lawrence's drive toward articulation extends as well to the structure of the novel.

We may return to Gudrun and Ursula for evidence pointing toward the larger patterns of the book. Gudrun has returned home from her art studies only *pour mieux sauter,* though she has no idea where such a jump might land her. The narrator uses this image to summarize the insecure and still undefined state of both sisters: "The sisters found themselves confronted by a void, a terrifying chasm, as if they had looked over the edge" (p. 4).

It is this chasm that most of the book is devoted to defining and ultimately to bridging. After *The Rainbow* we readily suspect that it represents an inadequacy or perversion of being, and once we suspect this much Gudrun's greater response to it (her cheek "was flushed with repressed emotion") makes us increasingly conscious of her difference from her sister. We may further expect Gudrun's inadequacy, whatever its ultimate source, to appear in her sexual experience. But what indicates the shift in Lawrence's concerns from *The Rainbow* to *Women in Love* is the immediate associations which the chasm accumulates. Within a page we encounter Gudrun's horror of the collieries: "Gudren, new from her

3. This is particularly obvious in the dancing which takes place in the "Breadalby" chapter. The appearance and behavior of the participants is an allegory of their internal or vital sufficiency.

life in Chelsea and Sussex, shrank cruelly from this amorphous ugliness of a small colliery town in the Midlands. Yet forward she went, through the whole sordid gamut of pettiness, the long amorphous, gritty street. She was exposed to every stare, she passed on through a stretch of torment" (p. 5). At first, this seems unnecessary anguish, simply an indication of Gudrun's unstable state of mind. But the insistence on the defaced countryside, where "sooty cabbage stumps stood shameless," soon takes on more ominous implications.

> "It is like a country in an underworld," said Gudrun. "The colliers bring it above-ground with them, shovel it up. Ursula, it's marvellous, it's really marvellous—it's really wonderful, another world. The people are all ghouls, and everything is ghostly. Everything is a ghoulish replica of the real world, a replica, a ghoul, mad, Ursula. [p. 5]

As the book develops, Gudrun's remarks about the underworld acquire a double significance: the collieries become the major symbol for a dead or dying civilization, and the colliers are men who have given up their souls to "the mechanical principle." At the same time the psychological underworld which the very quality of Gudrun's response captures here, is itself explored as an explanation of how the replacement of vitality by mechanism is possible. Not only are the collieries dirty and productive of death, but they possess, at least for Gudrun, a horrible fascination which unfolds as several varieties of sensual experience. She indulges repeatedly in a kind of madness that contains the same qualities which she perceives in the colliers, especially their "aboriginal" detachment (p. 6). The important differences between Gudrun and the colliers lie primarily in the subtlety and thoroughness with which she develops her demonic propensities.

By introducing the collieries at the outset of this book, then, Lawrence indicates his intention to explore the connection between dead civilizations and dead souls which he brought up in Tom Brangwen's collieries in *The Rainbow*. He is to do this with a thoroughness that makes the objections to the similar scenes in

The Rainbow irrelevant here; if those earlier scenes seemed forced, these are thoroughly related to almost every other aspect of Lawrence's exploration of "death in the mind." And that relatedness lies, as we shall see, precisely in the sort of connections which made the first Tom Brangwen so impressive. Thus, although the polemic force of *Women in Love* is if anything greater than that of the social passages in *The Rainbow,* it brings with it none of the concomitant irritations. In *Women in Love* Lawrence is able not only to explore the relation between the psychological and ontological which dominated *The Rainbow,* but to incorporate the social and intellectual into his ontology. And this brings us back to the first chapter and another incipient pattern.

Gudrun, whose responses to the collieries have been strikingly intense, reaches yet another level of intensity when she encounters her future lover, Gerald Crich. First she is struck by his "northern" beauty.

> But about him also was the strange, guarded look, the unconscious glisten, as if he did not belong to the same creation as the people about him. Gudrun lighted on him at once. There was something northern about him that magnetised her. In his clear northern flesh and his fair hair was a glisten like sunshine refracted through crystals of ice. And he looked so new, unbroached, pure as an arctic thing. [pp. 8-9]

This seems as great a contrast to the underworld of the colliers as is possible. Yet as Gudrun's excitement mounts we begin to suspect similarities quite as striking as the differences that dictate this arctic imagery:

> His gleaming beauty, maleness, like a young, good-humoured, smiling wolf, did not blind her to the significant, sinister stillness in his bearing, the lurking danger of his unsubdued temper. "His totem is the wolf," she repeated herself. "His mother is an old, unbroken wolf." And then she experienced a keen paroxysm, a transport, as if she had made some incredible discovery, known to nobody else on earth. A strange transport

took possession of her, all her veins were in a paroxysm of violent sensation. "Good God!" she exclaimed to herself, "what is this?" And then, a moment after, she was saying assuredly, "I shall know more of that man." She was tortured with desire to see him again, a nostalgia, a necessity to see him again, to make sure it was not all a mistake, that she was not deluding herself, that she really felt this strange and overwhelming sensation on his account, this knowledge of him in her essence, this powerful apprehension of him. [p. 9]

Beneath his icelike glisten lies a sinister, wolflike power, and it is this darker power which seems to induce Gudrun's transport. Obviously the violent response is sexual and mysterious, and insofar as these qualities are emphasized it follows the pattern of the early or initial encounters of each of the three pairs of lovers in *The Rainbow*. And, again as in *The Rainbow,* this response has an ontological dimension. But *Women in Love* extends the relevance of such responses still further until they have both cosmological and structural implications.

The two sides of Gerald which Gudrun notices here become the two sides of the book: they may roughly be labeled the light and the dark because of the patterns of imagery which carry many of the themes relevant to each. One way of considering the progression of the book is to organize it dialectically as a movement from one of these patterns to the other; almost a hundred pages are devoted to final integration in which the themes of darkness become increasingly revealed and identified with the themes of light. (I hope to make this pattern clearer shortly.) Gerald is the only figure who fully embodies both these patterns, and this is Lawrence's only book in which his metaphysics exert equally direct control over both characterization and structure. Yet *Women in Love* is not a book about metaphysics; like all Lawrence's novels, it is about human need and its relation to the unknown.

Perhaps the most obvious instance of Lawrence's increased concern for articulation is Hermione Roddice, the book's most

important minor character. She invites such categorization because, although she is no less vivid than either Gerald or Gudrun,
Lawrence almost explains her away in the first chapter. No sooner is she presented than she is analyzed in such a way that we
expect her dismissal; and, except for one brief return (in chap.
22), she is in fact dismissed before we are halfway through the
book. Yet Hermione is considerably more than a vehicle for Lawrentian dogma: she is crucial to the plot, for she presents an
obstacle which must be understood and surmounted as a condition for the only successful coupling in the book; and her peculiar
position in Lawrence's larger patterns of negation gives her certain important insights into the difficulties of other characters.
Finally, her very defects are in some sense shared by everyone
else in the book. Perhaps this is why Lawrence analyzes her so
early.

Hermione, like Gudrun, is presented with considerable attention to her clothing.

> Now she came along, with her head held up, balancing an enor-
> mous flat hat of pale yellow velvet, on which were streaks of
> ostrich feathers, natural and grey. She drifted forward as if
> scarcely conscious, her long blanched face lifted up, not to see
> the world. She was rich. She wore a dress of silky, frail velvet,
> of pale yellow colour, and she carried a lot of small rose-
> coloured cyclamens. Her shoes and stockings were of brownish
> grey, like the feathers on her hat, her hair was heavy, she drift-
> ed along with a peculiar fixity of the hips a strange unwilling
> motion. [p. 9]

Whereas Gudrun dresses in "dark blue silky stuff," set off by
emerald green (a rather brilliant effect), Hermione is in pale
yellow velvet set off by brownish grey. And whereas Gudrun is
beautiful and soft, Hermione is scarcely conscious, with a long
blanched face and a strange unwilling motion. Of the two Hermione is obviously the more dead, and our description of her is
soon extended into an analysis of her peculiar habits of repression. She is "a woman of the new school, full of intellectuality,

and heavy, nerve-worn with consciousness." She is a *Kulturträger,* "a medium for the culture of ideas." Her role among the intellectual and artistic avant-garde is meant to fortify her, put her "beyond reach of the world's judgment." Yet her desire for such invulnerability is of course an index of her insecurity, which Lawrence labels with terms by now quite familiar: "She always felt vulnerable. . . . It was a lack of robust self, she had no natural sufficiency, there was a terrible void, a lack, a deficiency of being within her" (p. 11).

This is a much more harsh and explicit judgment than any we encountered in the initial descriptions of Gudrun and Gerald. In it we find the basis for the charges that Lawrence was anti-intellectual, for Hermione's deficiency of being is obviously related to her tendency to intellectualize: "The pensive, tortured woman piled up her own defences of aesthetic knowledge, and culture, and world-visions, and disinterestedness." Yet to say that Hermione uses her mind to deny herself life is not equivalent to saying that her deficiencies are simply the result of the mind. The point is that she has put the mind to bad use; why she was trapped into doing so is not explained, just as the ultimate basis for the differences between Ursula and Gudrun are not explained. (I doubt, in fact, whether any novelistic characters are explained in this sense; ontological deficiencies are not reducible to psychological causes.) We need to be cautious, then, about making a simple equation between Hermione's habits and her deficiency of being, for it is precisely this relation that Lawrence wants to explore. And, as with all his major characters, such exploration has a thematic resonance amounting to a qualification of the judgments which are already apparently clear. Hermione, for all her consistent wrong-headedness, sufficiently shares her problems with the other characters to demand sympathy. If she is occasionally loathsome, she is also a victim.

Hermione's defenses are, of course, mainly against herself. Her "lack of robust self," though possibly a hereditary defect, is more properly viewed as a perversion of those same dark forces with which Gudrun found herself so fascinated. Throughout the book

Hermione's behavior, like Gudrun's, demonstrates a self-conscious and determined insistence on the importance of the will, both in relation to others (she quite unabashedly tries to bully people) and in relation to what she considers her true self (discipline is almost her trademark). In sexual matters this willfulness amounts to a pattern of domination and submission; she can only conceive of loving Birkin as a mother or a slave. In intellectual matters it involves insistence upon rationalization of desires sometimes demonic without realizing that the demonic element in fact exists. And in social matters it means justification of democracy, nationalism, materialism, and war.

We begin to see, then, that if Lawrence's book is meant to explore "death in the mind," Hermione provides the most obvious and pointed lessons as to how the mind can kill. Insofar as she does this, she stands at the "northern" extreme of the book, for she is more thoroughly involved in abstraction—which, as we shall see, is an inseparable element in the reduction of vitality to mechanism—than anyone else in the book. But abstraction presupposes something to abstract from; Hermione also has considerable sensual power, which in one scene breaks through her shell of abstraction completely.

Of the five characters introduced in the first chapter of *Women in Love,* Birkin is the most vaguely portrayed and probably remains the most indefinite character of the book, if by definition we mean predictability in terms of a stable psychological pattern. Yet there is good reason for this; both Ursula and Birkin carry on the Lawrentian quest for selfhood, and such a quest demands, as we saw in *The Rainbow,* a flexibility which calls stable personalities into question. Hermione, Gerald, and Gudrun all live out patterns without fundamental change, though Gerald at times comes close.[4] Ursula and Birkin search throughout the greater

4. This is not equivalent to the frequently heard charge that Lawrence's characters do not develop. It implies only that they develop the wrong way, extending themselves without removing or coping with their fundamental deficiencies. It certainly does not mean that their responses are always predictable, or that the patterns in which they are caught are Lawrentian theories which they merely illustrate.

part of the book for the correct pattern to follow, and even when they find it it remains tentative. Birkin's comparative elusiveness in this first chapter, then, is an indication that he, like Ursula, has a self as yet unrealized. There are only two clues to the nature of this self: first, it has something to do with the understanding to which Ursula initially responded; and second, it is somehow "clever and separate," for these are the qualities which the narrator tells us with irritation were "travestied" before the crowd.

From these notions, vague as they are here, grows Lawrence's most positive, and perhaps his most definite, formulation of the ideal marriage, which was, at least at this stage in his life, a prerequisite for self-realization. But again Lawrence's insistence on possibility will prevent his ideal from becoming a formula. Lawrence's hero, moreover, embodies that possibility in his role as an intellectual with unabashedly intellectual attitudes, pursuits, and even vocation (though this last does not satisfy him and is given up). To realize this much puts Hermione's stultifying mind in a slightly different light, just as it tends to put the notion of understanding at the center of the book, as the quotation from "The Reality of Peace" (see p. 215 above) implies it should be. As it turns out, in fact, the differences between Birkin's and Hermione's understanding indicate the difference between legitimate and illegitimate uses of the mind; Birkin's dependence upon her is in one sense a function of his adoption of her version of what understanding should be; and Ursula's job, or one of her jobs, is to set him straight.

The notion of understanding is in fact moving into a position parallel to the one that consciousness and knowledge took earlier. "There are ultimately only two desires, the desire of life and the desire of death. Beyond these is pure being, where I am absolved from desire and made perfect. This is when I am like a rose, when I balance for a space in pure adjustment and pure understanding."[5] This passage and the development which follows put understanding in the position held earlier by the crown—as a

5. *Phoenix*, p. 680.

meeting place of the two opposing forces, a place of transcendence. Lawrence again extends a word usually used to refer to some variety of rational process into the ontological realm. But in so doing he does not discard its usual meaning altogether. "God works in me (if I use the term God) as my desire. He gives me the understanding to discriminate between my desires, to discern between greater and lesser desire: I can also frustrate or deny any desire; so much for me, I have a 'free will,' in so far as I am an entity."[6] Where this second sort of understanding, an analytic faculty, merges with or divides from the more mysterious use, which denotes achievement of vital purpose, is an important concern of *Women in Love.* The mind, in fact, turns out to be much more useful in the process of fulfillment than Tom Brangwen found it. It is important to keep this hint in mind, for the discussion that follows will be largely concerned with exploring the wrong relations between sense, mind, and spirit—in order, of course, to gain some insight into the right ones.

Gudrun, as indicated earlier, is probably the most limited of the four characters whom we follow to the end of the book. Not only is she the least courageous in her exploration of vital possibility, she is finally Gerald's murderer.[7] She also provides an important part of Lawrence's indictment of the mechanical world by exposing the perverted sensuality in which mechanical people (the colliers) find satisfaction. And, like the other major characters, she furnishes certain insights into the relation of sense to mind, for which Lawrence provides a narrative mode symbolic in an almost Freudian manner, and which he finally explains for us in a perverse theory of art.

Perhaps the most striking scene in which Lawrence explores the quality of Gudrun's attraction to Gerald is the much-discussed subjugation of a mare in chapter 2 ("Coal Dust"). It has been pointed out that in this scene Gudrun identifies with the mare,

6. *LM*, p. 467 (16 July 1916).
7. Mark Schorer emphasizes that Gerald invited his destruction in "*Women in Love* and Death," in Spilka, *Critical Essays,* pp. 54-56.

which Gerald brutally and sexually assaults in order to assert his willful masculinity—or, according to Gerald's explanation, to teach it obedience.[8] This is true enough and itself implies a desire for submission on Gudrun's part similar to Hermione's desire to submit to Birkin, though of course Gudrun's approach to submission is anything but spiritual. But what is more interesting is the quality of Gudrun's response, which gradually gathers associations with the colliers. In Lawrence's unfolding of this incident we can also see significant changes in method and purpose from *The Rainbow*.

Gerald forces the mare to remain at a railway crossing despite her terror. "It seemed as if he sank into her magnetically, and could thrust her back against herself." Ursula responds with violent antagonism, calling Gerald a fool and urging him to let the mare retreat from the train. But Gudrun looks at him "with black-dilated, spellbound eyes," and as Gerald persists she approaches a state of mindlessness:

> But as strong as the pressure of his compulsion was the repulsion of her utter terror, throwing her back away from the railway, so that she spun round and round on two legs, as if she were in the centre of some whirlwind. It made Gudrun faint with poignant dizziness, which seemed to penetrate her heart. [p. 103]

> Gudrun looked and saw the trickles of blood on the sides of the mare, and she turned white. And then on the very wound the bright spurs came down, pressing relentlessly. The world reeled and passed into nothingness for Gudrun, she could not know any more. [p. 104]

Ursula's screams are unendurable because they disturb the trancelike state into which Gudrun is falling. She comes out of it before the struggle is over—"cold and separate, she had no more feeling for them." But the scene is impressed on her

8. Moynahan, *Deed of Life*, p. 86.

mind, "isolated and momentary, like a vision isolated in eternity."

This is a new version of the ecstatic loss of self of which all Lawrence's characters are capable. Like the ecstatic moments of Tom Brangwen, it follows a pattern of unendurable intensity, mindless release, and a return to the everyday world. And Gudrun, like Tom, has been changed by the experience. But here the similarities end. Whereas Tom's experience follows the model of religious ecstasies, with the subsequent (if temporary) achievement of peace and harmony, Gudrun's lapse has the quality of a demonic inversion of such experience. Her response seems keyed directly to the violence of the act, and the sight of blood sets off her movement into nothingness. When she returns to normal consciousness, moreover, she wants to reject the experience.[9] She is much more detached than she was before Gerald came along, "hard and cold and indifferent."

This indifference, however, is but a thin shell covering the intense desires which the scene has aroused. Once the train passes she suddenly springs into motion:

> The gate-keeper stood ready at the door of his hut, to proceed to open the gate. But Gudrun sprang suddenly forward, in front of the struggling horse, threw off the latch and flung the gates asunder, throwing one-half to the keeper, and running with the other half forwards. Gerald suddenly let go the horse and leaped forwards, almost on to Gudrun. She was not afraid. As he jerked aside the mare's head, Gudrun cried, in a strange, high voice, like a gull, or like a witch screaming out from the side of the road:
>
> "I should think you're proud." [p. 105]

Gerald responds to this with surprise and "wondering interest" and bounds off.

It should be obvious by now that Lawrence is developing an extended symbolic scene to indicate the demonic nature of the

9. Here, of course, she has much in common with Ursula in *The Rainbow*.

bond which is forming between Gudrun and Gerald. In its visual intensity the scene is quite unlike anything in *The Rainbow,* though it is perhaps close to some of the more intense scenes of *Sons and Lovers.* There is no attempt here to blur the boundaries between self and nature, as we saw happen (to very good effect, of course) in the early scenes of *The Rainbow.* Nor is there an attempt to imply a struggle for identity, as the ontological excursions of Will, Anna, and Ursula all do. Instead Lawrence depicts an unholy collusion, rooted in sexual response, related to the will, and clearly perverse. That it concludes with a witchlike cry of challenge, accompanied by the violent opening of a gate, is certainly no accident.

These differences point toward a more deliberately limited form of symbolism than we are accustomed to expect in Lawrence's writings. As George Ford has pointed out, this scene is similar to one in *Anna Karenina,* where a horse is killed with much the same ominous import for the future of the characters present.[10] One of the reasons that this parallel comes to mind is that much of the action in both scenes serves the symbolic function of foreshadowing the course of events. Gudrun's opening of the gate is an offering of release as well as a challenge; Gerald accepts the former but does not cope with the latter. The power that Gerald exercises over the horse he tries also to exercise over Gudrun, who really becomes witchlike to defeat it. This sort of symbolic function is not of the same order as the "constitutive symbols" which leave their referents vague. The consistently brilliant rendering of physical detail, though charged as always with ontological implication, does not really yield to the deeper meanings which it presupposes or implies; the emphasis lies more strongly on the psychological aspects of this emerging bond than on the ontological implications. Unlike Gudrun's initial response to Gerald, which sought answers to questions of the form "What does it all ultimately mean?" this scene more immediately seeks

10. Ford, *Double Measure,* pp. 211-12.

answers to the questions "What will happen?" and "What sort of sexual relationship is going to develop?"

This departure into a more vividly descriptive mode has a particular and appropriate function. It is more limited to the senses because the characters it depicts are themselves more limited by their senses than any of the major characters in *The Rainbow*, or even than Ursula and Birkin in this book. To depict responses strongly sexual and involved with sensual detail, Lawrence now gives us the detail itself. By this shift Lawrence avoids some of the difficulties of Ursula's more destructive moments; he takes us, in fact, further into the quality of the emotions here than was possible in those more ontologically oriented descriptions. When we finally come to the summation of what is indeed happening inside Gudrun, the same sort of visual articulation keeps her obsession with deliberate, willed, sexual domination strongly before us; it is all the more effective because it is also a visual summary of the scene we have just witnessed.

> Gudrun was as if numbed in her mind by the sense of indomitable soft weight of the man, bearing down into the living body of the horse: the strong, indomitable thighs of the blond man clenching the palpitating body of the mare into pure control; a sort of soft white magnetic domination from the loins and thighs and calves, enclosing and encompassing the mare heavily into unutterable subordination, soft-blood-subordination, terrible. [p. 106]

The highly elaborated sensual detail presented here is in fact characteristic of the dark side of this book, as is the visual symbolic mode which goes with it.[11] And if the nature of the subject matter itself seems to demand this type of writing, so does Lawrence's newly emphatic drive toward articulation.

11. See Angelo Bertocci, "Symbolism in *Women in Love*," in *A D. H. Lawrence Miscellany*, ed. Harry T. Moore (Carbondale, Ill., 1959), pp. 83-101, for a reading of the novel which argues that these symbolic scenes are central.

Gerald's torture of the horse contains details which also extend to the collieries and their meaning. He makes the mare stand to the horror of the train "with an almost mechanical relentlessness." The horse submits, as Gudrun secretly yearns to submit— although she, unlike the horse, responds with a delicious terror. The miners have already submitted. It is no surprise, then, that the fascination with the collieries which Gudrun revealed in the first chapter should come more into the open here.

> The girls descended between the houses with slate roofs and blackish brick walls. The heavy gold glamour of approaching sunset lay over all the colliery district, and the ugliness overlaid with beauty was like a narcotic to the senses. . . .
>
> "It has a foul kind of beauty, this place," said Gudrun, evidently suffering from fascination. "Can't you feel in some way, a thick, hot attraction in it? I can. And it quite stupefies me." [pp. 107-08]

The phrase "ugliness overlaid with beauty" might apply to Gerald and Gudrun as well as to the collieries. What they have in common is insistently brought out.

> Now she realised that this was the world of powerful, underworld men who spent most of their time in the darkness. In their voices she could hear the voluptuous resonance of darkness, the strong, dangerous underworld, mindless, inhuman. They sounded also like strange machines, heavy, oiled. The voluptuousness was like that of machinery, cold and iron . . . a wave of disruptive force . . . went to the brain and the heart, awaking a fatal desire, and a fatal callousness . . . She hated it, she knew how utterly cut off it was, how hideous and how sickeningly mindless. Sometimes she beat her wings like a new Daphne, turning not into a tree but into a machine. And yet she was overcome by the nostalgia . . . she craved to get her satisfaction of it. [p. 108]

Through passages like these Lawrence not only evokes the sensual darkness which dominates Gudrun's sexual responses (and thus the quality of those responses themselves), but he manages to establish at once the fascinating appeal of the miner's lives and the horrible cost that this fascination has for their humanity, thereby preparing the ground for the polemics which follow. In short, his theme of darkness expands and links itself with the idea of mechanization, which, ultimately, is a form of abstraction,[12] implying a kinship between this mode of experience and that represented by Hermione.

This string of associations is again characteristic of *Women in Love* but not of *The Rainbow,* where there is no such highly condensed movement from the psychological to the social. Nor has Lawrence sacrificed evocative power to this new firmness of control; the passages quoted are enforced by scenes of Friday night marketing, into which Gudrun is drawn almost in spite of herself. The crowd scenes are as realistic as anything in *Sons and Lovers.*

> The carts that came could not pass through. They had to wait, the drivers calling and shouting, till the dense crowd would make way. Everywhere, young fellows from the outlying districts were making conversation with the girls, standing in the

12. As the *Study of Thomas Hardy* makes clear, Lawrence's actual use of the term *abstraction* is subject to radically different evaluations. There are basically two ways in which one can be abstracted. All the major characters except Ursula are subject to abstract states of mental consciousness, states of inhibition. All are also susceptible to states of impersonality which may be labeled abstract, as when Birkin argues, "in a voice of pure abstraction," for a final self, "impersonal and beyond responsibility." This second association is not pejorative, though, as Lawrence's continued struggle to define states of impersonality implies, its precise value may remain ambiguous. Gerald, for example, gradually forced by Gudrun into the demonic state in which he attempts to strangle her, becomes temporarily "innocent and pure"; "a certain peace, an abstraction possessed his soul" (p. 441). Loerke, on the other hand, appears to Gudrun a couple of pages later as "single and, by abstraction from the rest, absolute in himself" (p. 443). Both Gerald and Loerke are certainly in an impersonal state, but we read Gerald's as a purification under duress and Loerke's as a final stage of corruption. The obvious lesson here for critics is to avoid making a "Lawrentian dictionary" and then dismissing repeated terms without sufficient attention to the context in which they appear.

road and at the corners. The doors of the public-houses were
open and full of light, men passed in and out in a continual
stream, everywhere men were calling out to one another, or
crossing to meet one another, or standing in little gangs and
circles, discussing, endlessly discussing. The sense of talk,
buzzing, jarring, half-secret, the endless mining, and political
wrangling, vibrated in the air like discordant machinery. And it
was their voices which affected Gudrun almost to swooning.
They aroused a strange, nostalgic ache of desire, something almost demoniacal, never to be fulfilled. [p. 109]

The pattern of courtship, talk, and movement gathers intensity
through the shortening of phrases until it is summarized in the
now familiar image of machinery, which is linked again with Gudrun's desire. There is also a convenient definition of the demonic
as a state of frustration, which makes it clear that whatever fulfillment may have to do with the senses, it cannot be equated with
the mindless and mechanical sensualism. (With the colliers mindless and mechanical go together, just as mindful and mechanical
would go together in Hermione.)

Before the chapter ends Lawrence has one more important
point to make about the quality of this world to which Gudrun is
so attracted. The word *nostalgia*[13] has been used repeatedly to
describe her desire, and its use is at least somewhat odd. It usually
means a sentimental response to something past, but what is past
for a young woman of twenty-four? "The same secret seemed to
be working in the souls of all alike, Gudrun, Palmer, the rakish
young bloods, the gaunt, middle-aged men. All had a secret sense
of power, and of inexpressible destructiveness, and of fatal half-
heartedness, a sort of rottenness in the will" (p. 110). Palmer is
Gudrun's kindred spirit, a man too "cold" and "destructive," too
much an "egoist," to care for women. Yet he wants Ursula, who
does not take to him. Obviously he perceives in Ursula a vitality
which he, Gudrun, and the colliers possess in diminished form,

13. This has been part of Gudrun's makeup from the first. See the
quotation on p. 232 above.

destructively powerful because its bare sensual nature is recognized, uninhibited by morality, yet fatally half-hearted and "rotten in the will." What creates the nostalgia, then, is an ineffectual yearning after a fullness of desire which they perhaps never had. In the more sophisticated, such as Gudrun and Palmer, animalism has yielded to egoism, and the rotten will concentrates its destructive power upon subserving that ego. But the will remains half-hearted before the prospect of facing itself in all its demonic potential. With Gudrun, in fact, it seems to gain in strength in proportion to her success in maintaining a domineering and artistically abstracted ego. The will then draws on her demonic propensities sufficiently to kill off Gerald, while the egoistic shell prevents Gudrun from facing the truth about herself.

Lawrence extends his analysis of a civilization he considered fundamentally perverted through an examination of bohemian life in London. Our attention is focused on a simplified and inferior counterpart to Gudrun, an artist's model named Minette,[14] who attracts Gerald with an intensity even more openly demonic than that of Gudrun.

> She looked at him steadily with her naive eyes, that rested on him and roused him so deeply, that it left his upper self quite calm. It was rather delicious, to feel her drawing his self-revelations from him, as from the very innermost dark marrow of his body. She wanted to know. And her eyes seemed to be looking through into his naked organism. He felt, she was compelled to him, she was fated to come into contact with him, must have the seeing and knowing him. And this roused a curious exultance. [p. 59]

Unlike Gudrun, Minette enjoys no delicious terror in the idea of submission to masculinity; she is calculatingly exultant as she

14. Her name was originally Pussum, but it was changed because of a threatened libel suit. See Ford, pp. 189-90 n.; and Robert L. Chamberlain, "Pussum, Minette, and the Afro-Nordic Symbol in Lawrence's *Women in Love*," in *PMLA* 78 (1963): 407-16.

considers this submission, and she proves herself capable of cal-
culated violence as well (she stabs a boorish young man who is
irritating her). The more she is abused, the greater her pleasure
seems to be. Her significance in the governing patterns of the
book, however, is only made clear some three hundred pages after
Gerald's first encounter with her.

> There is a phase in every race . . . when the desire for destruc-
> tion overcomes every other desire. In the individual, this desire
> is ultimately a desire for destruction in the self. [p. 374]

> Surely there will come an end in us to this desire—for the
> constant going apart—this passion for putting asunder—every-
> thing—ourselves, reducing ourselves part from part—reacting in
> intimacy only for destruction—using sex as a great reducing
> agent, reducing the two great elements of male and female from
> their highly complex unity—reducing the old ideas, going back
> to the savages for our sensations—always seeking to *lose* our-
> selves in some ultimate black sensation, mindless and infinite—
> burning only with destructive fires, ranging on with the hope of
> being burnt out utterly. [p. 376]

This is all from a letter which Birkin wrote to the bohemians to
get them to mend their ways before Gerald came on the scene. It
is mocked vociferously by them all, for by the time it is read
aloud in a cafe Birkin is out of favor, and the tone is, as they call
it, too much like "the Saviour of man." But it supplies us with a
link between what happens to Gerald and Minette and a little
African (or "West Pacific")[15] statue, and it outlines a set of
Lawrentian beliefs which were developed in "The Crown" and
which govern a great deal of this book.

The "reduction" of a "highly complex unity" to "ultimate
black sensation" is of course the "flux of corruption" of "The

15. In response to the same threats which changed Pussum to Minette,
"African" became "West Pacific," but it was changed back again toward
the end of the book.

Crown."[16] As is characteristic in *Women in Love,* its meaning is
extended to encompass the destructive tendencies not only of
individuals or social groupings but of whole civilizations. This
extension is most clearly and dramatically made through a small
carving which attracts Gerald's attention at a flat where he spends
the night with Minette.

> One was a woman sitting naked in a strange posture, and look-
> ing tortured, her abdomen stuck out. The young Russian ex-
> plained that she was sitting in child-birth, clutching the ends of
> the band that hung from her neck, one in each hand, so that she
> could bear down, and help labour. The strange, transfixed, rudi-
> mentary face of the woman again reminded Gerald of a foetus,
> it was also rather wonderful, conveying the suggestion of the
> extreme of physical sensation, beyond the limits of mental con-
> sciousness. [p. 67]

Just before he goes in to sleep with Minette, "the looks of her
eyes made Gerald feel drowned in some potent darkness that
almost frightened him." (p. 69). The next morning the statue has
an even more powerful effect: "It was a terrible face, void,
peaked, abstracted almost into meaninglessness by the weight of
sensation beneath. He saw Minette in it. As in a dream, he knew
her" (p. 71). This is all obvious enough to require little comment.
Minette, too, has been abstracted almost into meaninglessness by
the weight of sensation, and Gerald's fear of being drowned depends precisely upon his hazy recognition of this meaninglessness.
But Birkin extends the interpretation of the statue even further.

> "It conveys a complete truth," said Birkin. "It contains the
> whole truth of that state, whatever you feel about it."
> "But you can't call it *high* art," said Gerald.
> "High! There are centuries and hundreds of centuries of de-

16. See pp. 209-14 above; also "The Crown," esp. chap. 3.

velopment in a straight line, behind that carving; it is an awful pitch of culture, of a definite sort."

"What culture?" Gerald asked, in opposition. He hated the sheer barbaric thing.

"Pure culture in sensation, culture in the physical consciousness, really ultimate *physical* consciousness, mindless, utterly sensual. It is so sensual as to be final, supreme."

But Gerald resented it. He wanted to keep certain illusions, certain ideas like clothing.

"You like the wrong things, Rupert," he said, "things against yourself."

"Oh, I know, this isn't everything," Birkin replied, moving away. [p. 72]

Because Lawrence's books all plead, among other things, for a recognition and reintegration of the senses into human experience, this little statue has been taken by some as the focus of his values in this book. But others have denied this, and they are clearly right.[17] The statue represents a legitimate pursuit taken to its extreme, to a dead end. It is precisely because the culture it represents is finished that the statue can capture its final sensuality. By identifying mindless sensuality with a dead civilization, Lawrence both retains his attraction to the dark powers (embodied in art, the sensuality is supreme) and rejects their more modern, destructively final embodiments. Mindlessness is not the answer; Minette and the bohemians have not, unlike the culture behind the statue, experienced centuries of development in a straight line but have resorted willfully to the sort of experience the statue represents in an attempt to escape from themselves. In so doing they too represent a dying culture, but the principle behind its death is somewhat different. They are slaves to the mechanical principle quite as much as the colliers are. Although their response has been to reject the society which industrialism has built, it is, like the rituals of rejection of most

17. Ford (*Double Measure*, pp. 192-94) convincingly refutes Horace Gregory's contention that the statue represents hope.

bohemians, simply an inverted form of dependence. And this affinity, together with what we have noticed about the sensual nostalgia of the colliers' world, helps to explain why Gerald, the industrial magnate, is attracted to them and finally to Gudrun. For Gudrun, too, has moved in bohemian circles, and though she considers herself superior to them, she creates little statues which significantly share many of the qualities of this one.

The trouble with the bohemians, then, is that they are indeed caught in a "metaphysical antipathy"—of themselves. Their destructive tendencies imply a destruction of human meaning, and Birkin's letter suggests that the forces which lie behind this destructiveness are themselves metaphysical. As such they are not entirely explicable, but it is important to recognize that Lawrence believed in them, for this belief lies behind the fated quality of most of the characters in the book. Industrialism, with its mechanical principle, is certainly a great evil, but the perversions of life which result cannot be explained by the principle itself. For man created the principle and abused himself with it—how does one explain that? Only by certain metaphysical assumptions, which are now symbolized by the darkness and light we have been noticing, especially the darkness. Although the Lawrentian ideal seems to remain in a principle of balance, at the end of the book we are unable to find the elements of that balance in the extremes implied by the apparent opposition between sensuality and intellectuality. Both are mainly destructive in this book and are finally identified with one another, just as in "The Crown" Lawrence tended to collapse his forces of light into reductive processes dominated by dark and sensual images.[18]

18. Similar arguments appear in his letters as well: "And of death you gather death: when you sow death, in this act of love which is pure reduction, you reap death, in a child *born with an impulse towards the darkness,* the origins, the oblivion of all" (*LM,* p. 468; italics mine). An earlier version of the scene in the classroom even identifies the "analytic adventure" with a plunge into sensuality:

If we are out on the analytic adventure, we must penetrate the darkest continent. But we might as well know all the time what we are about,

Once we recognize that Lawrence means to have a destructive ultimate dominant in this book, the negative results of what are clearly ontological excursions on the part of Gerald and Gudrun become more easily comprehensible. The sensuality which came to dominate the sexual activity of Will and Anna in *The Rainbow* here becomes both worse and farther-reaching; it dominates not only Gerald and Gudrun, but the society, culture, and civilization of which they are a part. And as is hinted by the descriptions of the miners, the difficulty is compounded by the willful use of, as well as the willful refusal to recognize fully, this demonic undercurrent. The abstract will both directs and hinders a destructive propensity in man which, if let loose, might result in a catastrophe which would be also a purgation (see pp. 205-14 above). What is perhaps most horrible to Lawrence is the fact that industrialism has brought demonism, bad enough in itself, into something like a stasis. This is why miners are *"almost* demoniacal," and it is at least part of the reason why the destruction of Gerald is not simply fated but accompanied by a strong sense of frustration and waste.[19]

---

and not begin to lie to ourselves. . . . And if we have to push on into the darkest jungle of our own physical sensations, and discover the sensuality in ourselves, we need not pretend we are being simple animals . . . the adventure of knowledge is not finished for us till we have got back to the very sources, in sensation, as one traces back a river. . . . it is a form of immediate anthropology, we study the origins of man in our own experience. [This passage is taken from the earlier corrected typescript at Texas, p. 47; Roberts's listing, E441d.]

Here Birkin seems merely to be claiming the necessity for honesty. But his rhetoric reveals a fascination with and hope for the ontological sort of knowledge as well. Birkin, like Lawrence, is not clear what role analysis of these emotions is supposed to play. Lawrence tried to write his way through the problem by creating the novel itself; Birkin, as we shall see, manages to argue and analyze his way out of the need for analysis.

19. Gordon (*D. H. Lawrence as a Literary Critic,* p. 90) has pointed out that in Lawrence's later work the demonic became a form of revenge for life forces which have been thwarted: "Particularly during his so-called power period (1920-25), he believed that vital being had become so oppressed that it must assume a demonic role as a nemesis to an evil civilization." Gordon cites evidence from both Lawrence's critical writings and his fiction; Romero in "The Princess" is probably the best example. See also

Lawrence is also able to dramatize his ideas about destruction in a thorough and detailed manner. Just as certain images from "The Crown" have striking analogues in the cathedral chapter of *The Rainbow,* others have a striking effect upon the form which certain passages take in *Women in Love.* For example, a passage in Birkin's letter speaks of the "desire for destruction in the self":

It is a desire for the reduction-process in oneself, a reducing back to the origin, a return along the Flux of Corruption, to the original rudimentary conditions of being. . . . And in the great retrogression, the reducing back of the created body of life, we get knowledge, and beyond knowledge, the phosphorescent ecstasy of acute sensation. . . . And if, Julius, you want this ecstasy of reduction with Minette, you must go on till it is fulfilled. But surely there is in you also, somewhere, the living desire for positive creation, relationships in ultimate faith, when all this process of active corruption, with all its flowers of mud, is transcended, and more or less finished. [p. 375]

This has interesting similarities to Gudrun's perception of some water plants:

Gudrun had waded out to a gravelly shoal, and was seated like a Buddhist, staring fixedly at the waterplants that rose succulent from the mud of the low shores. What she could see was mud, soft, oozy, watery mud, and from its festering chill, water-plants rose up, thick and cool and fleshy, very straight and turgid, thrusting out their leaves at right angles, and having dark lurid colours, dark green and blotches of black-purple and bronze. But she could feel their turgid fleshy structure as in a sensuous vision, she *knew* how they thrust out from themselves, how they stood stiff and succulent against the air. [p. 111]

Kingsley Widmer ("Our Demonic Heritage," in *A D. H. Lawrence Miscellany,* ed. Moore, pp. 13-28), whom Gordon cites; and especially Clarke, *River of Dissolution,* chaps. 3, 4. Clarke makes it clear that Lawrence was often inclined to approve strongly of tendencies like those described here, although he also withdrew his approval in much of his later work.

Gudrun is "absorbed in a stupor of apprehension of surging water-plants." Her savoring of the sensual detail, almost over-whelmingly phallic, is of course meant to convey that Gudrun herself is one of the flowers of mud. The voluptuousness of the passage, moreover, illustrates the degree to which Lawrence was willing to go to give his ideas flesh, and it is once again character-istic (in kind, though nothing quite matches it in its degree of phallic detail) of the highly sensuous modes of description which he uses to convey his themes of darkness. Into this darkness, however, soon comes a light.

> Gerald was her escape from the heavy slough of the pale, under-world, automatic colliers. He started out of the mud. He was master. She saw his back, the movement of his white loins. But not that—it was the whiteness he seemed to enclose as he bent forwards, rowing. He seemed to stoop to something. His glisten-ing, whitish hair seemed like the electricity of the sky. [p. 112]

By an extraordinarily persistent use of images Lawrence conveys, perhaps even too clearly, how deceived Gudrun is in thinking that Gerald's whiteness provides her escape.

> And as if in a spell, Gudrun was aware of his body, stretching and surging like the marsh-fire, stretching towards her, his hand coming straight forward like a stem. Her voluptuous, acute ap-prehension of him made the blood faint in her veins, her mind went dim and unconscious. And he rocked on the water per-fectly, like the rocking of phosphorescence. [p. 113]

Here, indeed is the "phosphorescent ecstasy of acute sensation." The prurient quality of these descriptions is of course quite de-liberate, for they are meant to convey—and they do convey—the reduction upon which the letter elaborates. In Gerald's starting from the mud, his incorporation of marsh fire, and his imagistic metamorphosis into a phallic plant, we have strong hints that the whiteness of the master is only a mask for the sensual darkness in which Gudrun is trapped. It is because Lawrence is so capable of assimilating metaphysical doctrine to a dramatic medium that he avoids the "superimposition of a theory" which he abjured in his introduction to this novel.

Lawrence's drive toward articulation, which is evident in the thoroughness with which he embodies visually and symbolically certain lessons about sensuality, is also expressed in an abundance of talk. Even Gerald has a *"passion* for discussion" (p. 22), and in an early scene with Hermione and Birkin he engages in an argument that ranges over a number of issues which Lawrence conceives as very closely related: nationalism, materialism, individualism, and, though the word itself is not used, war. The scene passes quickly, but the fundamental differences among the speakers are dramatized here just as effectively as they are in the more visual, symbolic scenes we have been examining. Here the basic issue is the relation of the individual to the social order, as in the scenes which dramatize Gudrun's and Gerald's affinities with the colliers. But here the talk carries an analysis of the book's themes, a rare occurence in *The Rainbow*. And in *Women in Love* talk gains a peculiar force because its value is itself one of the central thematic concerns of the book.

The value of talk is essentially the value of worrying things into consciousness. We have already seen something of this in the scene between Gerald and Birkin before the African statue; there Birkin was explaining that the statue represented a culture of "ultimate *physical* consciousness," "mindless" but still completely articulated in the statue itself and therefore available to Birkin's analysis. It is precisely this analysis that Gerald resents. "He wanted to keep certain illusions, certain ideas like clothing." In Gerald's response we find what is perhaps Lawrence's main reason for including as much talk as he does.

Everyone in the book has a propensity to wear ideas like clothing. For both Gerald and Hermione, especially Hermione, ideas are essential as a covering for an ultimate nakedness. On the other hand, ideas are not safe; they have a capacity to reveal as well as to clothe, and Hermione is continually being trapped by them. (This is what happens at this early dinner party, where she makes

a half-comic admission of murderous tendency.) Lawrence plays
on these basic functions of language throughout his book. This is
especially evident in Birkin, who tries continually to talk his way
through self-deception to a kind of fundamental honesty. That he
largely succeeds is strong evidence that Lawrence has placed the
analytic functions of the mind in an honorable position, certainly
a more central one than in *The Rainbow*. Yet the problems involved are not simple, for the ultimate experience remains essentially mindless, and Birkin often preaches against certain mental
attitudes. To complicate matters further, Birkin is not always
right, and he characteristically overstates when he is.

In the third chapter, "Classroom," Lawrence takes up these
problems directly. The classroom is Ursula's, but Birkin and Hermione, who invade it, do most of the talking. A vicious argument
develops in which Hermione parodies Birkin's plea for a return to
sensuality. She begins by asking Birkin "Do you really think the
children are better for being roused to consciousness?" "A dark
flash went over his face, a silent fury. He was hollow-cheeked and
pale, almost unearthly. And the woman, with her serious, con-
science-harrowing question tortured him on the quick" (p. 33).
The violence of his response indicates that not only Hermione but
the question itself is harrowing. In what follows Hermione develops a Wordsworthian argument against analysis. "Isn't it better
that they should remain unconscious of the hazel, isn't it better
that they should see as a whole, without all this pulling to pieces,
all this knowledge?" (p. 33). But she carries it to a pitch that
would certainly have made Wordsworth uncomfortable:

> They thought she had finished. But with a queer rumbling in
> her throat she resumed, "Hadn't they better be anything than
> grow up crippled, crippled in their souls, crippled in their feel-
> ings—so thrown back—so turned back on themselves—incapa-
> ble—" Hermione clenched her fist like one in a trance—" of any
> spontaneous action, always deliberate, always burdened with
> choice, never carried away." [p. 34]

Her repulsive gestures are not merely rhetorical hints that she is going too far, but indications that for her as well as for Birkin the matter is crucial. As she goes on, it becomes increasingly evident that she is talking about her own condition.

"It is the mind," she said, "and that is death." She raised her eyes slowly to him: "Isn't the mind—" she said, with the convulsed movement of her body, "isn't it our death? Doesn't it destroy all our spontaneity, all our instincts? Are not the young people growing up to-day, really dead before they have a chance to live?

"Not because they have too much mind, but too little," he said brutally. [p. 34]

Birkin's brutality emerges in a direct attack upon Hermione, in which he insists with hysterical persistence (it frightens Ursula to see how Birkin and Hermione "hate" each other) that for Hermione consciousness is in fact everything. His attack upon her is so direct and so intense that we almost lose our sense that the argument is important in itself. But it is. Just before he launches into his attack Birkin does meet Hermione's argument sensibly, explaining what he means by "too little mind." " 'Are you *sure?*' she cried. 'It seems to me the reverse. They are over-conscious, burdened to death with their consciousness.' 'Imprisoned within a limited, false set of concepts,' he cried" (p. 34). Birkin's hysterical tone is, among other things, due to his struggle to find out for himself which concepts are true and which are false.

In what follows it becomes reasonably clear that Birkin has not even succeeded in his attack on Hermione, although if we can separate out his own rage and insecurity he comes pretty close. Before he is through he reduces her entirely to a "voluntary consciousness," with even "animalism" entirely "in the head." We can gauge the degree of overstatement by noticing Lawrence's description of this animalism, which Birkin's attack fosters. The queer rumbling in Hermione's throat and the trancelike clenching of the fist, while repulsive enough, are also sensual in a sense that Birkin's rage will not allow. Her response to the flowers which

Ursula was using to teach plant reproduction has a characteristically heavy, almost prurient quality.

"Little red flames, little red flames," murmured Hermione to
herself. And she remained for some moments looking only at
the small buds out of which the red flickers of the stigma
issued. [p. 31]

"Now I shall always see them," she repeated. "Thank you so
much for showing me. I think they're so beautiful—little red
flames—"
Her absorption was strange, almost rhapsodic. Both Birkin
and Ursula were suspended. The little red pistillate flowers had
some strange, almost mystic-passionate attraction for her. [p.
31]

The quality of these responses is not simply "all mental." But the
more subtle distinction between the sensuous and the sensual,
which Birkin offers when he cools down, is helpful: for Birkin the
sensual response is the honest one; sensuous refers to the sensual
mediated by self-consciousness. What is wrong with Hermione is
not that she has no sensuality, nor that she has repressed it beyond recognition, but that she cannot sufficiently release it from
the ideas which she has learned to consider relevant. Her mystic-
passionate attraction is reminiscent of Miriam's in *Sons and
Lovers* and leads to another Lawrentian vice, spiritualism. And
since spiritualism inverted is demonism, it turns out later, that
Hermione is also subject to that.
But if these are the right concepts for Hermione. which are
appropriate for Birkin himself? His distinction between the sensual and the sensuous also puts him on the wrong side, at least if
we accept the definition of sensual. Ursula breaks in and asks if
Birkin "really wants sensuality."

"Yes," he said, "that and nothing else, at this point. It is a
fullfillment—the great dark knowledge you can't have in your

head—the dark involuntary being. It is death to one's self—but it is the coming into being of another."

"But how? How can you have knowledge not in your head?" she asked, quite unable to interpret his phrases.

"In the blood," he answered; "when the mind and the known world is drowned in darkness—everything must go—there must be the deluge. Then you find yourself in a palpable body of darkness, a demon—"

"But why should I be a demon—?" she asked. " 'Woman wailing for her demon lover'—" he quoted—"why, I don't know." [p. 36]

Birkin is a good way off from any such deluge, and when he finds something like it, it contains no demon. And although the actual experience is in fact mindless, he prepares the way for it by a lot of talk. The fact that the sensual darkness here appears demonic to him is evidence that he, like both Hermione and Gudrun, is still caught in a false concept of himself.[20]

If my analysis is correct, neither Birkin's nor Hermione's arguments remove the necessity for the struggle toward consciousness which Lawrence mentions in his foreword. There is not only nothing against it but nothing that can be done about it. As Birkin says of the children, "consciousness comes to them, willy-nilly." What Hermione illustrates is not that consciousness is bad but that it can have a perverse dominance over the other parts of a human being. The implication is that one must somehow learn to leave it behind when it interferes with religious or ultimate experience, but that if such experience is a goal, the more you understand about what's keeping you from it the better. Most of what Birkin says and does from this point in the book on is best seen as such an attempt at self-knowledge, in the most definite sense of knowledge possible.

The paradoxical nature of Birkin's search—that it is an intel-

20. Lawrence probably is not fully convinced himself that the demonic is a dead end. See pp. 240-41 n. 19 above.

lectual search for a mindless self—need not lead to confusion. It does not, at any rate, confuse Lawrence; it offers him a way of keeping Birkin alive as a character. The force of this scene, as well as that of many others which follow, depends upon Lawrence's skill in presenting these "Lawrentian" arguments as drama, and the obvious way to do this is to play off what people say against what they are. Both Birkin and Hermione are insufficiently aware how much their violence is an indication of inner inadequacy: Hermione has, as we have seen, a kind of sensual intellectualism (an inadequate compromise between real passion and real thought); Birkin's shrill espousal of a doctrine of self-obliteration reveals something of the same trouble, even though it turns out to have more promise than Hermione's anti-intellectual pleading, which is both too simple and too timid. Our awareness of these tensions constitutes, of course, our dramatic interest in the scene. In Lawrence's arguments silly things are often said but trivial things seldom, for the words always have an important relation to the characters' needs. It is for this reason that argument can and often does break into open violence, and the continual presence of that violence, with its intricately extended associations in the darker parts of the book, keeps the talk from being dry. With Birkin, whose conversation functions as both doctrinal revelation (of the proper direction of his search) and a mask for his own inadequacy (his attack on Hermione is also an attack on a part of himself which he has not fully admitted yet), the tension between word and feeling often amounts to an irony that even approaches humor (see pp. 266-68 below).

Lawrence's own struggle for consciousness takes yet another turn in Gerald. Of all the characters in this book, he is the only one whose growth is traced from childhood, whose family is portrayed in detail. Besides the symbolic modes in which his sensual power is revealed and scenes of dialogue in which a great many of his attitudes (especially his social attitudes) are revealed, we find a lengthy chapter devoted almost entirely to the narrator's explanation of how Gerald came to be. If we consider Lawrence's ability to convey his meaning in dramatic modes like those we have examined, the length and thoroughness of the chapter "The Industrial Magnate" may well seem a bit strange.[21] Yet there is good thematic reason for it. As I mentioned above, Gerald is the only character to embody fully both aspects or faces of the destructive powers to which *Women in Love* is largely devoted. As such he provides our main insight into their relation, even though all the other characters furnish, in their own ways, similar implications as to the identity of Lawrence's abstract and sensual modes of destruction. When we remember as well that industrialism and the society that condones it are the main villains of the book, it is all the more obvious why Lawrence chose to explain Gerald as thoroughly as he did.

Gerald is heir to qualities of both his parents. In his childhood his mother's rebellious intensity seems to dominate. He ignores the industrialism which his father helped create and rebels against authority in general. "Life was a condition of savage freedom" (p. 214); he holds to this through school ("which was so much death to him"), through war, through travel "into the savage regions" of Africa. But in the course of this essentially rebellious career he also learns to use his mind: "he wanted to see and to know, in a curious objective fashion." Finally, upon returning to the mines, he has a vision: "His vision had suddenly crystallized. Suddenly he had conceived the pure instrumentality of mankind. There had been so much humanitarianism, so much talk of sufferings and feelings. It was ridiculous. The sufferings and feelings of individuals did not matter in the least" (p. 215). This, of course, is a "vision of power"; "he was the God of the machine." In this vision he connects his mother's dark power with his father's quest for an ideal order. To see precisely what this means in the book we need to notice what the elder Crich has come to stand for.

In Thomas Crich Lawrence captures more clearly than before his conviction that Christianity is finished. Crich's devotion to

---

21. Ford (*Double Measure,* p. 166), at least, has found it "somewhat labored."

the ideal of charity sacrifices spiritual reality to an impossible ethic.

> He had been so constant to his lights, so constant to charity, and to his love for his neighbour. . . . To move nearer to God, he must move towards his miners, his life must gravitate towards theirs. They were, unconsciously, his idol, his God made manifest. In them he worshipped the highest, the great, sympathetic, mindless Godhead of humanity. [p. 207]

Christian charity and humility can all too easily lead to "creeping democracy." The process is interesting, and it reveals a point crucial to Lawrence's whole approach to social matters. The ideal of charity which Crich cherishes has rather startling results when the miners themselves become converted to it.

> Seething masses of miners met daily, carried away by a new religious impulse. The idea flew through them: "All men are equal on earth," and they would carry the idea to its material fulfilment. After all, is it not the teaching of Christ? . . . "All men are equal in spirit, they are all sons of God. Whence then this obvious *disquality?*" It was a religious creed pushed to its material conclusion. [p. 217]

The real God, then, becomes the machine itself, for it produces the material fulfillment which the miners come to see as a result of the Christian insistence upon equality before God. "Somewhere," to be sure, "Thomas Crich knew this was false." But he does not know why, and neither does his son, although his son sees more clearly how to take advantage of this sad end to which a spiritual ideal has come.

What has happened, of course, is a false translation of spirit into matter.

> Mystic equality lies in abstraction, not in having or in doing, which are processes. In function and process, one man, one part, must of necessity be subordinate to another. It is a condition of being. But the desire for chaos has risen, and the

idea of mechanical equality was the weapon of disruption which should execute the will of men, the will for chaos. [p. 218]

It is doubtful whether Lawrence ever really believed that even mystic equality existed.[22] Certainly any measurable equality was for Lawrence equivalent to chaos, because he firmly believed that "being" was as various as the individuals who possessed it, and that to level it in any way was to pervert it or destroy its meaning. At one point in his career he himself made a kind of translation of spiritual realities into principles of government, and he came up with something startlingly like fascism—even though actual fascism, which he saw beginning in Italy, repelled him.[23] There are, of course, many difficulties involved in translating religious beliefs into the material world, and Lawrence was very far from solving them. But his conviction that the relationship between the unknown and life as each man must live it must be taken into account, that to ignore it is to invite disaster, gave him an excellent position from which to criticize a materialistic society, whose continued and determined procedure has been to ignore or deny that such relationships exist, or to insist that material advances automatically contain spiritual panacea.

22. He spoke at times as if the terms *equal* and *unequal* were simply irrelevant when ontological matters were under consideration. Raymond Williams ("Lawrence's Social Writings," in Spilka, *Critical Essays*, pp. 62-74) considers this evidence that Lawrence insisted too radically upon the separation of "the material issues and issues of feeling," and there is good evidence for this view in Lawrence's essay "Democracy" in *Phoenix*. See also *Women in Love*, pp. 96-97. But the evidence of the novels is overwhelmingly in favor of relating those material issues, the issues of everyday life, to the ultimate needs of the individual.

23. Bertrand Russell came to call him a fascist after his death. Lawrence's letters to him, in response to which Russell says he considered suicide, took place at the height of Lawrence's agonies over the war. At that time Lawrence drew up a plan which does have a fascistic flavor in its insistence upon authoritarian government by those innately superior. See *LM*, pp. 352-56, 366-67. A useful summary of Lawrence's differences from Russell can be found in James L. Jarrett, "D. H. Lawrence and Bertrand Russell," in Moore, *A D. H. Lawrence Miscellany*. See also Russell's *Autobiography* (London, 1968), 2: 20-24, 53-54.

Gerald's vision, then, is in a peculiarly Lawrentian sense a real one. The miners have, by their adoption of a mechanical equality, flattened out what religious capacities they might have had. Gerald's seeing them as "pure instrumentality" is indeed an onto-logical insight. It is ironic, however, that this insight is also a step in his reducing himself to a mere function. Though he sees more clearly than his father that the men have somehow lost their full range of human response, he does not recognize that his own impulse to power is only a more intense form of the same leveling process. He makes the same translation which his father led the miners to make; but from a more philosophic position.

> In his travels, and in his accompanying readings, he had come to the conclusion that the essential secret of life was harmony. He did not define to himself at all clearly what harmony was. The word pleased him, he felt he had come to his own conclusions. And he proceeded to put his philosophy into practice by forcing order into the established world, translating the mystic word harmony into the practical word organisation. [p. 220]

For Lawrence the mystic word *harmony* must refer, if it refers to anything, to the transcendence achieved by opposing forces which the crown symbolized, which understanding came at one point to mean. It has nothing whatever to do with this use of the word *organization*. And this organization, while it directs Gerald's own dark powers, will finally stifle them. Perhaps the most un-fortunate characteristic of machines is that, once they are perfect-ed, they run by themselves. So Gerald, like his colliers, comes to the point where his will, at first crucial to the formation of the machine, is no longer necessary. And since by then he has become almost exclusively a "willing animal," he is not necessary himself.

By this translation, then, Gerald has managed to reconcile the organization which his father created with the sensual powers of his mother. His satisfaction is the same satisfaction we no-ticed Gudrun sharing with the miners, a submission to a me-chanical order which provides easy sensual release. If the chap-ter "Coal Dust" shows us the quality of that release, this chapter shows us its rationalization in the minds of Gerald and the miners.

> They were exalted by belonging to this great and superhuman system which was beyond feeling or reason, something really godlike. Their hearts died within them, but their souls were satisfied. It was what they wanted. Otherwise Gerald could never have done what he did. . . . This was a sort of freedom, the sort they really wanted. It was the first great step in undoing, the first great phase of chaos, the substitution of the mechanical principle for the organic. [p. 223]

Once again Lawrence's language seems to insist upon the fated nature of the whole process, as if the forces behind it were more than anyone could resist. And whatever we think of the metaphysics behind all this, it has as usual psychological plausibility. Slaves, especially unwitting slaves, are free to substitute self-indulgence for self-responsibility.

This long chapter, then, explores in detail the relation between dead civilizations and dead souls which *The Rainbow* treated too sketchily. Through his explanation of the false translations of both Gerald and his father, Lawrence provides a way of answering philosophical and psychological questions which *The Rainbow* evaded. It is not necessary to believe with Lawrence that all of civilization was coming to express mysteriously destructive forces to make the state of the Criches and the colliers plausible, though we must at least take these beliefs into account if we are to understand the full meaning of these scenes. What is most peculiarly Lawrentian here is what we have been noticing all along—the psychological explanations merge into ontological explanations. And with Gerald it is particularly important to realize this, for otherwise it is difficult to feel the sympathy for him which Lawrence surely intended us to feel. If we simply mark him off as slightly twisted, cruel, warped by inadequate parents, fond of power, and deceived as to what that power will cost, he seems too much a monster. But if we realize that Gerald's difficulties reflect an ultimate inadequacy with which he is agonizingly and pathetically trying to cope, we can sympathize with his quest. Although Lawrence makes us feel that Gerald is indeed inviting his own destruction, he also convinces us that Gerald wants intensely to live—certainly more than either Hermione or Gudrun. Of the three he is most willing to face up to his problems, and he therefore shows us the possibility of conquering them. It is because such possibility exists that Gudrun can be said to murder him.

We have already seen that Gerald and Gudrun have much in common. They are both, as Birkin puts it, "flowers of dissolution" (p. 164);[24] they possess a willful, sensual power of demonic tendency. Yet their capacities for life are not identical. One critic has maintained that "life for one is death for the other," but, though this is true to the extent that both at times seek a dominant position, Gudrun emerges as less capable of life than Gerald.[25] In their relationship Lawrence develops a pattern of considerable psychological subtlety, and through this pattern he affirms that even characters as obviously alike as Gerald and Gudrun have different capacities for being.

If it is Gudrun's challenge at the railway crossing which rouses Gerald's interest, it is her dance before Scotch bullocks which leads to his first declaration of love. Like Anna's dance, this is a dance of self-assertion. But it is not so clearly egotistical, nor does it celebrate anything so positive as the cycle of birth. It seems more a moment of demonic release in which sexual excitement and violence are inseparable from an urge to assert an absolute power. The secret power which Gudrun discovers in herself is strongly reminiscent of the black, sensual power which Ursula recognized in the horses, a power from which she fled but which Gudrun welcomes. When Gerald appears, Gudrun's urge for

24. This remark is part of an elaboration of the "black river of corruption," which expresses much the same ideas as the letter to the Bohemians. Birkin embarks on this explanation shortly after Gudrun's dance, probably to give the reader perspective on the dance itself.

25. Daleski, *Forked Flame*, p. 160.

violence comes into the open; she rushes among the cattle, scatters them, and finally strikes Gerald across the face.

Once again the destructive ultimate, the mysterious force of doom which runs beneath the surface of the book, has bubbled to the surface. Upon receiving the blow, Gerald too is caught in it. "He became deadly pale, and a dangerous flame darkened his eyes." " 'You have struck the first blow,' he said at last, forcing the words from his lungs, in a voice so soft and low, it sounded like a dream within her, not spoken in the outer air. 'And I shall strike the last,' she retorted involuntarily, with confident assurance. He was silent, he did not contradict her" (p. 162). But, as prophetic as this is, neither of them realizes what is happening. Gudrun becomes gentle, and Gerald, whose emotions are at an almost uncontrollable pitch, blurts out that he loves her. Gudrun, for all her abandonment in the dance, remains in control throughout. Her sequence of response is like that of her ecstasy before the mare, and it sets a pattern for most of her later ecstasies with Gerald. She briefly loses herself in a moment of intensity (this moment can be either demonically assertive or painfully submissive), refuses to admit the experience fully to her conscious mind after it passes, and returns to a cold state of control, both of herself and, if he is malleable (as he usually is), of Gerald. The second step makes the third, detached state possible; to refuse to admit fully one's demonic vitality allows one to direct it by the will. Gerald is more likely to be crushed and helpless by these assaults from below.[26]

26. As if to provide another reason, one more obviously psychological, for Gerald's insecurity, Lawrence brings the scene between Gerald and Gudrun to an end by reiterating information he gave much earlier. "He walked on beside her, a striding, mindless body. But he recovered a little as he went. He suffered badly. He had killed his brother when a boy, and was set apart, like Cain" (p. 163). In the context of what has just passed, this seems abrupt and somewhat lame. It helps, perhaps, to provide a pat explanation of why Gerald is so worried about and affected by death (not only his father's, but the prospect of his own) and why he moves unwittingly toward self-destruction. But even if it does, it is secondary to his sheer terror over his failure to grasp himself. If suppressed guilt over killing

The prolonged effects of this scene on Gerald are strikingly different from those on Gudrun. From her position of detachment she gradually tightens the sexual bond, kissing and visually caressing Gerald while she paddles the canoe (Gerald has caught his hand in some machinery).[27] Gerald, once his swooning state dies down, feels a new peace; his submission to Gudrun allows him escape. "His mind was almost submerged, he was almost transfused, lapsed out for the first time in his life, into the things about him. For he always kept such a keen attentiveness, concentrated and unyielding in himself. Now he had let go, imperceptibly he was melting into oneness with the whole. It was like pure, perfect sleep, his first great sleep of life" (p. 170). Here we sense a possibility in Gerald which is never evident in Gudrun. The key to it seems to be submission and surrender of the will, as a child surrenders to a mother. Several times Gudrun is able to bring Gerald to this state, but she always does it reluctantly, without knowing what she is doing or against her will altogether. In refusing to allow Gerald this healing experience, she finally goads him to destruction.

A short time later Gudrun herself momentarily realizes that Gerald somehow contains more possibility than she does. She has a kind of vision as he climbs back into the boat after searching vainly for his drowned sister.

Then he clambered into the boat. Oh, and the beauty of the subjection of his loins, white and dimly luminous as he climbed over the side of the boat, made her want to die, to die. The beauty of his dim and luminous loins as he climbed into the boat, his back rounded and soft—ah, this was too much for her,

---

a brother contributes to Gerald's tenuous state, it does not explain it as it is repeatedly portrayed.

27. When described summarily, this scene seems much more blatantly symbolic than it actually is. Lawrence presents almost a panorama of activity on the water, and this rendering of light and movement, along with the continuing account of the sexual tension itself, keeps both Gudrun's paddling and Gerald's machine-mutilation happily subordinate.

too final a vision. She knew it, and it was fatal. The terrible hopelessness of fate, and of beauty, such beauty!

He was not like a man to her, he was an incarnation, a great phase of life. She saw him press the water out of his face, and look at the bandage on his hand. And she knew it was all no good, and that she would never go beyond him, he was the final approximation of life to her. [p. 173]

This is an insight which she emphatically rejects at the end of the book, but the events bear out its truth. Not only does she fail to go beyond him, she never really accepts him. It is characteristic of Gudrun to link physical beauty with fate, for her concentration on the sensual is a kind of fate in its exclusiveness. Gerald's dim and luminous loins, like the African statue, are a final vision. Gudrun sees this and realizes in an intuitive flash that all are linked with death, but she does not understand why.

In the chapter portentously titled "Death and Love," the differences between Gerald and Gudrun are brought to a climax. As his father nears death, Gerald exerts his will to triumph over it. But a "great dark void" is at the "centre of his soul." To fill it he turns to Gudrun, asking her straightforwardly for sympathy. She has a kind of reverence for his self-possession, aside from the sexual attraction which has been developing for some time. He walks her home and slips his arm about her waist. "But then, his arm was so strong, she quailed under its powerful close grasp. She died a little death and was drawn against him as they walked down the stormy darkness. He seemed to balance her perfectly in opposition to himself, in their dual motion of walking. So, suddenly, he was liberated and perfect, strong, heroic." Gudrun's responses are more ambivalent: "The exultation in his voice was like a sweetish, poisonous drug to her. Did she then mean so much to him! She sipped the poison" (p. 321). This ambivalence is developed at length. She longs for an intimate embrace but fears it as well. While Gerald strips himself before her, telling her she is everything, she can only manage an increasingly intense mixture of exultance and doubt.

In contrast, Gerald needs nothing more than Gudrun's willing physical presence to transform him. The implication is both that he is desperate for the most fundamental human contact and that he has a capacity to receive it. "His arms were fast around her, he seemed to be gathering her into himself, her warmth, her softness, her adorable weight, drinking in the suffusion of her physical being, avidly. He lifted her, and seemed to pour her into himself, like wine into a cup" (p. 323). For a moment Gudrun almost lets herself reach a similar state, but her glory in possession soon returns, and the "desirable unknown" gradually becomes "descendentalized."

> She reached up, like Eve reaching to the apples on the tree of knowledge, and she kissed him, though her passion was a transcendent fear of the thing he was. . . . How perfect and foreign he was—ah, how dangerous! Her soul thrilled with the complete knowledge. This was the glistening, forbidden apple, this face of a man. . . . He was such an unutterable enemy, yet glistening with uncanny white fire. She wanted to touch him and touch him and touch him, till she had him all in her hands, till she had strained him into her knowledge. Ah, if she could have the precious *knowledge* of him, she would be filled, and nothing could deprive her of this. [p. 324]

> Ah, her hands were eager, greedy for knowledge. But for the present it was enough, enough, as much as her soul could bear. Too much, and she would shatter herself, she would fill the fine vial of her soul too quickly, and it would break. [p. 325]

Surely this is as much self-deception as it is insight on Gudrun's part. Her desire for knowledge is largely a delight in the forbidden, and she therefore hovers in a curious middle ground between the sort of knowing which Tom Brangwen has of Lydia and the more limited sense in which Hermione wants to know. The more Gudrun insists that she can have her knowledge in her hands, the more we realize that she is trying to attach an ontological significance to the merely physical. The difference between the "firm cup" which Lawrence uses to represent Gerald and the "fine vial" which is Gudrun reflects the difference in their capacities to contain life. It is not that the sensual and the ontological have no legitimate connection, but that Gudrun needs to retain an illusion of control, both of Gerald and, more fundamentally, of herself. This is why the pornographic element, the relish of the forbidden, is always present; to avoid admitting the reality of her need, she presents it to herself as the all-too-commonplace desire for forbidden fruit. That she almost recognizes true possibility is implied in her perception that Gerald's otherness is important (at least this fits the positive doctrine that emerges from the book). But as usual she relies upon the wrong concepts, the limited concepts of sense divorced from its deeper meanings.

When the sexual consummation finally comes, it is not demonic at all. For Gerald it is a resurrection, a purgation of death, a healing, the finding of a mother; for Gudrun it is "an ecstasy of subjection, throes of acute, violent sensation" (p. 337). In rendering it Lawrence uses the highly detailed, realistic mode of *Sons and Lovers,* creating an intense suspense in the fear of discovery by the Brangwen family (Gerald barges, boots muddy from his father's grave, right into the Brangwen house and Gudrun's bedroom) but moving, as always, into an exploration of his more transcendental themes. An increasingly detailed account of Gerald's undressing suddenly switches to the psychological-ontological mode Lawrence characteristically uses to describe sexual experience.

Quickly he pulled off his jacket, pulled loose his black tie, and was unfastening his studs, which were headed each with a pearl. She listened, watching, hoping no one would hear the starched linen crackle. It seemed to snap like pistol-shots.

He had come for vindication. He found in her an infinite relief. Into her he poured all his pent-up darkness and corrosive death, and he was whole again. It was wonderful, marvellous, it was a miracle. This was the ever-recurrent miracle of his life, at the knowledge of which he was lost in an ecstasy of relief and wonder. The terrible frictional violence of death filled her, and she received it in an ecstasy of subjection, in throes of acute, violent sensation. [p. 337]

Gerald's need is so great that Gudrun's mere physical cooperation, given the significance he has already attached to her as his savior ("If there weren't you in the world, then I shouldn't be in the world, either"), brings him the peace he seeks. For Gudrun, however, the sexual act emphatically does not provide new life. Her violent sensations give way to "perfect consciousness," and she looks into the darkness and sees nothing. She cannot sleep.

Why Gudrun is brought to a state of "violent active superconsciousness" can only be explained by assuming that she is radically deficient in a way Gerald is not. For once she seems to have given up her will; Gerald's appearance was overwhelming, his needs so apparent and intense as to be "supernatural." "She sighed. She was lost now. She had no choice." And even though Lawrence fully supplies the usual psychological reasons for difficulty—they are hidden in her room, in hearing distance of the whole family—in the context of everything we know about Gerald and Gudrun such reasons are not nearly sufficient. Clearly Gudrun, as was implied from the first, is beyond hope of the "right" response. She cannot surmount "this awful, inhuman distance which would always be interposed between her and the other being!" Gerald's very presence becomes nauseating to her, and though she recognizes that "her passion for him was not yet satisfied, perhaps never could be satisfied," she feels "old, old." She can only think that "one must preserve oneself"; to this she devotes the rest of her efforts.

For Gerald the experience is a real completion, but it does not imply that he is suddenly self-sufficient. "He was a man again, strong and rounded. And he was a child, so soothed and restored and full of gratitude. And she, she was the great bath of life, he worshipped her. Mother and substance of all life she was. And he, child and man, received of her and was made whole" (p. 337).

Not only does this imply a dependence which we have reason to think Gudrun will abuse, but it entirely circumvents the demonic sensualism which is undeniably present in Gerald when he is in control of his will. If Gudrun were willing to play the mother and offer Gerald the tenderness which he has apparently never had, there might be hope that he would achieve a satisfactory independence in time, which in turn would enable him to seek the ultimate about which Birkin preaches. But this assumes a different Gudrun from the one we know. What in fact happens is that she, in her effort to preserve herself from the agonizing views of eternity which submission to Gerald bring, exploits the violent bond which they have already formed, makes him depend on it, and then removes it. Of course he kills himself when she does.

The development of the bond between Ursula and Birkin is even more complicated than that between Gerald and Gudrun. Or at least it takes more surprising turns, especially in the arguments through which Ursula and Birkin try to define it. This is because of the intellectual nature of Birkin's search, which is also Lawrence's search. Everything about the self must be questioned if one is to discover what it is. The pattern which emerges, then, is dialectical in at least two ways; the arguments develop intellectual oppositions, and beneath the verbal battles lie more fundamental oppositions, which the words may either reveal or mask. The resolution of words does not necessarily coincide, of course, with the resolution of emotional states (see pp. 244ff. above). But the relation of words to emotional states is on the whole more positive than negative. If Birkin's fault is talking too much, certainly that talk is good for him. Through it he not only releases certain inhibiting tensions but also discovers why they are inhibiting; through it he not only gets Hermione out of his system, he also converts Ursula.

From a distance none of this looks very complicated. It is fairly clear from the outset that Hermione and Birkin will separate and that Ursula and Birkin will come together. It should not, then, be difficult to sort out the stages of progress. But confronting some of the arguments does not readily yield such stages; in any given scene everyone speaking is likely to be partly right and partly wrong, and it is not always obvious how the arguments line up. The "Classroom" scene which we have already examined gives some indication of this, but it is one of the clearest in the book. There Ursula and Birkin oppose Hermione for reasons which the rest of the book largely bears out as valid. Matters become more complicated when, for example, Hermione and Ursula line up against Birkin, especially if we keep in mind that Ursula's role is to wean Birkin from Hermione. Yet it is largely these complications which make the arguments worth reading. Most unsympathetic readings of this book tend to slight the complexity of both the evolving drama and the ideas themselves. Once they are taken into account it is difficult to maintain that Lawrence is using his novel as a pulpit, that he is forcing Lawrentian dogma on the reader.

Perhaps the most dramatic function of Birkin's talk is its tendency to foster a violent emotional outburst: "I want every man to have his share in the world's goods, so that I am rid of his importunity, so that I can tell him: 'Now you've got what you want—you've got your fair share of the world's gear. Now, you one-mouthed fool, mind yourself and don't obstruct me' " (p. 97). Birkin is continuing in chapter 8 the argument about individualism (the value of "intrinsic otherness") which cropped up in chapter 2. These words have a curious effect on Hermione. "She heard his words in her unconscious self, *consciously* she was as if deafened, she paid no heed to them" (p. 97). Birkin's words come at the end of a series of outbursts in which he asserts himself somewhat vindictively (as he comes to recognize) against Hermione and her insistence upon spiritual equality. In this distinction between her conscious deafness and unconscious hearing, Lawrence indicates that she is willing not to listen and perhaps does not even receive Birkin's ideas into her head, but that his opposition affects her despite all her resistance. Very soon afterward she has a paperweight of lapis lazuli in her hand. "Terrible shocks ran over her body, like shocks of electricity, as if many volts of electricity suddenly struck her down. . . . Then swiftly, in a flame that drenched down her body like fluid lightning and gave her a perfect, unutterable satisfaction, she brought down the ball of jewel stone with all her force, crash on his head" (p. 98). This is Hermione's "voluptuous consummation," her single release into the dark, sensual world which has been forcing expression in her heavy movements and animal noises. There is no better example in the book of the indirect connection between word and deed, between talk and action, that is assumed in all Lawrence's arguments. By the time Hermione ceases to hear Birkin's talk she has fallen back on language as gesture, on its subconceptual function as a vehicle for antagonism. She responds directly to Birkin's attack, finally rendering his words irrelevant.

Perhaps this is just another way of saying that Lawrence's arguments always reflect something about his characters' ultimate states, but it has some use in indicating how closely his dialectics are related to his more symbolic modes. In one sense his scenes of argument, abstract though the issues may be, are really nonintellectual; the characters usually respond as much to the implied attitude or emotional state of the speaker as to what he says, and almost every argument that gathers any steam dissolves or explodes in ad hominem irrelevancies. Yet these "irrelevancies" often reveal more about the emotional realities than the "logical" argument does. And since the narrative modes which deal most directly with emotion are those symbolic modes which are attached to the darker themes of the book, argument readily and naturally yields to the symbolic scene, which in turn provides a kind of commentary on the issues and emphasizes their relation to the rest of the book.

Hermione's attempted murder of Birkin develops into just such an extended symbolic scene. Her attack is both an unwitting refutation of Birkin's charge that she is too spiritual and a final affirmation that he is right. In that it is her only truly mindless act, following the sequence of sexual consummation ("electric" arousal, a climax of "voluptous bliss" when striking the blow, a drugged sleep afterward), it proves that her darker half is very much alive. But as a symbolic gesture it is an attack upon the restricting mind and its patterns of escape (both her own and Birkin's), for she directs an object of beauty at Birkin's head. When it is over, she ironically thinks of it as a pure, spiritual act. Unlike the more successful varieties of sexual consummation, this one brings no real change to her everyday self, just as Gudrun's and Gerald's sexual acts fail to create a lasting change, especially in Gudrun. Birkin, however, transforms the attack into a rite of purgation by taking off his clothes and forcing his naked body against the flora,[28] acting out a release from Hermione and all she stands for. He sees very little of her after this, and Ursula is left almost a clear field.

But Hermione still remains a friend; she continues to symbolize, even when absent from the action, Birkin's own willfulness. So a great deal more argument is necessary, most of it more controlled than the outburst which led to Hermione's violent act. This often requires from the reader not only constant attention to underlying emotional currents but a determined intellectual analysis of what is said. Lawrence's full meaning emerges only after the arguments are carefully weighed, not only against the known biases of the speakers but against each other.

For example, the most vexing of Birkin's false concepts is "the dominant principle," which allows him to condone Gerald's treatment of the horse and which lines him up with Hermione against Ursula. Although he attacks Hermione for her "obscene will," Birkin describes Gerald's mare in this fashion: " 'And of course,' he said to Gerald, 'horses *haven't* got a complete will, like human beings. A horse has no *one* will. Every horse, strictly, has two

28. This is certainly bizarre and perhaps even mad, but it is madness with a method in it. Birkin is obviously in revolt against the world of people who hide violence from themselves and let it break out in viciousness. To be sure, it is an extreme form of rejection to "love the vegetation," as Birkin says he would do if he had an island to himself. But I doubt that it is more absurd than saying "thou" to a tree, as Martin Buber would have us do, and for reasons quite similar. For Lawrence, too, trees have a distinct being which one can profitably recognize, and in this scene they represent uncorrupted nature as well.

wills. With one will, it wants to put itself in the human power completely—and with the other, it wants to be free, wild' " (p. 132). Ursula objects: "Why should a horse want to put itself in the human power?" Birkin replies that the impulse to do so is "perhaps the highest love-impulse: resign your will to the higher being." When Ursula jeers, he adds, "and woman is the same as horses." Ursula responds to this by striking up a friendship with Hermione, which lasts just long enough to condemn Birkin for the same reasons he condemned Hermione in the classroom, for thinking that "everything must be realised in the head."

Of course the scene is full of overstatement; it is clear from Ursula's growing revulsion to Hermione, even while they work out their condemnation of Birkin, that Hermione's insistence upon spirituality is excessive, but there is certainly truth in the charge that Birkin's love for analysis is getting the better of him. What it comes down to is another false concept, which implies that the female should submit to the male as higher being. Birkin's definition of love as this form of submission will not suffice, either for Ursula or for his own later formulations. Yet the idea of submission to some form of higher being is not in itself wrong, if we are to judge by what follows. It is just that higher being does not translate into male domination of female; it comes to mean mutual submission of each to the unknown. What Ursula responds to negatively is simply Birkin's egotism, which he expresses through his neat formulation of his own superiority. Yet her agreement with Hermione that Birkin is being irreverent simply by defining matters is itself a kind of false conceptualization, for the fault is not so much in Birkin's attempt to define as in what he comes up with. Hermione as usual keeps insisting that holiness is being destroyed, and Ursula finds this oppressive. Furthermore, Ursula is held to Birkin by "some bond, some deep principle."

It is the nature of this deep principle which Ursula helps Birkin to discover, by getting him to admit that a willed approach to love is not the proper way to arrive at his impersonal goals. Yet she, too, must finally admit that her insistence upon love has an

egotistic element which must be expunged. These two admissions
come to pass gradually, through the sort of argumentative scenes
we have been analyzing. We can understand neither adequately if
we do not consider what the characters say as seriously as how
they act.

This pattern of qualification, often intricate, lends itself to
comic effect. People who characteristically overstate, however
serious their motives, cannot altogether escape appearing comic;
it is to Lawrence's credit that his alter ego Birkin is effectively
mocked, even while straining toward his most Lawrentian pronouncements. This is perhaps most obvious in the "Mino" chapter. On her way to tea Ursula falls into a "dream world" whose
nature is described by an image already familiar from *The Rainbow:* "She had fallen strange and dim, out of the sheath of the
material life, as a berry falls from the only world it has ever
known, down out of the sheath on to the real unknown" (p.
136). Birkin, too, is "moved outside himself"; everything seems
ready for the "ultimate experience" toward which they presumably yearn. But Birkin seeks it the wrong way. He asks for an
"irrevocable" pledge with a "clang of mistrust and anger in his
voice" and begins to preach at her on the theme of "the real
impersonal me," repeatedly referring to "the stars" to illustrate
the impersonal balance he seeks. Ursula, who still wants an old-
fashioned sort of romantic love, interprets all this as a form of
selfishness, as a plea for masculine supremacy like that which
Birkin seemed to be making in his discussion of women and
horses. Birkin is very earnest, and this makes Ursula uncomfortable; so it would make us, if Lawrence did not allow her to under-
cut it repeatedly.

"You are very conceited, Monsieur," she mocked. "How do
you know what my womanly feelings are, or my thoughts or
my ideas? You don't even know what I think of you now."

"Nor do I care in the slightest."

"I think you are very silly. I think you want to tell me you
love me, and you go all this way round to do it."

"All right," he said, looking up with sudden exasperation.
"Now go away then, and leave me alone. I don't want any more
of your meretricious persiflage." [p. 139]

Birkin is once again the petulant child about whom Hermione
complained. What he is preaching is not, of course, silly in itself,
once we separate the doctrine from the overblown manner in
which he pushes it on Ursula. His request for a pledge is a legitimate demand for ethical commitment, and his insistence upon
separateness does not need star imagery to support it. But he is
unsure both of his emotional situation and of the force of his
doctrines, so as usual he overstates. This overstatement is particularly evident in his analysis of a little scene in which his cat Mino
cuffs and dominates a female cat that strayed in from the
woods.[29] He argues that Mino is seeking a "pure stable equilibri-
um" and is creating order for the stray cat's "chaos," again implying masculine domination. Birkin driven to make absurdly
phrased statements such as "I am with him entirely. He wants
superfine stability." This Ursula immediately interprets as
bossiness.

Ursula, though too egotistic as well, effectively reduces Birkin
to absurdity by instantly spotting the insecurity underlying his
insistence. In his awareness of the comedy inherent in Birkin's
overseriousness, Lawrence goes far in meeting the objections that
he is forcing his doctrine down the reader's throat. His relation to
Birkin's "star-equilibrium," whatever it may have been in his
expository writings, remains here healthily tentative. As Ursula's
criticisms unfold, it becomes clear that in this sense the ideas
themselves are neither affirmed nor denied; with the usual (and

29. Critics tend to read scenes like these with great solemnity, missing
the humor that is surely present. See especially Daleski (*Forked Flame*, p.
173), who takes Lawrence to task for not making the scene more powerful.
See also David J. Gordon's "*Women in Love* and the Lawrentian Aesthetic," in my anthology, *Twentieth Century Interpretations of "Women
in Love"* (Englewood Cliffs, N.J., 1969), pp. 50-60, for the more forceful
objection that the humor is inconsistently maintained and "sometimes
crude."

here surely deserved) ad hominem twist, she focuses on Birkin's inability to practice what he preaches.

> "I don't trust you when you drag in the stars," she said. "If you were quite true, it wouldn't be necessary to be so far-fetched."
>
> "Don't trust me then," he said, angry. "It is enough that I trust myself."
>
> "And that is where you make another mistake," she replied. "You *don't* trust yourself. You don't fully believe yourself what you are saying. You don't really want this conjunction, otherwise you wouldn't talk so much about it, you'd get it." [p. 144]

But if Birkin and the ideas he preaches are mocked, some of those ideas gradually emerge as more adequate than others. His submission, even though it contains ironic reservations, affects his later preaching. The significant change is toward a more human acceptance of Ursula, which is reflected in the disappearance not only of parables of domination and submission but of an acceptance of even the old-fashioned sort of love as a starting point toward the "impersonal beyond." The argument—and now I mean Lawrence's argument—goes on, not in spite of but because of the emotional qualification and apparent irrelevancies into which it falls.

After the famous scene in which Birkin throws rocks at the moon's reflection,[30] he finally becomes sufficiently self-critical

---

30. After reading Colin Clarke's analysis of this passage (*River of Dissolution,* pp. 100-04), I discarded my own, which came very close to his reading. Clarke qualifies Hough and others by arguing that the rock throwing is most fundamentally an attack on Birkin's own egoistic rigidity (and Ursula's too). I would only add a manuscript passage which indicates that Lawrence was struggling with the same uneasy mixture of femininity and individuality that we saw in the *Study of Thomas Hardy:*

Antemis—Tanit—Mylitta—Aphrodite—be damned to her. She's really supreme now—if you should begrudge it her—damn her. All is two, all is not one. That's the point. That's the secret of secrets. You've got to

to realize the error of his way. He first achieves a simple awareness of the inconsistencies in his preaching, which reflect the
basic conflict within himself. "He thought he had been wrong,
perhaps. Perhaps he had been wrong, to go to her with an idea of
what he wanted. Was it really only an idea, or was it the interpretation of a profound yearning? If the latter, how was it he was
always talking about sensual fulfilment? The two did not agree
very well" (p. 245). His egotism had arisen from a split between
mind and body similar to that of Gerald. This is something which
Hermione has seen all along but which Birkin has been unwilling
to admit.[31] Once he understands this much, Birkin can go on to
analyze what he does want more cogently. He reflects at length
about sensuality and the African statue which embodies it for
him and realizes more clearly than before that this way is destructive, a "lapse from pure integral being." Tired by speculation, his
"strained attention gave way." "There was another way, the way
of freedom."

There was the paradisal entry into pure, single being, the
individual soul taking precedence over love and desire for
union, stronger than any pangs of emotion, a lovely state of
free proud singleness, which accepted the obligation of the
permanent connection with others, and with the other, submits
to the yoke and leash of love, but never forfeits its own proud

---

build a new world on that, if you build one at all. All is two, all is not
one. In the beginning, all was two. The one is the result. That which is
created is One. That's the result, the consummation. But the beginning is
two, it is not one. And created is two, the whole is two, it is not one.
There you've got it. I wonder what the Priscillianists really made of it?"
[Typescript, p. 302; Roberts's listing, E441D]

Birkin identifies mythological figures who have in common associations
with the moon and fertility as representatives of a primal unity. He resists
this unity because it seems possessive, female, uncreative. But if "the whole
is two," he does not know how to formulate the duality "creatively"
himself. As his repeated outbursts about domination show, he and Lawrence both have trouble reconciling the idea of submission with the idea of
individual distinctness.

31. See *Women in Love*, p. 289.

individual singleness, even while it loves and yields. [p. 247]

Birkin has finally come to accept Ursula's version of love, romantic though it may be, as related to his own more transcendental endeavor. He has seen the necessity of relating his religious yearnings to the real world; up to this point he has been preaching from a standpoint of rejection of the more mundane aspects of love, a hopelessly idealistic position. This way of freedom is also idealistic, but it represents a real integration of attitude which makes experience of the ultimate at least possible. Philosophically, of course, difficulties remain; the relation of obligation to the yoke of love is not clear, nor is it clear how submission can preserve proud individual singleness. These are not only Birkin's difficulties but Lawrence's as well. Yet this does not mean that the doctrine is nonsense. In what follows Lawrence tests it by making Birkin try to act it out, and in some measure he succeeds. The extent and manner in which he fails reflect not only the problems of putting visions into flesh but the whole problem of arguing oneself into visions in the first place.

Birkin has arrived at the truest formulation of his goal by a double process of debate (with himself, with Ursual) and of action, both in emotional interchange with Ursula and in symbolic action (rolling in the vegetation and attacking the moon). His manner of working out his problems is, of course, strikingly different from anyone's behavior in *The Rainbow,* and those differences reveal significant changes in Lawrence's concerns and methods. For example, not only is Birkin more articulate than Tom Brangwen, but he is from the first more detached from every aspect of the real world. The only sort of significant relationship that Birkin has and Tom does not is social, and he repudiates it increasingly throughout the book. Birkin, therefore, is thrown upon his own resources much more, and he can only order them mentally, despite his recognition that the mental can be deathly. This fundamental shift in the Lawrentian hero is particularly evident in Birkin's relation to nature, which is illustrated in the two symbolic scenes. Where Tom Brangwen depended upon nature for his very being, Birkin, much more the modern man, approaches it with a mixture of desire and rebellion. He seeks connection with it because of his revolt against humanity, he preaches about its beauty and superiority to man, but he never connects with it in the sense that Tom does. Instead he approaches it for self-definition and release from his problems. He is even guilty of a form of pathetic fallacy, despite his continued insistence upon singleness, for he obviously sees in nature what his needs compel him to see, not necessarily what is there. He rolls in the flowers to cleanse himself and apparently rejoices in a mysterious affinity with them; but such rejoicing is evidently a response to violent trauma rather than a new direction, and in this sense it is mad. The rock-throwing scene also develops a personal crisis without attempting to suggest meanings in nature. There is no vital infusion from or association with natural forces, only a struggle symbolic of inner tensions.

In the figure of Birkin, then, Lawrence takes up most directly the problem of alienation which is supposed to be the mark of the modern age. Of all the Lawrentian characters Birkin is the most *déraciné,* the most intellectual and argumentative, and probably the most stubborn in his insistence that his alienation will not come to nothing. It is in this stubbornness that whatever heroism he has resides. With the exception of Ursula, all the other characters in this book refuse to admit fully the degree to which they too are alienated from the vital issues in which, as Lawrence argues, our only salvation lies. Like Birkin, they do not connect with nature; of all Lawrence's novels, this is the only one without one or more pastoral figures. Unlike Birkin, however, the characters in this book recognize no necessity for natural contact, unless we consider Hermione's straining at the flowers such a recognition. They are all eminently civilized, and their civilization is itself an emblem of their doomed natures. Birkin's stubbornness, spiritual in motivation and intellectual in form, allows him to recognize the degree to which civilization is dead and to alienate himself from a world already alienated from life, transforming rootlessness into possibility. In this sense he goes beyond the heroes of a Kafka or Camus; his problem is not lack of faith but lack of freedom in which that faith can be realized.

This lack of freedom is, as we have seen, a problem that can be approached intellectually, and so Birkin continually struggles for consciousness. Finally there comes a point where a conscious struggle toward an unconscious state becomes an obstructing paradox; nothing short of a leap of faith will suffice to take Birkin beyond it. Presumably Birkin has had the necessary faith all along; when the time and opportunity come he manages to put his struggle for consciousness aside. The continued argument between him and Ursula gives way to a scene of consummation. But if Birkin succeeds, something goes wrong with Lawrence's rendering of that success. As we watch the scene develop we shall see that Lawrence's own mental habits, which are in many ways responsible for the impressive success of this book as a whole, are not so successfully put aside as Birkin's.

Many of the critics have noticed that at least parts of the scenes of consummation are not successful.[32] We can conveniently see why they fail by applying the same sort of analysis to Lawrence's descriptive technique as we have been using on Birkin's arguments. After the most violent argument in the book (Ursula expatiates on Birkin's "foulness," which she says that he pretends is "purity"), both Birkin and Ursula seemed purged, and settle into a new state of peace. Birkin feels a "passionate tenderness" and becomes "smiling and transcendent." When they stop at an inn for tea, Ursula, too, loses her aggressiveness. "She recalled again the old magic of the Book of Genesis, where the sons of God saw the daughters of men, that they were fair. And he was one of these, one of these strange creatures from the beyond, looking down at her, and seeing she was fair" (p. 304). This, of course, is a direct echo of Ursula's yearning in *The Rainbow.* Precisely what Ursula and Birkin are going through eludes strict definition, but it is at least clear that it is something neither has experienced be-

32. See, e.g., Hough, *The Dark Sun,* p. 82; also Leavis, *D. H. Lawrence,* pp. 178-79.

fore. "This was release at last. She had had lovers, she had known passion. But this was neither love nor passion. It was the daughters of men coming back to the sons of God, the strange inhuman sons of God who are in the beginning" (p. 305). Obviously Ursula's religious quest is being fulfilled, just as Birkin's hunger for the free experience of the beyond is about to be fulfilled. The lovers move from the violence of conflict to the tenderness of love to, finally, the unknown. It is only unfortunate that the final moments, unlike Tom Brangwen's transcendent moments, become somewhat obsessively and therefore bathetically localized.

> She traced with her hands the line of his loins and thighs, at the back, and a living fire ran through her, from him, darkly. It was a dark flood of electric passion she released from him, drew into herself. She had established a rich new circuit, a new current of passional electric energy, between the two of them.

> It was a perfect passing away for both of them, and at the same time the most intolerable accession into being, the marvellous fullness of immediate gratification, overwhelming, outflooding from the source of the deepest life-force, the darkest, deepest, strangest life-source of the human body, at the back and base of the loins. [p. 306]

This almost works; we are almost convinced that the electric passion is something qualitatively different from and more significant than anything the lovers have experienced before. But Lawrence seems to have overestimated the flooding force of his prose. Transcendental forces cannot be convincingly located at the back and base of the loins. Even the slightest attempt to visualize this place brings bathos, and the scene unfortunately demands that it be visualized; Ursula is kneeling before Birkin, caressing "the full, rounded body of his loins." The flesh, especially this flesh, is recalcitrant when called upon to embody mystical forces.

In more general terms, Lawrence seems to have violated some of his own dicta, or at least some of Birkin's. Back in the scene with the cat he explained the impersonal and final realm of being this way: "There is no standard for action there, because no understanding has been reaped from that plane. It is quite inhuman—so there can be no calling to book, in any form whatsoever—because one is outside the pale of all that is accepted, and nothing known applies. One can only follow the impulse" (p. 138). Bearing this passage in mind, we can see that Lawrence's inadequacies in conveying the nature of this inhuman experience are precisely parallel to Birkin's inadequacies throughout the book; when nothing known applies, a description that takes the trouble to place an ontological force or state is a form of false conceptualization. Birkin and Ursula may have learned to put those parts of the mind which interfere with religious experience behind them, but Lawrence himself has not, or at least not quite.

This difficulty continues to appear as the lovers move toward the sexual consummation which marks their union as complete. The basic fault is still a form of overarticulation. One encounters in passing, "He looked at her with his strange, non-human singleness." It is almost embarrassing, moreover, to find the star-equilibrium, which Ursula mocked for being too preachy and lacking in conviction, passed on here without a hint of irony: "They would give each other this star-equilibrium which alone is freedom." "She was next to him, and hung in a pure rest, as a star is hung, balanced unthinkably." When the lovers finally come together, these too-familiar labels become less obtrusive, and the pulsation of Lawrence's prose almost catches us up in the experience as it has done many times before. But still it does not quite work.

They threw off their clothes, and he gathered her to him, and found her, found the pure lambent reality of her for ever invisible flesh. Quenched, inhuman, his fingers upon her unrevealed nudity were the fingers of silence, the body of mysterious night upon the body of mysterious night, the night masculine and feminine, never to be seen with the eye, or known with the mind, only known as a palpable revelation of living otherness.
    She had her desire of him, she touched, she received the

maximum of unspeakable communication in touch, dark, subtle, positively silent, a magnificent gift and give again, a perfect acceptance and yielding, a mystery, the reality of that which can never be known, vital, sensual reality that can never be transmuted into mind content, but remains outside, living body of darkness and silence and subtlety, the mystic body of reality. She had her desire fulfilled. He had his desire fulfilled. For she was to him what he was to her, the immemorial magnificence of mystic, palpable, real otherness. [p. 312]

The difficulty remains in the didacticism which Lawrence slips in along with emotional and physical detail. A more successful moment of transcendence from *The Rainbow* provides a helpful comparison.

His blood beat up in waves of desire. He wanted to come to her, to meet her. She was there, if he could reach her. The reality of her who was just beyond him absorbed him. Blind and destroyed, he pressed forward, nearer, nearer, to receive the consummation of himself, be received within the darkness which should swallow him and yield him up to himself. If he could come really within the blazing kernel of darkness, if really he could be destroyed, burnt away till he lit with her in one consummation, that were supreme, supreme.

Their coming together now, after two years of married life, was much more wonderful to them than it had been before. It was the entry into another circle of existence, it was the baptism to another life, it was the complete confirmation. Their feet trod strange ground of knowledge, their footsteps were lit-up with discovery. [*Rainbow,* p. 87]

It might be claimed that the language used here is just as abstract as that in the earlier passage, so that both succeed or fail for the same reasons. The strange ground of knowledge is in itself no more dramatic than a palpable revelation of living otherness. But the former strikes us as much less obtrusive and insistent. The scene from *The Rainbow* unfolds through Tom Brangwen's mind, which remains the consistent focus, even though Lawrence is employing his usual mode halfway between narrator and character. What we sense are Tom's strainings and Tom's rewards. The scene with Birkin and Ursula really has no comparable focus; their experience is seen more from the outside. Part of this effect is simply a result of the greater frequency of transcendent language throughout the scene, which acts against our sense that the experience is unfolding. The narrator tells us quite early that the ultimate in otherness is upon them, and he continues to insist on this. The rhythm of the prose will not quite overcome this insistence.

The best way to regard these difficulties is to see them as a struggle for consciousness which did not quite succeed. Birkin's remark that merely insisting upon something does not make it happen applies even more to Lawrence than to Birkin. For Birkin is allowed to stop defining; Lawrence was not quite able to stop, or he did not stop soon enough. If the nature of religious experience is by definition beyond definition, other, less explicit means must be found for conveying it. Lawrence often appears quite aware of this, both in his treatment of similar scenes and in much of Birkin's talk. That he could not always act upon this awareness seems to indicate a personal insecurity about the doctrine itself, analogous to the insecurity he effectively conveys in Birkin.[33]

We have at several points noticed that the two "destructive ultimates," manifested on the one hand in habits which are mental, abstract, and inhibitory of sensual release and on the other hand in a demonic sensuality which delights in disregarding such habits, have a relation to one another which approaches identity. Sensual propensities mask tendencies toward "abstract willing," as in Gudrun, and insistence upon consciousness and knowledge masks tendencies for purely sensual gratification, as in Hermione or in Birkin himself. In the last three chapters of the book Lawrence works out these implied relationships more fully and brings

33. The later novels provide ample evidence for insecurity about Lawrentian doctrine.

them to logical conclusions. Birkin's earlier reflections might well serve as a preface to this part of the book:

There remained this way, this awful African process, to be fulfilled. It would be done differently by the white races. The white races, having the Arctic north behind them, the vast abstraction of ice and snow, would fulfil a mystery of ice-destructive knowledge, snow-abstract annihilation. Whereas the West Africans, controlled by the burning death-abstraction of the Sahara, had been fulfilled in sun-destruction, the putrescent mystery of sun-rays. [p. 246]

This is Birkin's only explicit identification of the two main streams of destruction. It leads him not only to his discovery of the way of freedom but to reflections on Gerald. "Birkin thought of Gerald. He was one of these strange white wonderful demons from the north, fulfilled in the destructive frost mystery. And was he fated to pass away in this knowledge, this one process of frost-knowledge, death by perfect cold? Was he a messenger, an omen of the universal dissolution into whiteness and snow?" (pp. 246-47). The answer to the first of these questions is a qualified yes; the second is left open.

As Birkin's prophetic questioning implies, the major part of these last chapters is devoted to Gerald and Gudrun. It is they who have unfinished business; Gudrun's determination to preserve herself will not allow resolution by submission, and Gerald has yet to follow his demonic propensities to some sort of conclusion. Ursula and Birkin have come to a significant resolution; they cannot, therefore, endure the essentially destructive atmosphere of the "snows of abstraction" in Switzerland and leave for a warmer climate, returning only when the struggle between Gerald and Gudrun is over. But for Gudrun the mountains bring a new sort of religious experience.

In front was a valley shut in under the sky, the last huge slopes of snow and black rock, and at the end, like the navel of the earth, a white-folded wall, and two peaks glimmering in the late

light. Straight in front ran the cradle of silent snow, between
the great slopes that were fringed with a little roughness of pine
trees, like hair, round the base. But the cradle of snow ran on to
the eternal closing-in, where the walls of snow and rock rose
impenetrable, and the mountain peaks above were in heaven
immediate. This was the centre, the knot, the navel of the
world, where the earth belonged to the skies, pure, unapproach-
able, impassable.

It filled Gudrun with a strange rapture. She crouched in front
of the window, clenching her face in her hands, in a sort of
trance. At last she had arrived, she had reached her place. Here
at last she folded her venture and settled down like a crystal in
the navel of snow and was gone. [p. 391]

Gudrun's place is the ultimate in dead ends. Her response to it
excludes Gerald, who, when he finally gets her to look at him,
finds in her eyes "terror and a little horror." She is rapturous but
hardly joyful. "He knew that there were tears in her eyes, her
own tears, tears of her strange religion, that put him to nought."
The reason for her tears is revealed after she comes back to the
inn, as she watches darkness fall on those same peaks.

Blue evening had fallen over the cradle of snow and over the
great pallid slopes. But in the heaven the peaks of snow were
rosy, glistening like transcendent, radiant spikes of blossom in
the heavenly upper world, so lovely and beyond.

Gudrun saw all their loveliness, she *knew* how immortally
beautiful they were, great pistils of rose-coloured, snow-fed fire
in the blue twilight of the heaven. She could *see* it, she knew it,
but she was not of it. She was divorced, debarred, a soul shut
out. [pp. 392-93]

Gudrun's strange religion might be called an ultimate form of
nihilism. Like her own soul, the walls of snow are eternally cold,
unresponsive, shut-in. Her tears and horror are due to her realization that this finality is a reflection of her inner self, or rather her
lack of one. They are indications that even an ontological recog-

nition of purity and beauty amounts to a destruction of the essentially human. This is why, when Gudrun sees and knows (again, not in an intellectual but in an ontological sense) these peaks of negation transformed by the fires of heaven, she is divorced, debarred, a soul shut out. Despite her recognition that this is her place, Gudrun is unable to respond with the completion for which she obviously yearns.[34]

Lawrence's rendering of Gudrun's relation to these icy wastes is brilliantly original. It is simply inadequate to dismiss this relation as symbolic, just as it was inadequate to dismiss Tom's relation to natural forces as symbolic. Gudrun's religious trance is an indication of no simple recognition that these icy wastes are like herself, an emblem of her final denial of vital possibility; it means also that she mysteriously partakes of that nullity, responds to it with a religious intensity thay by its very nature is self-defeating. If this seems like unalloyed and unacceptable mysticism, it can be argued that Lawrence not only prepares us for it so that it seems inevitable but also manages to dramatize it convincingly.[35]

Gudrun's final responses to the snowy wastes can be seen as logical extensions of her qualities of coldness, unresponsiveness, and especially aestheticism, upon which we have only touched earlier. She is, after all, an artist by vocation, and the walled-in navel of the world is where that vocation leads in Lawrence's view of things. For Gudrun's view of art, as well as her practice as an artist, are also expressions of the inadequacy we have examined in her sexual relations. Here, for example, is the sort of thing she creates:

"That is hers, those two wagtails in Hermione's boudoir—you've seen them—they are carved in wood and painted."

"I thought it was savage carving again." "No hers. That's what they are—animals and birds, sometimes odd small people in

34. Although much more negative, this yearning resembles Tom Brangwen's desire for a continually ultimate state; they both presuppose the impossible absence of all human limitation.

35. Again, Vivas's notion of a "constitutive symbol" may be helpful here.

everyday dress, really rather wonderful when they come off. They have a sort of funniness that is quite unconscious and subtle." [p. 87]

The speakers are Gerald and Birkin at Breadalby. Birkin goes on to explain that Gudrun does not take her art seriously: "She won't give herself away—she's always on the defensive." For "won't" read "can't," and the relationship of Gudrun's world to the dead end in the mountains begins to emerge. It is also significant, of course, that her work resembles the savage carving of the African woman in labor. Birkin's description of that carving emphasized its abstraction of sensuality, which itself had the finality of a dead end. The missing link in the progression from her subtle and savage carving to her place in the snow is made clear in her discussions and affinity with the "sewer rat" and industrial artist, Loerke, who shows her, when she is desperate, how to regard art with a type of seriousness that Birkin could not have foretold at Breadalby.

Loerke is at one point or another likened to most of the repulsive animals in the Lawrentian repertoire. As a corrupted sensualist he is "farther along" than any of the others, hating yet serving "the ideal"—the social and mechanical ideal. He preaches about the beauty of the machine and decorates factories with friezes. In him Lawrence obviously brings together his themes of sensualism and mechanical abstraction in a particularly vivid manner; if Loerke is lacking in recognizable humanity, he is strikingly effective as a symbolic figure, embodying in his dwarflike body and obscene propensities all that is repulsive in the dying civilization that this book portrays. It is he, of course, who takes Gudrun from Gerald and therby shares in Gerald's "murder." He manages this by offering her further escape in new forms of sensual abstraction, from obscene mockery of all human achievement to a theory of utter divorcement of art from life. This theory is particularly attractive to Gudrun at a time when Gerald is making demands for life that she cannot and will not fulfill.

It is a work of art, it is a picture of nothing, of absolutely nothing. It has nothing to do with anything but itself, it has no relation with the everyday world of this and other, there is no connection between them, absolutely none, they are two different and distinct planes of existence, and to translate one into the other is worse than foolish, it is a darkening of all counsel, a making confusion everywhere. Do you see, you *must not* confuse the relative work of action with the absolute world of art. [p. 421]

Gudrun and Loerke have a particular fondness for the art of old and sensual cultures (or at least cultures which Lawrence so regarded), not only West African but Aztec, Mexican, and Central American. "They kindled themselves at the subtle lust of the Egyptians or the Mexicans." This amounts, finally, to a rejection of all real possibility of vitality. "The suggestion of primitive art was their refuge, and the inner mysteries of sensation their object of worship. Art and Life were to them the Reality and the Unreality" (p. 439).

A less Lawrentian position would be difficult to conceive. But in it we can find partial explanation for Gudrun's susceptibility to the overwhelming beauty and nullity of the frozen landscape. If her religion is an ultimate in nihilism, it is also an ultimate in aestheticism and is self-defeating for the same reasons. For Ursula, who despite her usual feminine impulsiveness is Lawrence's spokesman, the relation of art to life is just the reverse of that to which Gudrun and Loerke adhere; she argues that the former is an inevitable expression of the latter, and that it is impossible for the artist to escape his responsibility to life. This, of course, is precisely what Gudrun and Loerke seek to do: Gudrun through rejecting Gerald, and Loerke through continuing to reject any moral claims upon him (besides preaching false doctrine, he is guilty of homosexuality and sadistic tastes for young girls). Once we are aware of the extremes to which these aesthetic propensities go, Gudrun's intensity of response to sunsets on the mountains becomes a bit clearer.

They climbed together, at evening, up the high slope, to see the sun set. In the finely breathing, keen wind they stood and watched the yellow sun sink in crimson and disappear. Then in the east the peaks and ridges glower with living rose, incandescent like immortal flowers against a brown-purple sky, a miracle, whilst down below the world was a bluish shadow, and above, like an annunciation, hovered a rosy transport in mid-air.

To her it was so beautiful, it was a delirium, she wanted to gather the glowing, eternal peaks to her breast, and die. [pp. 437-38]

This has the religious overtones of the earlier trance, but it brings out a sensual element in Gudrun's response which is closely related to all the forms of sensual indulgence she has discovered throughout the book. A shift to Gerald's point of view reveals that her delirium is both an escape from his claims and a sexual thrill. "He wished the peaks were grey and unbeautiful, so that she could not get her support from them. Why did she betray the two of them so terribly, in embracing the glow of the evening? Why did she leave him standing there, with the ice-wind blowing through his heart, like death, to gratify herself among the rosy snowtips?" (p. 438).

Through his brilliant descriptions of the landscape, Lawrence makes almost any degree of intensity plausible. Gudrun's sensitivity to the beauty of the sunset need not be corrupt in itself. Yet we know from her relationship with Loerke, from her rejection of Gerald, from her delirium and search for gratification, and from the earlier scene on the pallid slopes that her "religion," though it may represent a real search for completion, is corrupt. Her very entrancement with beauty cannot be fulfilling, though it seems to come closer than anything else, Gerald included; it must remain inadequate because it is a final response based upon a final deficiency. Regarded either psychologically or ontologically the situation is not simple, but Lawrence successfully conveys both the intensity of her responses and their inadequacy, having provided for us a whole pattern of inadequacy to explain it. It is here, if anywhere, that Gudrun comes closest to integrating her fondness for abstraction and control with her need for sensual abandonment. And again psychological terms can largely account for what is happening: Gudrun's yearning for the beautiful and the icy is among other things a clear death wish, a desire to escape from a situation that has become almost intolerably revealing of her own sexual and moral inadequacy; her religious ecstasy might be dismissed as a form of masochism, a desire for self-immolation with the usual sexual dimension. But this language is inadequate in describing what Lawrence has in fact achieved, which is as usual a feat of evocation, the portrayal of emotions and behavior which are both convincing and comprehensible from his own point of view. He has provided an intricate pattern of need and failure extending to all corners of his book, in which we can find ample intellectual underpinning, and he has managed to convey through sheer descriptive force an element of vision which grows naturally from that underlying pattern. We can hardly ask him to do more.

Gudrun's inadequacies take a horrible toll on Gerald, whose needs are proportionate to his superior capacities. She has the consistent advantage of knowing where she is incapable of going; her self-preservation requires his destruction. His progression toward suicide has the same logical quality as Gudrun's movement toward Loerke and the "snows of abstraction." Its first stage is simply a burst of sensual vitality, a release from England's inhibitions in a setting whose very bareness seems to foster revelation of one's essential qualities.

> "Gerald! Oh, my word, he came out like a dandelion in the sun! *He's* a whole saturnalia in himself, once he is roused. I shouldn't like to say whose waist his arm did not go round. Really, Ursula, he seems to reap the women like a harvest. There wasn't one that would have resisted him. It was too amazing! Can you understand it?"
>
> Ursula reflected, and a dancing light came into her eyes.
>
> "Yes," she said. "I can. He is such a whole-hogger." [p. 384]

Gudrun finds this promiscuity immensely attractive; despite its hyperintensity, it is an indication of real vitality. But it is a power out of proportion, and both Gerald and Gudrun are at moments slaves to it.

> The passion came up in him, stroke after stroke, like the ringing of a bronze bell, so strong and unflawed and indomitable. His knees tightened to bronze as he hung above her soft face, whose lips parted and whose eyes dilated in a strange violation. . . . He was super-humanly strong and unflawed, as if invested with supernatural force. [p. 392]

It is this force which brings Gudrun back from her tears in the snow; as in the scene in her bedroom she helplessly submits. " 'I shall always love you,' he said, looking at her. But she did not hear. She lay, looking at him as at something she could never understand, never: as a child looks at a grown-up person, without hope of understanding, only submitting" (p. 392). But this child-like state of submission is neither fulfilling to Gerald nor endurable to Gudrun. When she fully realizes that he is "naturally promiscuous," it seems to her the writing on the wall; "the deep resolve formed in her, to combat him. One of them must triumph over the other" (p. 403). Gerald's need and his concomitant sensual power are simply too great; they bring her out of herself to a realization of her emptiness. Both as a response to her resistance and as an inevitable movement of release from his willed existence, Gerald becomes increasingly demonic.

In his most abstract and wolflike moments Gerald comes close to winning; in this sensual, unconscious state, a phenomenon rather than a human being, he almost pushes Gudrun into madness, or at least so she fears. She is combing her hair before a mirror, "part of the inevitable ritual of her life," and he is simply watching. She becomes panicky:

> She started. It took all her courage for her to continue brushing her hair, as usual, for her to pretend she was at her ease.

She was far, far from being at her ease with him. She beat her brains wildly for something to say to him.

"What are your plans for to-morrow?" she asked nonchalantly, whilst her heart was beating so furiously, her eyes were so bright with strange nervousness, she felt he could not but observe. But she knew also that he was completely blind, blind as a wolf looking at her. It was a strange battle between her ordinary consciousness and his uncanny black-art consciousness. [p. 405]

Gerald's demonic qualities have reached a kind of perfection; again there seems to be an implication that if he could follow them to their logical end, if Gudrun could somehow meet him in his dark consciousness, something like a purgation might take place. But Gudrun regards this possibility as immediately destructive. She outwits him by sending him after something in her bag, and the moment passes.

Obviously Birkin's prediction that Gerald will fulfill the "destructive frost mystery" is coming to pass. In giving him all the qualities of abstract dark sensuality of the African statue, Lawrence neatly merges his two destructive streams, emphasizing their identity. But Gerald is also a good deal more than a symbolic figure throughout these last scenes; there remains a suggestion of real possibility and therefore real tragedy. His blindness, of which Gudrun takes such effective advantage, is both a sign of his purification or reduction in Lawrence's ontological scheme and a symptom of a real helplessness and human need. If to Gudrun he is a phenomenon which threatens to destroy her, Lawrence also makes it clear that the same need which led him from the graveyard to her bedroom continues to make him dependent upon her. Gerald finally realizes that she will destroy him if he lets her and speculates that, if he could achieve a state of self-sufficiency comparable to hers (he never understands that she is the more deficient of the two of them), he would be free of danger. "But then, to have no claim upon her, he must stand by himself, in sheer nothingness. And his brain turned to nought at the idea" (p. 436). His solution is to accept the inevitable destruction, for even though it leads to final annihilation it is at least better than sheer nothingness.

> A strange rent had been torn in him; like a victim that is torn open and given to the heavens, so he had been torn apart and given to Gudrun. How should he close again? This wound, this strange, infinitely-sensitive opening of his soul, where he was exposed, like an open flower, to all the universe, and in which he was given to his complement, the other, the unknown, this wound, this disclosure, this unfolding of his own covering, leaving him incomplete, limited, unfinished, like an open flower under the sky, this was his cruellest joy. Why then should he forego it? Why should he close up and become impervious, immune, like a partial thing in a sheath, when he had broken forth, like a seed that has germinated to issue forth in being, embracing the unrealised heavens. [p. 437]

The fact is that Gudrun, through her very physical acquiescence, has to some extent met his need and released a possibility for completion with which she cannot cope.

Throughout all this Gudrun, moving closer toward Loerke, becomes increasingly analytic. She spends nights of insomnia analyzing Gerald's possibilities as an organizer and ruler but dismisses them because her experience with society only leads her to cynicism. He would need her help, and she would not give it. Loerke encourages her in developing a cynical and ironic attitude toward everything which might encroach upon her, especially Gerald himself. Once the aesthetic doctrine is promulgated, with its inversion of art and life, Gerald can be dismissed with relief as "bagatelle." She repeatedly and openly accuses Gerald of being incapable of love, which is true enough to hurt him (but even truer of herself). Finally, close to hysteria, she reduces Gerald's very kisses to the ticks of a clock. Gudrun even realizes that Gerald needs to be mothered, but she dismisses this as an intolerable responsibility. The whole stream of consciousness has the quality of a nightmare. Gerald in turn feels a growing urge to murder her and finally attempts it. It is a measure of her torture of him that we read through this outburst with relish, hoping he will succeed. His soul laughs, and he reaches "at last to take the apple of his desire."

> He took the throat of Gudrun between his hands, that were hard and indomitably powerful. And her throat was beautifully, so beautifully soft, save that, within, he could feel the slippery chords of her life. And this he crushed, this he could crush. What bliss! Oh what bliss, at last, what satisfaction, at last! The pure zest of satisfaction filled his soul. He was watching the unconsciousness come into her swollen face, watching her eyes roll back. How ugly she was! What a fulfilment, what a satisfaction! How good this was, oh how good it was, what a God-given gratification, at last! He was unconscious of her fighting and struggling. The struggling was her reciprocal lustful passion in this embrace, the more violent it became, the greater the frenzy of delight, till the zenith was reached, the crisis, the struggle was overborne, her movement became softer, appeased. [p. 463]

The obvious sexual nature of this attempted murder fits neatly into the pattern Lawrence has been elaborating. What Gudrun could not consistently give Gerald (abandon, release of her will), he will take by rape. She has repeatedly expressed a fear that his sexual demands would destroy her, that she might die, yet at the same time her most profound experiences have contained a yearning for annihilation. But Loerke interrupts with a sardonic comment ("Monsieur! ... Quand vous aurez fini—"), and Gerald is overwhelmed with contempt and disgust. So Gudrun survives, though her death would have been quite as logical as Gerald's; Gerald, stripped of defenses by the two of them, escapes his nausea by self-immolation.[36] He leaves behind a pair who have

36. It is interesting to speculate whether finishing off Gudrun might have freed Gerald, as the maimed soldier in "The Crown" implies is possible (see pp. 212-14). I think probably not, but it is here that Lawrence

between them merged virtually all the aspects of mental and sexual experience against which this book is directed: though ostensibly bohemian, they unabashedly serve industrial society; they depend for existence upon analytic defenses against emotional and ontological inadequacies; they revel in a peculiarly self-conscious and prurient form of sensuality, living by what Lawrence later defined as pornographic principles;[37] and they justify all this by a creed which denies life in favor of a peculiarly limited art.

Thematically, then, the only loose ends lie in the open-ended nature of the relationship between Ursula and Birkin. As with all Lawrence's successful couplings, there is no such thing as complacency in success. What views we do get of them after they reach the continent are not all positive, despite the enduring peace which they have achieved. While still at the resort they go through the purgation of shame which has by now become part of the Lawrentian pattern of marriage.[38] Even this does not result in a final form of union; nothing can, because of the inherently unstable nature of the realm of being itself. As lovers, moreover, they are not always in accord and not always sexually successful. But this, too, is part of Lawrence's expectation; there is no such thing as an infallible pattern of fulfillment, in any realm whatsoever.[39] There are still no easy answers, even though Birkin's way of freedom seems to be a reasonable way to describe Lawrence's view of a successful relationship between a man and

---

comes closest to carrying through the demonic release which has obviously been on his mind.

37. See "Pornography and Obscenity."

38. This has led to great fuss over *Lady Chatterley's Lover,* where the physical acts in question have received great attention. But the main point is that whatever Lawrence's heroes are doing with their sexual parts, their intention is to remove whatever self-conscious inhibitions may remain. This does not necessarily work, as Will and Anna Brangwen, among others, have shown.

39. Allen Friedman, in his *Turn of the Novel* (New York, 1966), argues convincingly that this sort of openness is a characteristic of the modern novel, reflecting a characteristically modern attitude toward experience. See esp. chap. 6, which is devoted to Lawrence.

woman. And Lawrence's terms have a great deal in common with theological views of marriage which are much more obviously traditional. The pledge, the submission, the release into the unknown with the aim of reaching, in the words of a character of Forster's, "more than I am myself" have strong affinities with certain forms of Christian theology.[40] The view of marriage which Ursula and Birkin support is in fact the most generally satisfactory one that Lawrence ever expressed. His next novels unfortunately revert to the pattern of domination and submission which it took so long to remove from Birkin's speculation. But that is another story.[41]

40. Martin Jarret-Kerr, in *D. H. Lawrence and Human Existence* (2d ed. London, 1961), devotes most of his book to exploring these affinities, but I believe his approach too easily accommodates Lawrence's ideas to a Christian existentialist position.

41. There is one other unresolved problem which I have deliberately ignored because I do not now intend to go on to the next novels. That is the relationship of Gerald and Birkin, about which I remain uneasy. In general I agree with Hough's view that Lawrence did not fully face up to the homosexual elements which clearly come across in the "Gladiatorial" chapter; he consistently sought to dismiss them with idealistic phrasing about friendship that was somehow physical but not sexual. What he dramatizes of the physicality I cannot accept as not sexual. Earlier versions of the novel, moreover, indicate more open admission of what most of us would call homosexual yearnings (see *Phoenix II,* where an early opening chapter is printed). The whole problem remains a bit confused and is referred to with a hanging question in the last sentence of the book. It causes trouble in the novels which follow, but it did not seem to me necessary to pursue it here, both because I cannot see how it illuminates the dominant patterns which I have been analyzing and because it offers no distinct and important lessons about Lawrence's method. For a defense of the whole relationship, see Spilka, *The Love Ethic of D. H. Lawrence* (Bloomington, 1955), chap. 7. Cf. Hough, *The Dark Sun,* p. 85; and Ford, *Double Measure,* pp. 198-207.

Conclusion

We have noticed repeatedly that Lawrence, confronted with conflicting values, sought to relate them dialectically, both in the fictional process and in his analytic formulations. Charles Feidelson, Jr. has called attention to the similarity between such a procedure and the symbolist's search for unity:

> The dialectician closely approaches the symbolistic point of view. The language in which he works is an autonomous realm of meaning; place the focus of attention in objects outside the medium, and his function simply disappears. Confronted with the divisiveness of logic, the fact that we can define a word only as meaning *this, not that,* he assumes that "opposition can occur only between the parts of a *whole.*" His search for the inclusive statement is an act of faith in a unity which is prior to logical exclusion and which appears in the human capacity to entertain contradictory propositions.[1]

Lawrence's faith in such a unity never seriously wavered. This is perhaps why he himself was able to entertain so many contradictory propositions. He seems to have been quite aware, at least by the time he wrote *The Sisters,* that all his formulations of duality were the result of phenomenal limitation and not reflec-

1. Charles Feidelson, Jr., "The Symbolistic Imagination," in *Symbolism and American Literature* (Chicago, 1953), p. 68. The phrase in quotations is from M. J. Adler, *Dialectic* (London, 1927), p. 165.

tions of a noumenal schism. In the midst of his far-ranging divisions of all things into male and female in the *Study of Thomas Hardy*, Lawrence inserts a word of caution: "But it must first be seen that the division into male and female is arbitrary, for the purpose of thought. The rapid motion of the rim of a wheel is the same as the perfect rest at the centre of the wheel."[2] But this truth is not one that man can comprehend directly. The "infinite rest of inertia" is the same as "the infinite rest of speed, the two things having united to surpass our comprehension." To our comprehension, then, the world is everywhere divided, even when we consider it metaphysically. The closest we can come to describing the ultimate unity is to call it a relation, especially a relation between man and his universe. And when pressed to show where such a relation exists, we can point—or at least Lawrence pointed—toward works of art as well as living things, insisting that an ultimate balance could be intuited, though it was grounded in a "fourth dimension."[3]

Lawrence's progress as a novelist might well be viewed as a continued attempt to understand this incomprehensible unity. Of course there are great problems involved in such an attempt, as Lawrence was well aware.

2. *Phoenix,* p. 448.

3. See Gordon, *D. H. Lawrence as a Literary Critic,* pp. 54-55. Occasionally this ultimate balance seems implicit in the "vital flame" itself. For example, here is a portion of Lawrence's exposition of the "law of life" in "Reflections on the Death of a Porcupine":

> 3. The force which we call vitality, and which is the determining factor in the struggle for existence, is, however, derived also from the fourth dimension. That is to say, the ultimate source of all vitality is in that other dimension, or region, where the dandelion blooms ... not to be reckoned in terms of space and time.
>
> 4. The primary way, in our existence, to get vitality, is to absorb it from living creatures lower than ourselves. It is thus transformed into a new and higher creation. . . . The best way is a pure relationship, which includes the *being* on each side, and which allows the transfer to take place in a living flow. . . .
>
> 5. No creature is fully itself till it is, like the dandelion, opened in the bloom of pure relationship to the sun, the entire living cosmos. [pp. 210-11]

It is novelists and dramatists who have the hardest task in reconciling their metaphysic, their theory of being and knowing, with their living sense of being. Because a novel is a microcosm, and because man in viewing the universe must view it in light of a theory, therefore every novel must have the background or the structural skeleton of some theory of being, some metaphysic. But the metaphysic must always subserve the artistic purpose beyond the artist's conscious aim. Otherwise the novel becomes a treatise.[4]

We have seen a few instances where Lawrence's most analytic novel did approach a treatise, but on the whole such lapses have been successfully and often brilliantly avoided. Although the metaphysic has increasingly emerged, for the most part it has been subservient to the "artist's conscious aim." And this aim, though involved from the first with a quest for being, has been primarily to show the phenomenal struggle which every man must undergo to find it—to point out, dramatize, and weigh those forms and values which allow it to be realized or which thwart it. From one point of view the dialectical approach might be seen as a second best; Lawrence's increasing use of symbolic scenes implies a search for a symbolic mode which can resolve the Many under the aspect of the One. Failing in such a discovery, bound to the world of the Many, Lawrence may have settled on his continually changing oppositions as the only compromise available. But to stress such an explanation would be to distort his emphasis on the principle of individuation, which is itself a phenomenological commitment.

It would seem that Lawrence's insistence on identifying the supreme ontological reality with individual life (in *Fantasia* he explicitly derives the material cosmos from individual life) is inconsistent with his belief in the equal reality of otherness, necessary for relationship. But Lawrence does not worry the solipsistic dilemma philosophically, as Nietzsche and Sartre do,

4. *Phoenix,* p. 479.

because, empirically, in blood consciousness, we are aware both of the reality of our creative identity and of the reality of otherness: aware of them as primary data.[5]

Through these novels this primary awareness, which the dialectic is designed to reveal and finally to relate to the "theory of being," becomes increasingly a structural principle.

In a sense, then, Lawrence's task as a novelist entails a continual struggle for relation. From the most abstract height this struggle may be viewed as the perennial problem of the One and the Many, but in terms of his writing it amounts to a double commitment to the "primary data" of experience, discrete by nature, along with an equally powerful need to reveal larger wholes by which the divisions implicit in discreteness may be overcome. The very nature of this problem, together with Lawrence's particular methods of attacking it, make anything like a final resolution impossible. The philosophical or theological resolutions must finally rest in the inconceivable (though not, perhaps, impossible) moment of transcendence, somehow both in this world and beyond it, immanent and individual, yet also transcendent, without boundary, out of time. Lawrence's formulations must therefore be paradoxical, usually dualistically so. In writing novels these basically religious questions raise technical problems of a very difficult sort, mainly because a consummatory movement into the beyond must be made to emerge from human, phenomenally bound, recognizably definite characters. The general pattern of this problem is of course a familiar one; Frank Kermode has recently called our attention to it by pointing to the modern novelist's difficulties in attempting to accept and embody radical

5. Gordon, p. 60. Gordon has also called attention to Lawrence's persistent tendency, even in 1929, to formulate an "ultimate symbol" (see Nehls, *Lawrence: A Composite Biography*, 3:297). But it is revealing that the same conversation Gordon cites contains this qualification: "What was wrong with all the religions was that they had always 'plucked the lily,' had found one or another symbol and had clung to it, refusing to relinquish it as its vitality was exhausted. Yet a symbol, he had found, lasted only about twenty minutes—he didn't know why; then it had to be replaced by another."

contingency: an apparently universal need for the eschatological paradigms remains. Chaos can never be made "human."[6] Both mere experience and absolute transcendence are not conceivable and are therefore chaos to the novel reader. Character types and transcendent formulas, however, resolve chaos too easily, especially to most modern sensibilities. The novelist must find a meaningful area of movement between them, an area whose boundaries seem to diminish with time and with increased sophistication in his audience. A religious novelist must further be able to suggest final answers and imply them nondogmatically, or at least with minimal dogmatism. His technical problems may be directly proportional to the intensity of his need to make this sort of suggestion.

With Lawrence the need for coherence does not lead to any simple set of answers. He accepts willingly his phenomenal limitations and in fact seeks to transform them into new possibility. The primary data of which Gordon speaks are part of a world of flux and conflict, a world inherited from the Romantic movement through evolutionary and vitalistic theory somewhat infused with symbolism.

> The idea of harmony *in spite of* conflict, or simple reconciliation of apparent or superficial conflict, is a staple Greek and Roman, Medieval and Renaissance idea. The idea of harmony, or at least of some desirable wholeness or sanity or salvation, only *because of* or *through* some kind of strife of contraries . . . is [profoundly different] —the difference, for example, between Satan and Prometheus.[7]

For the most part Lawrence avoids satanic posing, but the element of wholeness through conflict is persistently present throughout his work.[8] With this sort of dynamic precedent he

---

6. Frank Kermode, *Sense of an Ending* (New York, 1968), passim.
7. W. K. Wimsatt, *Hateful Contraries* (Lexington, Ky., 1965), p. 21.
8. We may of course discover ambivalence toward this formulation as well, since the need for resolution always entails some degree of rejection

was bound to have trouble formulating a satisfactory harmony, but without it he may have had even more trouble writing novels, for a harmony in spite of conflict could not be so easily embodied in the literary form most persistently and tenaciously devoted to the vagaries of the phenomenal world.

―――――

of the conflict, and Lawrence, like Blake, insists on the value of the conflict itself.

INDEX

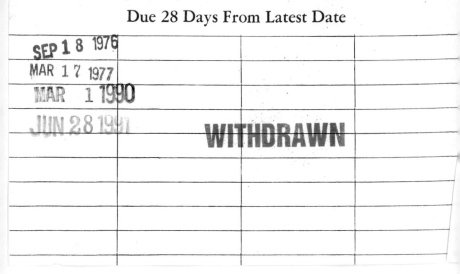